Contingent Loves

Contingent Loves

Simone de Beauvoir and Sexuality

EDITED BY

Melanie C. Hawthorne

University Press of Virginia

Charlottesville and London

The University Press of Virginia

Printed in the United States of America
First published in 2000

∞ The paper used in this publication meets the minimum requirements of the American National Standard for Information Sciences—Permanence of Paper for Printed Library Materials, ANSI Z39.48-1984.

Library of Congress Cataloging-in-Publication Data
Contingent loves : Simone de Beauvoir and sexuality / edited by Melanie C. Hawthorne.
p. cm.
Includes bibliographical references and index.
ISBN 0-8139-1916-9 (cloth : alk. paper) — ISBN 0-8139-1974-6 (paper : alk. paper)
1. Beauvoir, Simone de, 1908—Views on sex. I. Hawthorne, Melanie.
PQ2603.E362 .Z625 2000
848′.91409—dc21 99-042990

Contents

Acknowledgments

There are many people who helped bring this book to fruition and to whom thanks are due. First, Yolanda Patterson, for suggesting this project to me; Nancy Essig at the University Press of Virginia, and the readers of the manuscript who made so many valuable suggestions for revision; Steven Oberhelman, head of the Department of Modern and Classical Languages at Texas A&M University, for his continued support of my research; and last but not least, the "proud peanuts" of my writing group, without whom this project would never have been finished and to whom this book is therefore dedicated.

Contingent Loves

Introduction

MELANIE C. HAWTHORNE

As the existentialist philosophers of mid-twentieth-century Paris famously asserted, a person's life can be fully assessed only after that life is over. It comes as no surprise, then, that in the years since her death in 1986, philosopher and novelist Simone de Beauvoir has been the subject of numerous evaluations that attempt to assess her life and account for her contributions to intellectual thought. Beauvoir occupies a central place in the canon of great thinkers and writers of the twentieth century. Like her predecessors of the nineteenth century, such as Victor Hugo and George Sand, her life spanned the century itself (1908–86). As a major novelist, philosopher, feminist theorist, and political activist, she has had her life and work scrutinized from every imaginable perspective, always with thought-provoking results. Far from exhausting the possibilities, such ongoing commitment to the exploration of Beauvoir and her work attests to the importance of her contributions and opens up new perspectives for further consideration.

Beauvoir's monumental career offers many areas for study, and a steady flow of work had already begun to appear during her lifetime, but her death made possible the kind of judgments and analysis precluded by a life still unfolding. One of the first such ground-breaking studies was Deirdre Bair's biography, based on firsthand interviews with Beauvoir but not published until 1990, four years after Beauvoir's death.[1] Beauvoir was such an inspiration to so many that it may be difficult to avoid a hagiographic tone when recounting her life, but Bair steered a difficult course. On the one hand she recognized Beauvoir's brilliance and significance, yet she also broaching troubling questions and blind spots about the occasional gaps between what Beauvoir said and what she did. Following the publication of the biography in the United States and its translation in France, there was an outpouring of response. Many people, especially women, confronted certain details about Beauvoir's life for the first time and learned that their idol might have had feet of clay. In particular, what had seemed like a model relationship with Jean-Paul Sartre—a lifelong mutual commitment that offered an alternative to marriage and promised intellectual fulfillment—turned out to be far more emotionally fraught and intellectually one-sided than previously realized. Now it became apparent that this model relationship had problems. The asymmetry of the open relationship in which Sartre felt free to take other lovers while Beauvoir found casual physical relationships difficult;[2] Beauvoir's jealousy of Sartre's dalliances that she felt compelled to hide and deny; the lack of sexual intimacy after the 1920s;[3] Beauvoir's role as Sartre's unacknowledged amanuensis[4]—these imperfections were suddenly irrefutable. The reactions ranged from fascination and curiosity to disillusion to anger and resentment, particularly on the part of women who had comforted themselves with the belief that Beauvoir was proof that alternatives to unhappy and unsatisfying relationships were possible. Bair summarized the reactions in an article in the *New York Times Magazine:* "how do we go on without an ideal to look up to, now that we know that Simone de Beauvoir made the same mistakes and the same doubtful choices as all the rest of us?"[5]

Sartre, in writing to Beauvoir, had made a distinction between "contingent" and "essential" love, opposing their "essential," enduring love to the "contingent," casual loves each of them experienced with other partners in their more ephemeral affairs. Sartre's letter has always sounded like a fairly transparent attempt to give a high-minded, philosophical grounding to his own preference for sexual freedom. Although, ironically, the distinction invokes the existentialist rhetoric of "engagement" (often translated as "commitment") to avoid sexual commitment, Sartre's wish to explore multiple partners is justified by an appeal to the vocabulary of existentialism and is cast in terms that Beauvoir could not refuse without appearing to be a jealous, bourgeois wife. Sartre's self-serving rhetoric is ultimately less surprising than Beauvoir's apparent willingness to be duped by it. It does not, after all, take a sophisticated reader to see through it, and one can imagine any Lovelace or Valmont wishing he had thought of such a pretty phrase. Yet this perspective of the enduring bond with Sartre overriding the transient, passing affairs has often dominated Beauvoir studies. The present volume acknowledges this perspective while challenging the often unexamined underlying rhetorical privileging of "essence" over "contingency."

In part, this is possible because recent publications have provided further information about Beauvoir's "contingent" relationships. The revelations of Deirdre Bair's biography, which focused mainly on the less successful aspects of Beauvoir's relationship with Sartre such as those described above, were followed by yet more revelations when documents thought to be lost were rediscovered and published shortly after Beauvoir's death.[6] A wartime diary and two volumes of letters to Sartre provided further insight into the early years of Beauvoir's relationship with Sartre and of World War II.[7] These highly personal writings—described by Hazel Barnes as a "poisoned gift"[8]—showed that despite Beauvoir's sometimes shocking honesty about her experiences, she was at times less than honest with both Sartre and herself about some of her feelings and relationships. These autobiographical sources reveal, among other things, some of Beauvoir's sexual relationships with women as well as relationships with men that she did not tell Sartre about (or told him about in an apparently selective way).[9]

As a number of contributors to this volume note, Beauvoir once stated that she "would have liked to have given a frank and balanced account of [her] own sexuality."[10] Taking this invitation to place sexuality at the center of Beauvoir's legacy, critics and readers now try to imagine what this account might have been as they struggle to deal with the posthumous revelations and the ways they add to or complicate it.

When it comes to reassessing Beauvoir's life, there is far more to be taken into consideration than anyone at first suspected. Biographical revisions have also benefited from the recent publication of other primary sources. The notebooks of Beauvoir's childhood friend Elisabeth Lacoin ("Zaza" in *Mémoires d'une jeune fille rangée* [Memoirs of a dutiful daughter]) have now been published, along with a memoir by Bianca Bienenfeld

Lamblin (referred to by the pseudonym "Louise Védrine" in Beauvoir's autobiographical writings).[11] Given the role of these women in Beauvoir's life and thought, such publications are bound to affect the overall interpretation. Beauvoir's relationship with Zaza structures the first volume of her memoirs, and the intensity of the feelings evoked there is hard to ignore. Surely if Zaza had been a male companion critics would not hesitate to describe the relationship as one of an early love lost. Zaza's premature death makes it impossible to know how the friendship might have evolved, but publication of her notebooks at least adds information to complicate Beauvoir's idealized image. Lamblin's settling of scores in her recent publication also provides a corrective, but it raises new issues for consideration, too. For example, if Sartre was indeed such an inconsiderate lover as Lamblin claims, perhaps Beauvoir was relieved to be freed from his sexual attentions by their pact of mutual nonfidelity.

Thanks to her posthumous publications, Beauvoir has continued to fuel debate about the place of sexuality in her work. Whether the focus is on the fact that Beauvoir's lifelong relationship with Sartre was sexually unsuccessful, or on the "infidelity" of both Sartre and Beauvoir, or on Beauvoir's sexual relations with women and her denial of them, the reader is obliged to confront the centrality of questions of sexual expression. Such matters go to the heart of Beauvoir's project to offer a new paradigm for women, her theoretical writings on feminism, her claim to write candidly about her own life, and her attempts to probe the condition of women in her fiction. They are relevant even to her politics and the continued accusations of collaboration during World War II.[12]

The areas treated by the new scholarship on Beauvoir are thus shot through with issues concerning the affective, personal, and sexual dimensions of Beauvoir's life and work,[13] whether they be her relationship with Sartre, the "contingent" affairs (with both men and women), or the more serious affair with Nelson Algren that threatened to displace Sartre—documented in Beauvoir's letters now published for the first time and even translated into French.[14] This is not surprising given Beauvoir's emphasis on sex and gender in her theoretical work *Le deuxième sexe* (The second sex), as well as in her autobiography. François Mauriac misogynistically wrote to one of the contributors to *Les temps modernes* that after reading *Le deuxième sexe,* "J'ai tout appris sur le vagin de votre patronne" [your employer's vagina has no secrets from me].[15] The remark was intended as an insult, but it underscored the fact that what both fascinated and repelled readers about Beauvoir's work was the element of self-revelation. For some, it was too shocking and personal, for others it was brave and iconoclastic; but as the fiftieth anniversary of its publication was celebrated in 1999, its enduring importance and relevance remained undisputed.

For Beauvoir, the intimate, the affective, and the sexual were at the heart of lived experience, the center of philosophical enquiry, and the core of the human condition. Sexuality was thus inextricable from politics, and for Beauvoir, the way to change other people's politics was to write about one's own emotional life. The use of self-revelation in Beauvoir's work, particularly sexual self-revelation, has thus always been important, but it took on a new force in the 1990s. Beauvoir was an important influence on the so-called sexual revolution of the sixties, participated in the second wave of feminism in the seventies, and lived to see the "sex wars" debate in feminist theory in the United States in the eighties, yet she surely could not have predicted the explosion of scholarly work on sex and gender in the nineties. This work draws heavily on feminist studies, with its emphasis on sex and gender as key categories of analysis, but also incorporates the skepticism of postmodern philosophy, anthropological and sociological insights on social constructionism, historical research on sexuality inspired by Foucault and others, and the insights of queer studies and activism in the age of AIDS.

Sartre's essential/contingent distinction derives from the existentialist framework: the recognition of the fundamental contingency of things in the world is at the heart of the existentialist moment, as described for example in Sartre's *La nausée* (Nausea). Yet the substance of the distinction—the difference between an immutable given and something that could have been otherwise—is precisely the distinction at the heart of the feminist debates about sexuality: how much of sexuality is predetermined (an essential given, a biological imperative) and how much could be different (contingent, socially constructed)? Social constructionism, one of the dominant models offered in opposition to essentialist forms of determinism, does not imply total freedom of choice: once a structure has been socially accepted, it is not always within the power of an individual to change it simply by an act of will. As Carole Vance has written, "Some suggest that if sexuality is constructed at the cultural level, then it can be easily reconstructed or deconstructed at the social or personal level. Not necessarily."[16] Judith Butler, a figure of major theoretical importance for this volume, speaks to the way social constructions can resist change when she describes a certain misreading of her work as commodifying gender, as suggesting that "I can get up in the morning, look in my closet, and decide which gender I want to be today."[17] Although social constructionism thus becomes constraining once implemented, it nevertheless recognizes that things might have been otherwise, that they are, in the vocabulary of Sartre, contingent. Sartre's distinction allows both models—the deterministic one of essential love and the contingent one of chance—to exist simultaneously. Although in matters of love he implicitly privileges the essentialist, in a suggestively nonessentialist moment, by proposing that the contingent love affairs are less important than the perduring relationship with Beauvoir, his gesture of tolerance of the two arguably mutually incompatible models of sexuality is fundamentally a utopian one. In the half century since the publication of *Le deuxième sexe,* feminist theory has fought over this terrain.

Theoretical work on sexuality in the 1990s is informed by feminist theory and poststructuralist philosophy that questions biological determinism as the foundation of the human gender system. In this perspective, "sex" is reserved for those biological configurations of the body that have to do with reproductive roles and the secondary (physical) characteristics associated with them. "Gender" refers to the social roles that get mapped onto dimorphically sorted human bodies, so that "females" become "feminine" and "males" become "masculine." Whereas human sexual (reproductive) dimorphism remains basically unchallenged, masculine and feminine attributes are held to be highly culturally specific and contingent.

Judith Butler's *Gender Trouble* (1990) has offered new paradigms in the fields of philosophy and literary theory. Butler's work, which has been described as using the performativity of language to evoke "an image of both the solidity and contingency of so-called hard facts,"[18] illustrates the way Beauvoir's work stands at the crossroads of a number of theoretical paths. Beauvoir was clearly a formative influence on Butler. In addition to figuring in Butler's early work on twentieth-century French philosophy,[19] Beauvoir is the subject of an article entitled "Gendering the Body: Beauvoir's Philosophical Contribution" in which Butler credits Beauvoir with having developed in *Le deuxième sexe* an "underacknowledged theory of gender identity" through which Beauvoir uses the sex/gender distinction to explore an existential understanding of gender.[20] Although Butler goes further in *Gender Trouble* to deconstruct the sex/gender opposition altogether (in part through a reading of Beauvoir), it is clear that the performative theory of gender Butler proposes in that work owes much to her reading of Beauvoir in this article, in which she explains that she takes Beauvoir's emphasis on "becoming" a woman to mean that "one is always in the process of becoming a gender."[21]

One of Beauvoir's greatest intellectual contributions, according to many contemporary feminist theorists, was her brilliant formulation of the insight into the social construction of femininity: one is not born a woman, one becomes one. But as Butler has pointed out, "there is nothing in her account that guarantees that the 'one' who becomes a woman is necessarily female."[22] Beauvoir has thus explained one aspect of theory only to raise questions about another.

Butler's work also shows how the issues loosely referred to as "sexuality" must be distinguished from the related yet conceptually different issues of sex and gender. Insofar as forms of sexual expression were traditionally presumed to follow from gender, which in turn followed "naturally" from sex, these concepts and the connections among them often went unquestioned. In Toril Moi's recent book, *Simone de Beauvoir: The Making of an Intellectual Woman,* for example, Moi makes the claim that "Beauvoir is the first thinker in France explicitly to politicize sexuality"; when it comes to explaining how Beauvoir accomplished this feat, Moi describes how "in the first volume of *The Second Sex,* Beauvoir sets out to assail and destroy patriarchal myths of femininity."[23] For Moi, the connection between gender roles and sexual expression is self-evident and requires no further explanation.

In the process of unpacking these concepts that marked feminist and queer theory of the 1990s, however, the points of articulation became the subject of interrogation and the point of departure for the present collection. These essays add to the continued reevaluation of Beauvoir's work, but also break new ground by treating the topic of sexuality (rather than merely the sex/gender system) in Beauvoir's life and work. Contributors to *Contingent Loves: Simone de Beauvoir and Sexuality* approach the topic in a variety of ways. The starting point for discussion is the important question of language, which, as postmodern philosophy has shown, is of central concern. Beauvoir wrote in French (her letters to Algren are an exception), but is known to many throughout the world only in translation. The significance of that superficially innocent fact lies at the center of the first article in this book, in which Luise von Flotow brings both her practical experience as a translator and her theoretical insights to bear on the translation of Beauvoir's work into English. It is already acknowledged that there are shortcomings in the (abridged) English translation of *Le deuxième sexe* by H. M. Parshley, but Flotow extends her attention to language to the complicated and ideologically charged task of rendering French sexual terms—both in slang usage and in descriptive passages—into English. Flotow argues that male bias has led to an unrecognized misrepresentation of women's sexuality in much of Beauvoir's translated work. As illustration, Flotow offers careful analysis of examples culled primarily from *La femme rompue* (The woman destroyed) and *Le deuxième sexe* as well as a cluster of fictional works that display a consistent pattern of misreading. Following Flotow's reminder of the way translation can skew Beauvoir's words, all quotations from Beauvoir's work in this book are given in both the original French and in English. (The exception is quotations from her letters to Nelson Algren, since she wrote these in English.)

Such questions of language are not limited to literary representation, however, and other articles in this volume examine the complexity of sexual expression evident in Beauvoir's own life. Serge Julienne-Caffié, author of *Simone de Beauvoir* (1966), responds both to Bair's biography and to Bianca Lamblin's recently published memoirs in his article on the theme of the triangular relationship. Noting that triangles dominated Beauvoir's life for only a decade (1933–43), he compares all the sources of information—fictional and nonfictional—in order to assess the role of this challenge to the bourgeois family in Beauvoir's development. His analysis suggests that while the triangular relationships were superficially similar, their deep structure was quite different.

A reevaluation of the representation of sexuality in Beauvoir's work also leads to a reevaluation of her place in the canon. While Beauvoir's stature as a twentieth-century novelist and philosopher remains unchallenged, questions of sexuality open up new perspectives, and my own contribution to this volume offers a reading of Beauvoir's recently published *Journal de guerre* (War diary) that relates this work to a series of French novels that stage homoerotic desire in a pedagogical setting. I argue that such a reading is justified both by the way this perspective enables us to read a puzzling aspect of Beauvoir's life (her relationships with her female students) and by the way it challenges sexual identities based on simple binaries of hetero and homo.

Writing in a more personal mode, Swedish journalist Åsa Moberg reads Beauvoir's fiction and more theoretical texts such as *Le deuxième sexe* as autobiographical projections of Beauvoir's sexual experiences, and looks in vain for some indications of positive sexual relations. She challenges the common perception that Sartre and Beauvoir's relationship broke with tradition, arguing that such a view is a misreading. While the emotional side of their relationship was indeed innovative, Moberg concludes, in sexual matters "they were very much a traditional double-standard couple."

Barbara Klaw draws on recent publications as well as unpublished sources in her analysis of Beauvoir's self-construction through her relationship with Nelson Algren. In this reading, Klaw argues that "Beauvoir" and "Algren" are fictional constructs and Beauvoir uses the exercise to explore stereotypical gender roles. Beauvoir experienced a conflict between the feminist philosophy she consciously adopted and the more traditional and patriarchal attitudes she grew up with and to some extent retained.

Questions about sexuality also extend to a reassessment of Beauvoir's theoretical writings. How do recent publications and critical debates affect the reading of central theoretical texts such as *Le deuxième sexe,* for example? Richard J. Golsan offers a new twist by interrogating not Beauvoir's sexuality, but Henry de Montherlant's. (Montherlant was one of Beauvoir's "case studies" in *Le deuxième sexe.*) Golsan rereads Beauvoir's attributions of misogyny in light of Montherlant's homosexuality as a form of countermythology, but concludes that while Beauvoir might have been wrong in certain ways about Montherlant, she was right about the general cultural climate.

Finally, Liz Constable offers compelling reasons to reread Beauvoir in a "post-Butler age." Judith Butler's powerful theoretical work on performative gender seems to have fixed Beauvoir's place as one whose insights into the social construction of gender are limited by her own blind spots about sex as a prediscursive (essential) category. When feminist theorist Julia Kristeva, a key figure in continental philosophy and in the feminist faction of *écriture féminine* that Beauvoir opposed, published her novelistic *roman à clef* about the lives and loves of her own intellectual generation, its title, *Les samouraïs,* was an obvious nod and tribute to Beauvoir's *Les mandarins.* Aside from such gestures of acknowledgment, however, postmodern philosophy may seem at first glance to have displaced Beauvoir as a central feminist theorist. Using recent work on the performativity of shame, Constable shows how Butler, too, has blind spots, moments of theoretical impasse when a return to Beauvoir can suggest new points of departure for analysis.

The new vision of Beauvoir that emerges from these considerations is that of a sexually complex person whose affective life cannot be summarized by labels such as "heterosexual" or "nonmonogamous" or other categories derived from traditional views of sexuality. What, for example, is the correct terminology in such a system for a person whose sexual preferences express themselves consistently in triangular configurations? Rather than answer such questions by invoking a set of pathologies or taxonomies reminiscent of nineteenth-century interventions into sexology, I intend these questions to disrupt the traditional patterns of seeing sexual behavior and its representations. Just as one is not born a woman, with all the cultural assumptions this implies, one is not born a sexually expressive subject (despite our culture's rhetoric of the "naturalness" of sex). Instead, one is constituted as a subject with affective and sexual preferences and forms of expression. Beauvoir's work—fictional, theoretical, and autobiographical—suggests some of the ways one becomes such a person.

The notion of contingent love evoked in the title of this collection suggests that current paradigms of sexuality are at best merely contingent, too, no more and no less culturally determined than the gender roles of which Beauvoir helped launch the critique. In a sense, then, these essays expand the scope of Beauvoir's social analysis. If we reclaim Sartre's description of love and sexual expression as mainly a matter of contingent factors, factors that might have been otherwise, Beauvoir's consent to such a characterization can be seen in a new light. Sartre intended to valorize essentialism over contingency, but existentialist philosophy associates the denial of contingency with bad faith. By accepting Sartre's words but evaluating them according to existentialist principles, Beauvoir can be seen not as acceding to self-deception, but as admitting the contingency of sexual expression. One is not born a sexual subject, she might have said, one becomes one.

Notes

1. Bair, *Simone de Beauvoir.*

2. Ibid., 200.

3. Ibid., 210–11.

4. Ibid., 567.

5. Bair, "Do as She Said, Not as She Did."

6. For the reception of Beauvoir's posthumous publications in the French press see Galster, "Une femme machiste et mesquine."

7. Beauvoir, *Journal de guerre* and *Lettres à Sartre.*

8. Barnes, "Simone de Beauvoir's Letters: A Poisoned Gift?"

9. Barnes claims that she "find[s] absolutely no evidence that Beauvoir significantly deleted or distorted in her letters to him" ("Simone de Beauvoir's Letters," 13), but Margaret Simons has noted slight differences between the way the same events were recorded in the *Journal* and in letters ("Lesbian Connections," 154).

10. Schwarzer, *After "The Second Sex,"* 84. Because these interviews were originally published in German (see the "translator's note," *After "The Second Sex,"* 7), I give only the English translation for all citations from this work throughout this book. To judge from the later, French, edition of the work (*Simone de Beauvoir aujourd'hui: entretiens* [Paris: Mercure de France, 1984]), some interviews were originally conducted in French, while others were in German.

11. See Lacoin, *Zaza: Correspondance et carnets d'Elisabeth Lacoin.* The identity of the pseudonymous "Louise Védrine" was revealed for the first time in Bair's biography; this, combined with Beauvoir's posthumous publications, evoked a response from Bianca Bienenfeld Lamblin (*Mémoires d'une jeune fille dérangée*). For studies of these publications, see Lacoste, "Elisabeth Lacoin's Influence on Simone de Beauvoir" and "An Intricate Relationship."

12. The question of Beauvoir's collaboration has recently been treated aggressively by Gilbert Joseph in *Une si douce Occupation* as well as more sympathetically and even-handedly by Susan Rubin Suleiman in *Risking Who One Is.*

13. Works on Beauvoir that have appeared since her death include: Brosman, *Simone de Beauvoir Revisited* (1991), a revised addition to the World Author Series; Crosland, *Simone de Beauvoir: The Woman and Her Work* (1992); Fallaize, *The Novels of Simone de Beauvoir* (1988), as well as the edited volume *Simone de Beauvoir: A Critical Reader* (1998); Forster and Sutton, *Daughters of de Beauvoir* (1989), a collection of essays by contemporary writers and thinkers about Beauvoir's influence on them; the Fullbrooks'

Simone de Beauvoir and Jean-Paul Sartre: The Remaking of a Twentieth-Century Legend (1994), which reassesses Beauvoir's contributions to the development of existentialism; Moi, *Feminist Theory and Simone de Beauvoir* (1990) and *Simone de Beauvoir: The Making of an Intellectual Woman* (1994); Monteil, *Simone de Beauvoir: Le mouvement des femmes* (1995); Ozouf, *Les mots des femmes* (1996); Patterson, *Simone de Beauvoir and the Demystification of Motherhood* (1989); Simons, *Feminist Interpretations of Simone de Beauvoir* (1995) and *Beauvoir and "The Second Sex"* (1999); and Tidd, *Simone de Beauvoir, Gender and Testimony* (1999). There also have been numerous articles and chapters in books. A special issue of *Yale French Studies* appeared in 1986 immediately following Beauvoir's death (though it had been in preparation before), and a cluster of articles on Beauvoir appeared in *Signs* 18.1 (1992). The Simone de Beauvoir Society publishes a regular newsletter as well as *Simone de Beauvoir Studies,* organizes a biannual conference, and regularly sponsors panels at the Modern Language Association's annual convention.

14. Beauvoir, *A Transatlantic Love Affair.*
15. Beauvoir, *La force des choses,* 205.
16. Vance, "Pleasure and Danger," 9.
17. Butler, "The Body You Want," 83.
18. Meijer, "How Bodies Come to Matter," 277.
19. Butler, *Subjects of Desire.*
20. Butler, "Gendering the Body," 253–54.
21. Butler, *Gender Trouble,* 256.
22. Ibid., 8.
23. Moi, *Simone de Beauvoir,* 190.

1

Translation Effects

How Beauvoir Talks Sex in English

LUISE VON FLOTOW

"TRISTAN est un con," exclaims Murielle in *La femme rompue* (1967) as she reviews all the failings of her ex-husband (92). The translation by Patrick O'Brian in Simone de Beauvoir's *The Woman Destroyed* (1969) reads "Tristan is a cunt" (94), giving the language of this timid yet angrily self-righteous middle-aged "bourgeoise" a distinctly different tone. In thinking about the book she could write, Murielle says "mon livre serait plus intéressant que leurs conneries" (90), which the translation renders "my book would be more interesting than all their balls" (92). What is happening here? How do "conneries" (idiocies) become "balls," and how does "con," the common French slang term for "idiot," become such a vulgar term in English? While it is true that "con" may once have been a neutral term for women's genitals, both the English and French terms have been appropriated by conventional language and denigrated to such an extent that they can hardly be used in any literal sense, as feminist translator and theorist Susanne de Lotbinière-Harwood has argued.[1] This is one reason why the use of the English term here and elsewhere in the text is striking.

From the conventional perspective of textual equivalence the translation of "conneries" as "all their balls" is somewhat more puzzling than the translation of "con"; it is not even a literal translation. It maintains the sexual nuance of the source text, yet skews the translation toward male sexuality.

This essay starts from the premise that every translation must change a text, a fact I accept. Translation as a textual operation that makes literary, scholarly, and pragmatic materials available across cultures is inordinately valuable; texts live on in translation, differently. The translation effect—the visible and verifiable changes a text undergoes in translation and the effect this has on its reception in a new culture—is, however, rarely discussed. I propose to focus on the translation of sexual terms and references to sexuality in a number of Beauvoir's texts. I will examine the translation, compare it to the source version, comment on the effect it creates in English, and speculate on possible explanations for the changes.

Comparatively little has been written about the English translations of Beauvoir's work. On the one hand this is surprising, considering the impact Beauvoir has had on postwar Anglo-American feminist philosophy and on the women's movement. On the other hand, this state of affairs reflects the common approach to translated texts, which is to read and discuss them as though they had been produced in the translating language and to ignore the translation effect. While this tendency may be "characteristic of the insensitivity to translation common to members of all imperialist cultures," as Sherry Simon has recently argued,[2] it is also the source of numerous problems of reception.

The commentaries and analyses that do exist on Beauvoir translations can be divided into three main types: full-scale essays such as Margaret Simons's work on *Le deuxième sexe* (The second sex) or Anne Cordero's study of *Mémoires d'une jeune fille rangée* (Memoirs of a dutiful daughter); occasional endnotes or footnotes in articles by critics such as Toril Moi and Barbara Klaw; and references to mistranslations in more general works focusing on gender and translation.[3] Most of the above address the issue from a feminist perspective, seeing an ideological patriarchal motivation in the apparent censorship and distortion of the source text. However, Terry Keefe's brief analysis of Beauvoir's 1972 interview with Alice Schwarzer, an expurgated version of which appeared in English in *Ms.* magazine in 1972 and was reprinted in *New French Feminisms* in 1980, takes a different tack;[4] it points to a deliberate manipulation of Beauvoir's text by the translator or publisher wanting to make her work attractive to mainstream American women. Keefe finds the translation distorted in questions "relating to sensitive and controversial matters of feminist ideology and strategy."[5] Among other things, Beauvoir's socialist ideas as well as passages on lesbianism and women with children were deliberately censored, which, Keefe implies, may have served the purposes of a capitalist venture such as *Ms.* Thus while analyses of Beauvoir translations are sparse, they all point to more than just changes in the translated text; they imply that no change is innocent, but is part of a (sometimes deliberate) ideological or cultural agenda on the part of the translation/translator. This is a more recent twist on the truism that every translation changes a text, and has been developed in some detail in contemporary work in translation and cultural studies.[6] The basic idea is that translation is part of a process of creating meaning, the circulation of meaning within a contingent network of texts and social discourses. If this is so, then the cultural and ideological contexts in which a translation is produced and marketed will have an effect on the way a text is prepared, consciously or unconsciously, for the new audience. Further, the translator's personality, identity, experience, and background will feed into the new text, also affecting the translated version.

Beauvoir's oeuvre in English would doubtless benefit from a thorough contextualizing and analysis: Who translated her? When? For what reasons? Into what type of cultural setting? And who commissioned and financed the translations? Such an analysis might consider the translations of her work as materials produced, contingently, at a specific moment and for a specific purpose, and might incorporate an analysis of, say, the conditions obtaining in the United States publishing and culture industries of the early 1950s when large parts of *Le deuxième sexe* were deleted and sex scenes in *Les mandarins* were considerably censored. How much pressure was exerted by the publishers to accommodate American definitions of "perversion," or did the translator simply conform to some internal censor? Such an analysis might also reveal what effect the British translations of most of Beauvoir's subsequent work have had on the English versions, and on the reception of her work. And some light might be cast on the type of translation effects attributable to Patrick O'Brian, an author best known for his naval novels, who came to be Beauvoir's most prolific translator. Finally, such a study might investigate how Beauvoir's almost exclusively male translators have consciously or unconsciously manipulated her texts, changing the voice and the perspective to reflect their own positions.

The present study of the translation of Beauvoir's discourses on primarily female sexuality deals with a topic that Beauvoir addressed directly and indirectly in many of her writings, and that has been the source of some concern to feminist critics. I will use Toril Moi's definition of the term "sexuality," which strikes me as wide enough for the topics I need to address. She writes: "By 'sexuality' I understand the psychosexual as well as the biological aspects of female sexual existence, or in other words, the interaction between desire and the body."[7] Moi's focus (and ostensibly Beauvoir's) is on women, which will also be my focus; as we shall see, however, the male translator may confuse the issue substantially. I have divided the field into three types of discourse: sexual terms used as expletives to express anger and frustration in a text such as *La femme rompue;* descriptions of sexuality in the more scholarly writing on sexual initiation in *Le deuxième sexe;* and "romantic" sex scenes in Beauvoir's fiction.

Why focus on the translation of sexuality at all? In doing so, I single out a field that is notoriously difficult to translate for reasons of cultural and generational differences—a *cas limite* that in some ways serves as a test of translation. One important reason is that anglophone Beauvoir scholarship has repeatedly turned to issues of sexuality and female eroticism in her work, and as Jo-Ann Pilardi shows, much of this scholarship has been critical of Beauvoir's "patriarchal" views on sexuality.[8] While such criticism may not derive entirely from the translations, they play a not negligible role in establishing the reception of Beauvoir in English. A second reason for focusing on sexuality is the importance of this theme in women's writing after Beauvoir, as well as the importance of the discussions that were raised over the translation of erotic writing by women. While translations of women's attempts to "write the body" in French *écriture féminine* may offer the most obvious examples of translation difficulties and cultural differences in this domain,[9] more standard forms of erotic writing by women have also proven difficult to transfer from one culture to another. Issues such as self-censorship and different target culture sensibilities and traditions serve to inhibit the translator.[10] Returning to Beauvoir allows us to peruse the translations of a comparatively early writing of women's sexuality.

From the Mouths of Angry Women

The "Monologue" from *La femme rompue* is a loose stream-of-consciousness text spoken by Murielle, a forty-three-year-old bourgeoise who is spending New Year's Eve alone. She is slightly off-balance and anxious about the impending New Year's Day visit by her son and ex-husband. She vacillates between vicious anger, self-pity, nostalgia, self-righteousness, hatred of her friends and family, and self-destructive behavior. Over the course of her monologue, we discover that her seventeen-year-old daughter, Sylvie, committed suicide some time ago; her second husband has left her, taking their son with him; her mother accuses her of having driven Sylvie to her death; and she is painfully lonely, although she hears and reacts angrily to the sounds of partygoers in the apartment above her and out on the streets.

The monologue is studded with crude references to sex. It is vulgar and intense. Murielle's fixation on sex—in this case mainly the sexual encounters that she imagines others engaging in—is an important refrain in the text and underscores her apparent distaste for sex. This distaste can be traced to childhood experiences such as standing in a crowd on Bastille Day, "pressée entre leurs corps juste à la hauteur de leur sexe."[11] It can also be seen in her references to her mother, whom Murielle suspects of engaging in incestuous sex with Nanard, Murielle's brother, of seducing Murielle's husband, and of paying for gigolos. Her anger is particularly visible in a passage where she links her mother's alleged lack of cleanliness with her lasciviousness; she says "elle ne se lavait pas pas ce que j'appelle se laver quand elle faisait semblant de se doucher c'était pour montrer son cul à Nanard" (105). Finally, railing at the party atmosphere in the streets and in the apartment house where she lives, Murielle angrily spells out what she sees as the purpose of these goings-on: sex; "ils le feront cette nuit même dans la salle de bain même pas allongés la robe retroussée sur les fesses suantes quand on ira pisser on marchera dans le foutre comme chez Rose" (91). Her tone is vicious, and expletives with sexual content are her self-lacerating weapons.

The English translation by Patrick O'Brian does not clean up Murielle's language. It does put a curious twist on it, though, which heightens its coarseness. Indeed, as in the example of the translation of "leurs conneries" as "all their balls," the translation masculinizes the language with numerous references to male sex organs. The translations of the citations above shall serve as examples of the new emphasis in the text brought about by the use of male-centered imagery and uninformed or derogatory references to women.

But first, a curiously male reference that sets the tone early in the piece: "I'll make a cock of it" (90). In this passage, Murielle is worried about the next day's visit with her son and ex-husband, and says "je raterai mon coup" (88). O'Brian, the translator, has presumably abbreviated the British term "cock-up," meaning "mess" or "failure," where he could well have written "I'll make a mess of it." He thus provides North American and British readers with a term that unmistakably connotes male genitals. This becomes a tendency of the translation: the crucial sentence where Murielle describes her childhood experience in the crowd of a July 14 event is even more indicative of a translation effect. The line "pressée entre leurs corps juste à la hauteur de leur sexe" is translated as "squashed between them just at *prick* level" (90, emphasis added). While this might be justified in that it underscores Murielle's apparent aversion to heterosexual sex, the translation again reveals a male perspective. Beauvoir's text clearly refers to both men and women; it goes on: "dans l'odeur de sexe de cette foule en chaleur," in no way indicating that this is a crowd of only men, but a crowd of people *in heat*. The translation "randy crowd" does not convey Murielle's crude reference to humans in the throes of animalistic physicality, a recurrent topic in Beauvoir's writing on sexuality.

O'Brian's use of the verb "to stuff" deserves mention. He uses it to translate "se coller des Boules Quiès mentales dans les oreilles" when Murielle's family "stuffs" earplugs into their ears to stop her nagging voice; to translate "me fourrer mes trucs dans le cul" when Murielle debates whether to insert the suppositories that her doctor has prescribed; and to translate the verb "baiser," whose tone in this text would probably best be reproduced by the English "fuck." Occasionally, O'Brian avails himself of the euphemistic and more friendly "make love," but not once does he use "fuck" where the vehemence of Murielle's monologue would warrant it. Again, the focus is male; in vulgar British parlance, men "stuff" women, and the translation evokes intercourse from an aggressive male perspective. Murielle says, "les nuits de fête où tout le monde rigole bouffe et baise les solitaires les endeuillés ont le suicide facile" (99). O'Brian translates this as "everybody laughing gorging stuffing one another"; in a later passage on the "youth of today," "ça s'entre-baise" (108) becomes "they stuff one another" (110). While an argument could be made that "stuff one another" at least has something reciprocal about it, it nevertheless remains a euphemism—and maintains a male slant. Might an English-speaking Murielle of that generation have selected the same euphemism?

Barbara Klaw has commented on the weakening of certain vulgar references to sex in Leonard Friedman's translation of *Les mandarins* (1954; The mandarins, 1956). She points out that in French, Nadine, the teenage daughter of one of the main woman characters, is quite bold and crude. Talking about her relationship with boys, she says to her mother, "Comment veux-tu que j'aie des histoires avec des types si je ne baise pas."[12] In English this statement becomes "How do you expect me to have affairs with guys if I don't go to bed with them?" (373). Klaw suggests that this should read "if I don't fuck."[13] Here, the toning down elides the effect of Nadine's crude discourse, a crucial aspect of her relationship with her mother and an element that reveals her own cynical and alienated condition. Though decades and cultures apart, both translations are thus reluctant to put the word "fuck" into a woman's mouth. O'Brian occasionally uses "fucking" as an adjective, but generally the solution is to take refuge in euphemisms or, as in *La femme rompue*, in semantic choices from a clearly masculine repertoire.

Finally, in two of the passages about Murielle's mother as an incestuous femme fatale, the translation seems oddly ill-informed, rendering the text far more crude than Beauvoir's. Setting the scene, O'Brian translates "son bordel de chambre" (89) as "her brothel of a room" (91), going to the surface meaning of "bordel" and ignoring the colloquial, though aggressive, use of the term: "messy." The sexual slurs Murielle utters about her mother thus appear justified when the mother is literally set in a brothel. Murielle's envy of her brother Nanard is evident in her comment "ça lève le coeur les mères avec leurs petits mâles" (89). In the translation, this becomes "it makes you really sick mothers with their little male jobs" (91). The term "jobs" is interesting here, evoking a tool or an instrument rather than a "little man." It renders the already heightened (brothel) scene more squalid. Similarly, the translation of the passage cited above, "quand elle faisait semblant de se doucher c'était pour montrer son cul à Nanard" (105), makes for an extremely debauched scene in English. O'Brian renders it as "when she pretended to use a douche it was only to show Nanard her backside" (108). In this version the mother does not take a shower, which would fit with the preceding comments on her lack of cleanliness, but performs a contraceptive operation in full view of her son.

It is easy to criticize translations. It is difficult to translate. Keeping this qualification in mind, it is still appropriate to point to the substantial effects that an apparent (and perhaps unconscious) male bias can have on a work such as Beauvoir's *La femme rompue*. Its vulgarity is heightened through literal translations and male sexual imagery, references to women's sexuality are misunderstood or misrepresented, and an aging bourgeoise starts sounding like a British sea captain.

The Terms of "Sexual Initiation"

H. M. Parshley's translation of *Le deuxième sexe* (1949; The second sex, 1952) has been extensively criticized for the way the text was selectively abridged.[14] Although Parshley wrote in his preface that the changes do not "involve anything in the nature of censorship or any intentional alteration or omission of the author's ideas,"[15] it has been shown that this claim is doubtful. However, we also know that Parshley worked under considerable pressure from the publisher Knopf and their attorneys to shorten and censor the text, and that he cut the text reluctantly.[16] While his translation of the chapter on sexual initiation in *The Second Sex* is in many ways painstakingly exact, the abridgements require commentary. Further, Parshley's tendency to render Beauvoir's language more polite by softening some of the coarser expressions is an important translation effect. Finally, his understated or poeticized translations of women's experiences substantially alter the tone of the entire text.

The third chapter of volume 2 deals with a girl's initiation into heterosexual sexuality, a traumatic event as Beauvoir describes it and one that she says contrasts significantly with the relative ease, clarity of purpose, and means with which young men experience sexual initiation.[17] For girls, sexual initiation is fraught with pain, confusion, uncertainty, and danger. The interplay between a woman's psychological and physical conditions, the effect that her upbringing and social conditioning have on her sexual responses, and the importance of the context within which she experiences sex are discussed at length. Beauvoir's analysis relies heavily on examples drawn from Wilhelm Stekel's *La femme frigide,* a French translation from German of a psychoanalyst's findings.[18]

The translation is not heavily abridged, but those elements that have been cut are of some importance. Beauvoir incorporates lengthy statements by women patients and descriptions of sexual encounters that she has culled from Stekel's work. These are often narratives told in the first person or accounts that include direct quotes from dialogue by the patients. For example, when Beauvoir argues that a woman's frigidity can be the result of psychological suffering about her abnormal or "ugly" body, she cites and paraphrases Stekel's patients: "Toute jeune fille porte en elle toutes sortes de craintes ridicules qu'elle ose à peine s'avouer dit Stekel. . . . Une jeune fille par exemple croyait que son 'ouverture inférieure' n'était pas à sa place. Elle avait cru que le commerce sexuel se faisait à travers le nombril. Elle était malheureuse que son nombril soit fermé et qu'elle ne puisse y enfoncer son doigt. Une autre se croyait hermaphrodite. Une autre se croyait estropiée et incapable d'avoir jamais de rapports sexuels."[19] The translation paraphrases Beauvoir and considerably abbreviates the passage: "According to Stekel, all young girls are full of ridiculous fears, secretly believing that they may be physically abnormal. One, for example, regarded the navel as the organ of copulation and was unhappy about its being closed. Another thought she was a hermaphrodite" (382). Of particular interest is Parshley's removal of the naive "ouverture inférieure," just as later in the text more vulgar expressions such as "tu as un grand trou" (143) are eliminated. In contrast to O'Brian, and in accordance with this more scholarly text, Parshley avoids all colloquial terms for genitalia. By doing so in these quotes from dialogues and patients' accounts, he strikes the individual woman from the narrative, making it a more academic treatise. In the passage above, the deletion of the reference to the girl handling or exploring her body, seeking to introduce her finger into her navel, removes the personal element from the text. It makes it less descriptive, more scholarly and detached. Subsequent accounts by Stekel's patients are also abridged to eliminate the subjective aspect. For instance, hurtful comments and situations that have rendered women sexually unresponsive and that they recount verbatim—"tu m'as trompé, tu n'es plus vierge," "comme tu as les jambes courtes et épaisses," "Mon Dieu, que tu es maigre" (143)—appear in elegant summary in the translation. Parshley writes, "her husband accused her of deceiving him *in regard to her virginity,*" "another husband made *uncomplimentary remarks* about how 'stubby and thick' his bride's legs were," "her husband brutally deplored her *too slender proportions*" (382). The politer, more literary formulations, here emphasized, as well as the quotation marks around "stubby and thick," indicate Parshley's distance from the text and, perhaps, his distance from such discourse. He reproduces the gist of these hurtful comments in a different language register, substantially undermining Beauvoir's point.

Such abridgements can have a more sinister effect. In several cases, the young women in question come across as coy, hypocritical, or hypersensitive, rather than wounded or insulted. In a section where Beauvoir discusses the danger of pregnancy as a reason for women's lack of sexual response, she cites the case of a young girl, pregnant at nineteen, who "demanda à son amant de l'épouser; il fut indécis et lui conseilla de se faire avorter, ce qu'elle refusa. Après trois semaines, il se déclara prêt à l'épouser" (159). The woman "punishes" her lover with frigidity for three weeks of "torment." Parshley's translation deletes the man's callous suggestion that the woman have an abortion: "becoming pregnant, she demanded marriage, but her lover hesitated for three weeks before acceding. She could not forgive him the three weeks of anxiety" (393). It is incomprehensible why this crucial piece of information should be deleted from the text, since it is vital to understanding the full extent of the woman's pain or torment (translated here as mere "anxiety"). Was abortion a greater taboo in 1950s America than in 1949 France or 1920s Austria, where the citation originates? In any case, the deletion of this brutal suggestion by the lover makes the girl's frigidity appear as a hysterical, exaggerated reaction.

Another example shows how the use of the English passive voice can remove the subject of the action and render a woman's decisions invisible. Again referring to the danger of pregnancy, Beauvoir writes: "Dans le mariage même, souvent la femme ne veut pas d'enfant, elle n'a pas une santé suffisante, ou il représenterait pour le jeune ménage une trop lourde charge" (149). Here the woman does not want a child because *she* is not strong enough or is worried about the economic burden this would represent. In the translation, the fact that such decisions need to be made and often are made by the woman is deleted through use of the passive voice and through elegant condensation: "And even in marriage a child may not be desired, for reasons of health or economy" (387). The woman's agency and her decision-making powers clearly written into the text by Beauvoir are removed through the translation. The female agent along with her concern for her own health and the couple's ability to support a child disappears.[20]

In *The Second Sex,* almost all of the citations from Stekel or other psychoanalysts and sexologists have been abridged or rendered more literary, and the same applies to Beauvoir's own writing. On several occasions Beauvoir refers to sexual arousal in men as "le rut" (131, 134, 147). According to a number of dictionaries, this term is applied exclusively to animals and refers to the period in which mammals are in heat. At each occurrence of the term, the English translation finds a way to soften the animalistic connotations: "sex excitement" (372, 375) and "masculine passion" (386). These euphemisms significantly understate Beauvoir's ironic commentary on the social and cultural representations that assign splendor and heroism to men's rut while ignoring or shaming women's interest in sex.

A similar situation arises when Beauvoir discusses contraceptive methods and their inhibitive effect on women's sexual interest. Beauvoir describes the woman having to "courir au cabinet de toilette pour chasser de son ventre le germe vivant déposé en elle malgré elle" (149). She argues that this postcoital technical operation puts a considerable damper on a woman's desire to participate in sex. She continues with an enumeration of the necessary gear: "La répugnance pour la poire à injection, le bock, le bidet est une des causes fréquentes de la frigidité féminine" (149). Again, the translation skirts the issue, rendering the situation less demeaning and thereby undermining Beauvoir's argument: the woman "takes measures to rid herself of the living sperm" (387), she doesn't "run to the toilet," and the technical equipment becomes simply "the apparatus of injection and cleansing" (387).

There doubtless are reasons for these changes. Are they due to a certain reticence on Parshley's part? To American prudishness or modesty? This may be debatable if we consider that Mary McCarthy's novel *The Group* appeared only a year later and included graphic descriptions of struggles with contraceptive gear. The important point is, however, that the translation effect renders Beauvoir's point far less concrete, less tangible, less credible.

Other minimal changes in the translation reinforce this tendency to understate the text: women's "refus" (133) to have sex becomes their "disinclination" (374); the fact that they may "se refuser à l'homme fait" (137) is transposed as women "avoid[ing] grown men" (377). Beauvoir's reference to the verb "baiser" as a vulgarity (134) is completely left out in the translation (375). Finally, a passage in which Beauvoir develops a description of a young woman as "une chose de chair sur laquelle autrui a prise" (143) is considerably weakened when this image of a "girl as a thing of flesh to which anyone can lay claim" is not translated at all (382). The deletion further weakens the subsequent point about a girl's physical experience of being handled and "livrée au mâle" (144); when Parshley translates this as "she is in his power" (382) rather than "she is delivered up to the male" he presents the situation as a fait accompli rather than a painful process in which the woman is handed over.

A final point in Parshley's translation has been briefly addressed in Toril Moi's *Simone de Beauvoir: The Making of an Intellectual Woman*.[21] Parshley's multiple translations of the term "aliénation" reveal what Moi describes as his "tendency to lose sight of the philosophical aspect of Beauvoir's arguments." On the topic of women's experience of true sexual arousal Beauvoir writes, "le désir du male est violent et localisé, et il le laisse . . . conscient de lui-même; la femme, au contraire, subit une véritable aliénation. . . . Cette fièvre la délivre de la honte" (155). She expands this idea later in the text, again stressing the notion of alienation: "On a déjà dit qu'elle désire en se faisant objet demeurer un sujet. Plus profondément aliénée que l'homme, du fait qu'elle est désir et trouble dans son corps tout entier, elle ne demeure sujet que par l'union avec son partenaire" (162). As Moi explains, the terms "aliénée" and "aliénation" are crucial to Beauvoir's philosophical idea that posits woman as a being divided against herself; here, she is both the object of the man's purposeful sexual activity and the subject of her own sexual interest and response. Moi writes of Beauvoir casting women as "subjects painfully torn between freedom and alienation" (155), a condition that seems exacerbated or particularly visible at moments of sexual involvement.

In the translation, "aliénée" and "aliénation" read "being beside herself" (397) and "really los[ing] her mind" (391), creating the impression that a woman in the throes of sexual intercourse goes slightly mad. The translation errs on the side of literalness and dictionary meaning, erasing Beauvoir's philosophical overtones and casting women as inherently mentally unstable. Its "effect is clearly to divest [Beauvoir] of philosophy and thus to diminish her as an intellectual," as Moi points out. But Moi comments insightfully, "the sexism involved in this process has more to do with the English-language publisher's perception and marketing of Beauvoir as a popular woman writer, with all the stereotypes that implies, than with the sexism of individual translators."[22] Moi's comment does not apply only to this "aliénation" example; she is responding to the more general charge that Parshley, the translator, was deliberately sexist. I would say that his sexism was cultural, an effect of his time, and greatly tempered by his learning and his scholarly aims. Nonetheless, the effect of the mistranslations and deletions, whether unconscious or deliberate, is felt on a number of levels: the text becomes less concrete, drawing less support from the narration of actual human experiences; it loses the personal, subjective element provided by these narrations and reads like an abstract, scholarly work; through the deletion of vulgarities and colloquialisms related to sex, it sacrifices liveliness and becomes drier, more tedious, though perhaps more tasteful. Finally, the misinterpretation of key terms such as "aliénation" causes important slippages of meaning. And yet, as Yolanda Patterson has pointed out, Parshley accomplished an enormous task in translating this work; it is the reader's job to remember that *The Second Sex* is a translation, and a translation is inevitably a different text.

(De)Sexing the Sex Scenes in Beauvoir's Fiction

Beauvoir's fiction is not studded with sex scenes. Indeed, it is quite a project to locate scenes where she evokes or describes "the interaction between [sexual] desire and the body," as Moi's definition goes, rather than the interaction between desire and the intellect. In the three works I have looked at—*L'invitée* (1943; She came to stay), *Les mandarins* (1954), and *Quand prime le spirituel* (When things of the spirit come first; a collection of early texts published by Gallimard only in 1979)—sex scenes and sexual desire are present, but are often expressed elliptically or used as the material for much intellectual agonizing.

L'invitée describes the attempt by an intellectual couple to set up and live a ménage à trois of sorts with a young, sexually inexperienced woman. It traces the development of this complicated relationship to its murderous end. The charged atmosphere of constantly changing allegiances and attractions where sexual desires, uncertainties, and jealousies as well as social inhibitions clash is the stuff of much discussion between Françoise and Pierre, the older couple, and between Xavière (the younger woman) and Françoise or Pierre. Xavière's young lover, Gerbert, who is also Pierre's student/disciple, appears tangentially and becomes important only when Françoise manages to seduce him.

Sex is obviously an issue in the text, but it functions primarily as a factor in the power struggles between the characters. For Pierre, it is often the source of condescending remarks: having made a play for the sexual favors of Xavière and persuaded her to kiss him, he describes her lying in his arms "avec un air de total abandon."[23] He, of course, is in complete control. For Françoise, things are more complicated. On the one hand her virtually platonic relationship with Pierre is important to her; on the other, she finds Xavière as well as the idea of a threesome attractive. Sex with Gerbert is a passing holiday fancy that confirms her powers of sexual attraction and conveniently annoys Xavière, bringing on the close of the story. Homoerotic desire between Françoise and Xavière is evoked though never consummated; its possibility, however, places Françoise in a more vulnerable position than Pierre. In the end, the reality of the threesome turns out to be psychologically untenable, precisely because sex is hardly engaged in yet is constantly available as a cudgel in the relations between the characters. An incident that demonstrates the psychological (self) abuse this instrument can trigger occurs when Françoise, overwrought and ill, is in the hospital; Pierre recounts his evening with Xavière, concluding that "elle aime bien ma conversation, mais elle souhaite les baisers d'un beau jeune homme," upon which "Le déplaisir de Françoise s'accentua; elle aimait les baisers de Pierre. Est-ce qu'il l'en méprisait?" (213). A throwaway comment by Pierre, admittedly preceded by a blow by blow account of his evening with Xavière, quickly takes on a painful and destructive meaning for Françoise, deepening her uncertainty and suffocating any sexual élan the text might develop.

The first American edition of *She Came to Stay* is derived from the British version first published in 1949 and presumably translated by Yvonne Moyse and Roger Senhouse. It follows the source text closely, and there is little in the way of translation effects in its rendering of the understated sex scenes.[24] At times, a certain impatience with Beauvoir's reticence becomes evident in the translation, as does a desire to provoke the reader by concretizing the activities being described. Thus, Pierre's comments about Xavière's "air de total abandon" is translated as "she lay in my arms in a state of complete surrender" (299). These two versions conjure up two different situations—in the French, Pierre knows there are histrionics involved in Xavière's "air of total abandon"; in the English, Pierre believes he has conquered her—her state (not air) is one of complete surrender. Meanwhile it is clear that they have spent the evening only "necking," as the translation of "embrasser" reads, and there has been no consummation. The English version may thus render somewhat more believable Pierre's aggressive recriminations when he confronts Xavière about her relations with Gerbert (358; 328). Another example of the English concretizing the allusive French occurs when Pierre and Françoise speculate on Gerbert's possible interest in Xavière. Françoise comes to the conclusion "je suis sûre que Gerbert ne lui fait pas la cour" (213). The English version renders this as "I'm sure Gerbert isn't making love to her" (195), significantly confusing the issue because the actual lovemaking occurs much later in the text.

In regard to Françoise and Xavière's relationship, the homoerotic interest also remains understated and vague in French: Françoise "sentait contre sa poitrine les beaux seins tièdes de Xavière, elle respirait son haleine charmante; était-ce du désir? Mais que désirait-elle?" (271). These questions are never answered clearly but are touched on in several ways, notably one page earlier when the two women go to a dance hall together. Xavière holds Françoise's arm because "elle ne détestait pas quand elles entraient dans un endroit, qu'on les prît pour un couple" (270). The English translation of this line reads "she did not dislike having people take them for Lesbians when they entered a public place" (246). Although the English version maintains the double negative of "elle ne détestait pas," thus also maintaining the careful approach to the subject, it is impatient, less euphemistic, in its rendering of "un couple" as "Lesbians." It pushes the text along, stating more precisely what Françoise spends considerable time agonizing over. Similarly, when Elisabeth, Pierre's sister, tries to shake off the memory of her physical passion for Claude, a former lover, by proclaiming "on ne m'a pas comme ça . . . je ne suis pas une femelle" (75), she implies that she can control her physical reactions to his embrace. The English substantially overstates this assertion: it reads "I'm not to be had like that . . . I'm not a bitch." Not only is the overstatement striking—a "femelle" is not a "bitch"—but the tone changes dramatically. "Bitch" in English generally refers to a bad-tempered, unpredictable, nagging woman, not a sexually responsive female. Moreover, the animalistic and/or biologistic connotations of "femelle" that are important to Beauvoir's theories about women's socially determined sexual inhibitions are replaced by a derogatory masculinist interpretation.

In *Quand prime le spirituel* (1979), translated in 1982 by Patrick O'Brian as *When Things of the Spirit Come First,* the situation is similar. Few sex scenes, few references to sexuality, much earnest demonstration of women's psychological and emotional initiation to their lot in life. The one scene of heterosexual intercourse on Marcelle and Denis's wedding night occurs early in the first story. While large parts of the translation follow Beauvoir's text closely, there is some tendency to use expressions that again foreground male sexual imagery—"les mains impérieuses [de Denis]" (28) becomes "masterful hands" (32), for example, and terms describing Marcelle's physical rush take on a curiously penile aspect: "so piercing a pleasure" (32) for "une jouissance si aigue" (29), "a jet of passion" (33) for "un transport passionné" (30), and "a shame whose stab was sweeter than the sweetest caress" (32) for "une honte dont la brûlure était plus douce que la plus douce des caresses" (28). On the whole, however, the translation reads as blandly as the French source text. For instance, the abortive lesbian sex scene in *Quand prime le spirituel* (240) is rendered in a tone similar to Beauvoir's French. It is experienced and described by Marguerite, Marcelle's younger sister, who is staying overnight with Marie-Ange: "elle [Marie-Ange] caressait ma poitrine" (241), she reports, choosing the euphemistic "poitrine" (chest/bust) over "seins" (breasts). The English reads "she fondled my bosom" (206), using a curiously Victorian term, doubtless an appropriate counterpart for the French euphemism.

The story is somewhat different in *Les mandarins.* Two graphic sex scenes occur early in the book, helping to situate the characters in relation to each other and to themselves; a love affair in Chicago receives some attention; and Nadine, the teenage daughter, keeps up a constant patter of sexual innuendo and information. The sex scenes involve Paule and Henri, a couple with a tenuous ten-year history who are on the verge of a breakup that Paule tries to stall with sexual histrionics (25); Anne, the psychiatrist, who agrees to have sex with Scriassine, a Russian "emigré" and political activist, partly in order to compete with her daughter Nadine's hyperactive sex life (72); and Anne and Lewis Brogan, who actually make passionate love (327). While these encounters are described more graphically than similar scenes in *L'invitée,* they are a miniscule part of the book, which is much more concerned with postwar politics and the positions held by French intellectuals. The fact that two graphic sex scenes occur within the first hundred pages of the five-hundred-page tome probably is one reason why it made it onto the list of books banned by the Catholic Church shortly after its publication in French.

The American translation considerably understates the sexual content of the cynical and passionless encounters early in the book as well as the passionate love scenes between Anne and Brogan. Censorship for cultural reasons is doubtless involved, as Barbara Klaw has pointed out. Citing Beauvoir's memoirs, Klaw refers to a talk Beauvoir recorded with the American publisher in which he said he "was happy with the translation of *Les mandarins* but apologized for having to cut some lines here and there: 'in our country, one can talk about sexuality in a book,' he explained to me, 'not about perversion.'"[25] It is interesting, however, that while actual descriptions of sex are toned down, and all references to oral sex are cut out of the translation, the imagery around the event is often heightened. For instance, in the course of Henri's dutiful lovemaking with Paule, he thinks "en elle il faisait rouge comme dans le studio trop rouge" (26). The English reads, "inside her it was red, a deep dark red as in the too-red living room" (30). The "deep dark red" is a melodramatic addition to the text, perhaps compensating for more lurid details that were censored for a mid-1950s American reading public. Similarly, in the Anne-Scriassine love scene, oral sex is censored (74; 83) but the baroque description of Anne's psychological response to this event is heightened: "j'allais échouer dans l'oubli, dans la nuit" (73) becomes "about to be stranded in oblivion, in the blackness of night" (81). Here, the added "blackness" of the night deepens the color of an otherwise rather pallid adventure.

It is inevitable that translation should change the way a text reads, yet it is odd that translations of Beauvoir often render the woman characters' roles or language slightly more vulgar. The love scene between Paule and Henri, for instance, emphasizes the routine aspects of their lovemaking: "il embrassa la bouche brûlante qui s'ouvrit sous la sienne selon la routine ordinaire" (25). The fact that the reference to this "routine ordinaire" is placed at the end of the French sentence increases its visibility and importance. In English, the focus is on Paule's demands rather than on the tired aspects of their lovemaking: "he kissed her burning mouth which, as always, opened greedily at the touch of his lips" (29). The adverb "greedily" clearly has been added to the text, a good example of a translation effect that imports the traditional topos of women's sexual insatiability and ignores the source text perspective. Later in the book, when Anne debates which man she might contact for companionship during her remaining week in the United States, she knows she has sex on her mind. Perplexed at her motivation, she says, "je me suis considérée avec scandale: je n'ai pas eu Philippe, alors je vais me jeter dans les bras de Brogan! Qu'est-ce que ces moeurs de femelle en chaleur?" (310). Like Elisabeth in *L'invitée,* she compares her interest in sex to that of a mammal in heat, but does not desist. The translation reads, "I looked inside myself and felt ashamed: I couldn't have Philip, so I was going to throw myself into Brogan's arms. What about those morals of a bitch in heat?" (332). Not only does this version turn the "scandale" into "shame," thus introducing a moralistic note not evident in the French, it again renders "femelle" as "bitch." The terminology is coarser, and the rhetoric more judgmental. Interestingly, in counterpoint, male sexuality is treated rather differently. In the scene between Paule and Henri, Henri tries to ignore Paule's histrionics, yet they are so disconcerting that "il lui semblait violer une morte ou une folle, et il n'arrivait pas à se délivrer de son plaisir" (26). Henri is so put off he is physically unable to come to a climax. In the translation, Henri has no such trouble: "It seemed to him as if he were raping a dead woman, or a lunatic, and yet he could not keep himself from enjoying it" (30). This is an odd reading, especially given the context, which makes it clear that Henri is complying with Paule for old times' sake, because he feels sorry, and he wants to get it over with as soon as possible. There is no enjoyment. Does the translation tell us something about 1950s male culture in the United States? Or is it an innocent mistranslation?

It is interesting to compare and analyze translations; in the work of comparing we see the many problems raised by cultural and linguistic transfer. However, to identify these problems is in no way to solve them. In the case of Beauvoir translations into English, and more specifically, the translation of sexual terms and references, issues of cultural sensitivity are encumbered by issues of gender stereotyping and cliché, perhaps made more severe by the fact that Beauvoir's translators were almost all men.[26]

What conclusions can be drawn, then, beyond the obvious one that a translation produces a different text? And how much of an impact can be assigned to the translation effects that I have identified? Does a translation that injects pleasure into an act clearly presented as unpleasurable reveal a motivation on the part of the translator? Or is it a mistake that anyone translating a text of more than five hundred pages could make? If the mistranslation of Henri's experience with Paule is innocent, it stands in contrast to other aspects of these translations, in particular those dealing with women's sexuality. The vulgarization of these aspects of the texts—the issue of the "douche" in *The Woman Destroyed,* the translations of "femelle" as "bitch" in *The Mandarins* and *She Came to Stay*—the systematic masculinization of sexual terms, and the use of censorship or euphemisms in English certainly indicate that writing and rewriting that explores or thematizes women's sexuality comes up against ingrained cultural beliefs. On the other hand, the tendency in English to get to the point and to concretize French euphemisms may contradict such an assertion. It is likely that the era in which the translations were completed affects how they read: the 1950s American translations by Friedman and Parshley are more likely to use euphemisms and to censor passages that might be viewed as perverted or vulgar, while a text such as *The Woman Destroyed,* produced in the Britain of 1969, uses more sexually provocative, though often misogynist or sexist, language.

This conclusion reflects my consternation at the changes I found in the English rewrites of Beauvoir. It will perhaps motivate careful reconsideration of other aspects of Beauvoir's work in English.

Notes

1. Lotbinière-Harwood, *Re-belle et infidèle,* 64–65.

2. Simon, *Gender in Translation,* 90.

3. Simons, "The Silencing of Simone de Beauvoir"; Cordero, "Simone de Beauvoir Twice Removed"; Moi, *Simone de Beauvoir;* Klaw, "Sexuality in Simone de Beauvoir's *Les mandarins*"; Lotbinière-Harwood, *Re-belle et infidèle;* Simon, *Gender in Translation;* Flotow, *Translation and Gender.*

4. Keefe, "Another Silencing of Beauvoir?"

5. Ibid., 20.

6. Bassnett and Lefevere, *Translation, History, and Culture;* Venuti, *Rethinking Translation;* Hermans, *The Manipulation of Literature.*

7. Moi, *Simone de Beauvoir,* 156.

8. Pilardi, "Feminists Read *The Second Sex.*"

9. Canadian writers and translators have discussed this issue at some length due to the intensive translation work that was triggered by feminist "writing the body" from Quebec. Gail Scott (1989) surmises that some of the difficulties in transferring erotic or sexualized material from French to English may stem from the difference in consciousness and conscience—the French Catholic writer can work with the notion of absolution in the confessional in the back of her mind while the more puritanical and rigid Anglo-Protestant has no such recourse. Other debates over these issues have been aired in a 1981 issue of *Yale French Studies,* addressed in terms of a critical problematic in collections such as *The Future of Difference,* ed. H. Eisenstein and A. Jardine (New Brunswick, NJ: Rutgers Univ. Press, 1983), analyzed subsequently by Bina Freiwald in "The Problem of Trans-lation: Reading French Feminism" in *Traduction Terminologie Redaction* 4.2 (1991): 55–68, and discussed at some length by Sherry Simon, *Gender in Translation,* 86–110.

10. Lotbinière-Harwood, *Re-belle et infidèle;* Flotow, *Translation and Gender.*

11. Beauvoir, *La femme rompue,* 88. Further references to this novel, as well as to the translation (*The Woman Destroyed*), will be given in the text. Since my point is to offer critical analysis of how Beauvoir has been translated, I will not automatically cite the standard published English translation after each French citation.

12. Beauvoir, *Les mandarins,* 350. Further references to this novel and its English translation will be given in the text.

13. Klaw, "Sexuality in Simone de Beauvoir's *Les mandarins,*" 216, note 8.

14. Simons, "The Silencing of Simone de Beauvoir."

15. Beauvoir, *The Second Sex,* x.

16. Patterson, "Who Was This H. M. Parshley?"

17. Moi repeatedly comments on Beauvoir's simplistic and sanguine view of male sexuality; see *Simone de Beauvoir,* 148ff.

18. A notice on the frontispiece of the English translation, *Frigidity in Woman in Relation to Her Love Life* (New York: Boni and Liveright, 1926), reads, "The sale of this

book is strictly limited to members of the medical profession, Psychoanalysts, Scholars and such adults who may have a definite position in the field of Psychological or Social Research." It may give some indication of an attitude still prevalent in 1950s America that motivated some of Parshley's abridgements.

19. Beauvoir, *Le deuxième sexe,* 142. Further references to this and to Parshley's translation will be given in the text.

20. Feminist analyses of English grammar, for example in Mary Daly's *Gyn/Ecology* (Boston: Beacon Press, 1976), have repeatedly pointed out the use of the passive voice to hide the agent of a particular action. Here the female agent is eliminated.

21. Moi, *Simone de Beauvoir,* 282, note 33.

22. Ibid., 281, note 19.

23. Beauvoir, *L'invitée,* 327. Further references to this and to the translation will be given in the text. In cases where two references are given together, the first refers to the French edition and the second to the English translation.

24. Although the first American edition clearly follows the British version closely, it diverges occasionally. For example, it understates the sexual activity between Gerbert and Xavière that the voyeuristic Pierre and Françoise comment on: In the American version, the two are suspected of "necking"; in the British version, they are "making love." Yet the American version overstates such activity in other places, notably in the translation of "faire la cour": the British version reads, "I'm sure Gerbert isn't making up to her"; the American says, "I'm sure Gerbert isn't making love to her." Finally, the American version is also more aggressive about Françoise's lesbian fantasies: "she did not dislike having people take them for Lesbians." The British version reads, "She did not dislike having people take them for a couple." Overall, it seems that the American version is more outspoken and direct; only the use of the term "necking" would contradict this. But both English-language texts are far less ambiguous and careful than the French.

25. Quoted in Klaw, "Sexuality in Simone de Beauvoir's *Les mandarins,*" 197.

26. Such a statement is obviously a controversial generalization; however, several instances in Canadian translation practice and criticism have shown how male translators simply do not see or do not understand certain slight differences that are important to the women writers they translate, or for the women characters. The most famous example is F. R. Scott's translation of Anne Hébert's *Le tombeau des rois.* Hébert had to point out to Scott that his translation of "En quel songe / Cette enfant fut-elle liée par la cheville / Pareille à une esclave fascinée?" as "In what dream / Was this child tied by the ankle / Like a fascinated slave?" ignored the fact that "this child" was a girl.

2

Variations on Triangular Relationships

SERGE JULIENNE-CAFFIÉ

IN 1929, when they were twenty-four and twenty years old, respectively, Jean-Paul Sartre and Simone de Beauvoir made a pact of mutual commitment giving their "necessary" relationship priority but setting one another free to taste "contingent" love affairs in "all transparency," meaning that they would talk to each other openly about them.

Until Beauvoir met Nelson Algren in 1947 during her first trip to the United States, it appears that this freedom was largely exercised by Sartre. The passing fancies that Beauvoir evokes in *L'invitée* (1943; She came to stay) and *Les mandarins* (1954; The mandarins) under the names of Gerbert or Scriassine, which refer to brief flings with Jacques-Laurent Bost and Arthur Koestler, can be deemed insignificant in Beauvoir's life compared to Algren and, later, Claude Lanzmann.

This is not to say that Beauvoir was completely faithful to Sartre. During the ten years from 1934 to the end of World War II, when Beauvoir decided to use the freedom granted her by the pact, she and Sartre participated in relationships involving other women. Although these relationships were not publicly discussed by the two at the time, evidence of triadic emotional relationships appears in their correspondence and in Beauvoir's novel *L'invitée*.

Recently, *A Disgraceful Affair* has offered for the first time a more detailed look at one of these relationships through the eyes of the third party, Bianca Lamblin, who was a friend of Sartre and Beauvoir's in the years 1937–40. Hers is a significant testimony of the triadic affair, honest in tone and sharpened by the suffering and rejection she experienced. It can be read not only as a commentary on a difficult and complex relationship seen through the eyes of a younger woman, but as one that provokes commentary on the personal history of Sartre and Beauvoir as well as on psychoanalysis, power, pedagogy, politics, and, of course, love. We are, in her case, at the top of a watchtower. We get the perspective of the third person that is missing in the other affairs, and a priceless connection to time, since this third person covers both the present (the 1980s) and the past of her friends. Above all, we see the deep impact on her entire life of that experience, overwhelming in all respects.

In this chapter I will examine the relationship with Bianca Lamblin in the context of others, especially the initial threesome shaped by Beauvoir and Sartre with Olga Kosakiewicz in Rouen from 1934 to 1937, to try to estimate the impact on Beauvoir's life of these triangular relationships—all curiously framed between 1934 and 1945. I want to restore the real life experience of the bold structure set in motion by Sartre and Beauvoir, with its emotions, its pleasures, and its dangers obviously at their peak with Bianca. My goal is to understand the motives, then the reservations, and finally the afterthoughts of all participants.

In 1945, aware that their past relationship might be mentioned by either Sartre or Beauvoir in their works, Bianca Lamblin made them promise that her name would never be used. Sartre and Beauvoir kept their word. After Sartre's death, Beauvoir refers to Lamblin by the pseudonym "Louise Védrine" in the 1983 publication of Sartre's correspondence, *Lettres au Castor et à quelques autres* (Witness to my life). When, after Beauvoir's death in 1986, Sylvie Le Bon began publishing the letters from Beauvoir to Sartre and her *Journal de guerre* (War diary) in 1990, she used the same pseudonym. It was not until the publication of Beauvoir's biography by Deirdre Bair in 1990 that the identity of Louise Védrine was revealed as Bianca Lamblin (her married name) or Bianca Bienenfeld (her unmarried name).

Lamblin makes it clear that she felt twice betrayed by Beauvoir: first, in the past, by what Beauvoir wrote about her in letters to Sartre in 1940; when the letters were published fifty years later it seemed to Lamblin that she had been manipulated by both Sartre and Beauvoir. She also felt betrayed by the attention Beauvoir paid to her from the time of their reunion in a quiet friendship from 1945 to Beauvoir's death in 1986: she suggests that it was nothing more than an attempt to appease her.

It was in order to be the subject of her own history, in which she recognizes herself as the reverse image of Simone de Beauvoir, that Lamblin presented the old relationship to the public in 1993 under the title *Mémoires d'une jeune fille dérangée* (A disgraceful affair),[1] in contrast to the title of the first volume of Beauvoir's memoirs, *Mémoires d'une jeune fille rangée* (1958; Memoirs of a dutiful daughter). The French title of Lamblin's text confirms the status of the relationship for her today: we are confronted by a filial link ("fille") now disavowed, "dérangée" meaning in French either "disgraced" or "disturbed," according to the context. More than forty years after their affair, it was Lamblin's turn to drop Beauvoir.

Let me review the story once again.

Lamblin was a student of Beauvoir's in 1937–38 in a Paris philosophy class. She was struck by Beauvoir's "obvious beauty," but even more relevant for her was Beauvoir's "brilliant, piercing, bold intelligence."[2] Beauvoir was the model who guided the young schoolgirl's intellectual development. Even before obtaining her high school diploma, Lamblin knew that she "wanted to get a degree in philosophy and teach, just like her [Beauvoir]."[3]

The love between the older and younger woman began during the summer of 1938 on the occasion of a trip to the Morvan. It would not be until the winter of 1939 that Sartre would come between them. Sartre, it would seem from Lamblin's reaction to him, was neither an accomplished nor especially concerned or sensitive lover. The affair with Sartre and Beauvoir, which ended abruptly in 1940 as Germany was invading, brought the young woman considerable pain. Being Jewish and fearing for her life at the hands of the Germans, Lamblin could not comprehend how her two friends could abandon her. Her suffering was compounded by their indifference to her plight, and evidently they did not try to contact her during the war. Although she recovered, thanks to the patience and tenderness of her future husband, Bernard Lamblin, whom she met at this time, the wound was reopened years later when the Sartre-Beauvoir letters were published in the 1980s and her name was revealed by Deirdre Bair in her biography of Beauvoir in 1990.

In September 1938, Beauvoir went to Quimper, in Brittany, to see her young lover Bianca. In October, when Bianca met Beauvoir again in Paris, she realized that something had changed without knowing what. In February 1940, Sartre sent her a letter announcing his breakup with her, an intention that, on her request, he confirmed to her in person while he was on leave in Paris. Bewildered, Lamblin confided in Beauvoir and took refuge more than ever in her philosophical studies at the Sorbonne. She saw the German Occupation in June as "the end of the world," at which time she left Paris in a car with her father and Beauvoir. Lamblin and Beauvoir parted company in Laval and would not be reunited until August in Paris.

In September 1940, Beauvoir told Lamblin of her affair with Jacques-Laurent Bost. Lamblin was "desperate beyond words, because my attachment to [Beauvoir] had been much deeper than my feelings towards Sartre."[4] She felt like a "drowning person," who clings to a "log" and is able to survive only "miraculously." As she said, "I clung instinctively to life and managed not to hit rock bottom."[5] Her trauma and sense of loss were deepened by the military defeat of France and all its frightening implications for French Jews. She took her abandonment by Sartre and Beauvoir as evidence of their insensitivity and selfishness.

Her distress was exacerbated by the fact that, as she wrote, "From the end of 1940 until the Liberation I remained completely cut off from them. They never worried about my fate or tried to get news of me."[6] Lamblin has to be thanked for mentioning the importance of this date. For history as for individuals, for her as for her friends and the following generations, the year 1940 marked the beginning of disaster. It was, to quote the only profound words ever uttered by Tixier-Vignancour, "a terrible year, which is not yet over."[7]

Bianca was able to escape the persecution of the Vichy government because of her marriage to Bernard Lamblin: she took her husband's name, which replaced her obviously Jewish unmarried name. With him, she participated in the French Resistance efforts and was part of the insurrection in the Vercors mountains. She did not come back to Paris to return to her philosophical studies until October 1945. All her maternal family were sent to concentration camps, among them her grandmother and her aunt Cécile, the mother of the future writer Georges Perec. In her account of these events and the pain at losing Sartre and Beauvoir, Lamblin mixes her first reaction to the events with her later reaction, when the wound was reopened as she read the published correspondence between Sartre and Beauvoir. The account has a dramatic intensity. Her words reveal the still close proximity between past and present in the fragile zone of the psyche where the wounds, losses, and blows to self-esteem have not yet healed.

Lamblin believes that her meeting with Sartre was initiated by Beauvoir to create another vicarious link with him. During the months between March 1939 and February 1940, the Beauvoir-Sartre-Lamblin triangle seems to repeat the pattern of the first triangle involving another young woman, Olga Kosakiewicz, although perhaps not with the same intensity described by Beauvoir in *L'invitée.* As proof of the relationship, Lamblin refers to several kinds of evidence. First, there were Sartre's letters in which he assures her of the triangle's future: "There is one thing I do know well, in any case, that *our* future is *your* future; there is no difference—and that Beaver [Beauvoir's nickname] lives in a world in which you are everywhere and always present."[8] In another letter he says, "Do you understand, my love, even if there was a war, there would be an *afterward,* for the three of us."[9] She also cites the fact that Sartre wrote daily letters to Beauvoir and two to three letters a week to her. She also mentions that she and Beauvoir exchanged letters written to them by Sartre.

Beauvoir, however, did not have the same view. In a conversation with Deirdre Bair, she said that the triangle was nothing more than the product of Lamblin's imagination. Lamblin evokes Beauvoir's jealousy when she quotes the revealing excerpt from Beauvoir's *Journal de guerre:* "Sartre would like to break with Védrine gently. I don't think he can, but I'm done worrying and feeling bitter for nothing. I'm not afraid of anything. I'm tangled up with Sartre once again, alone with him as in the days of Le Havre or Rouen before Kos. . . . So I'm happy."[10]

Lamblin also refers to a passage in a letter from Beauvoir to Sartre in which Beauvoir communicates her understanding that Lamblin was not an equal member of the triangle. Describing her anger at Lamblin for wanting to spend time with Sartre during his six-day army leave, Beauvoir wrote to Sartre about Lamblin: "le sang m'est monté au visage et je lui ai dit que je ne comprenais pas comment elle envisageait nos rapports, qu'elle avait l'air de prendre le trio pour une exacte division tripartite et que ça m'étonnait. . . . J'ai dit qu'elle se trompait, que ça ne serait pas comme ça" [flushing with anger, I told her I couldn't understand how she envisaged our relations; that she seemed to see the threesome as an exact tripartite division, which astonished me. . . . I said she was mistaken—that things wouldn't be like that].[11] In another part of this same letter, Beauvoir reveals to Sartre that Lamblin had not always assumed this equality; initially, she had seen them as a triangle with the base consisting of Beauvoir and Sartre and herself on "the projecting point," and not as "something perfectly symmetrical."[12]

In her book, Lamblin observes that she did not have precise memories of the arguments with Beauvoir over Sartre. She admits, however, that "it seems likely to me that my demands had increased and I had lost sight of what was real or possible." She recognizes that she had "forgotten Beauvoir's ferocious will to keep Sartre's 'necessary' love for herself" and was aware "of her absolute power over him."[13] Be that as it may, on 17 December 1939 Beauvoir wrote to Sartre urging him to back away from the relationship so as to dampen what to her seemed to be Lamblin's growing ardor. As Beauvoir puts it, "quand elle vous reverra elle sera reprise à plein, surtout avec la sexualité ça ira vite—si vous voulez arrêter l'histoire, c'est peut-être possible sans *désastre* mais non sans fracas" [when she sees you again, she'll be utterly smitten again. Especially with sexuality involved, that won't take long. If you want to stop the affair, that may be possible without a *disaster*—but not without a fuss]. Beauvoir counsels "beaucoup de dureté" [a lot of toughness]. "Diminuer lentement la passion des lettres, faire un revoir froid" [diminish the passion in your letters, say a cool "farewell"], she writes to Sartre.[14] At the end of December, Beauvoir comments on a letter from Lamblin sent to her by Sartre: "L'extrait de lettre de Védrine ne me semble pas si tiède, ni si vide—elle vous aime sûrement à plein, du moins par instants. . . . Je regrette de vous avoir tant dégoûté d'elle mais je le suis assez moi-même" [The extract from Bienenfeld's letter doesn't strike me as all that lukewarm, or all that empty. She certainly loves you with all her heart—at least intermittently. . . . I'm sorry to have put you off her so much, but that's pretty well how I feel myself].[15]

Beauvoir's letters of February 1940 refer to her own and Lamblin's reaction to the breakup. First, she writes about how Lamblin looked: "Il faut dire qu'elle était émouvante, toute contenue, grave, appliquée et silencieuse, me souriant de temps en temps et de temps en temps retenant ses larmes—elle était belle d'ailleurs hier. Ça m'a fait vache de penser au coup qui allait lui tomber sur la tête" [It must be said she was moving: all restrained, serious, attentive and silent, smiling at me every so often—and every so often restraining her tears. What's more she was beautiful yesterday. It struck me as rotten, thinking of the blow that was about to fall on her head].[16] Then, on 27 February, she writes of Lamblin's reaction to the breakup:

> Elle a lu vos lettres, elle s'est tenue avec un cran formidable, mais la colère la transfigurait—et vraiment je ne sais ce que vous aviez dans la tête, mais cette lettre avec ses encouragements moraux et ses protestations d'estime était inacceptable. . . . Védrine l'a senti ainsi et en a déchiré à belles dents chaque phrase—et elle était humiliée que vous n'ayez même pas pris le soin de lui expliquer correctement les choses. Humiliée à l'écoeurement par les lettres passionnées que vous lui écriviez quinze jours plus tôt—ça m'a été sinistrement désagréable.
>
> [She read your letters, she restrained herself with astounding guts—but she was transfigured by anger. And honestly, I don't know what got into your head. That letter, with its moral exhortations and its protestations of esteem, was quite unacceptable. . . . Bienenfeld felt it that way, and tore every sentence apart with gusto. And she was humiliated that you didn't even take the trouble to explain things to her properly. Humiliated and disgusted by the passionate letters you were writing to her only a fortnight earlier. I found it desperately unpleasant.][17]

Why such duplicity from Beauvoir, such suggestibility in Sartre? Why so much casualness on both sides? Why such deep despair in Lamblin? The answers to these questions can only be shallow and uncertain without full knowledge of the first triangle initiated by Sartre and Beauvoir to breathe air into their relationship and, paradoxically, to cement more firmly their mutual bond.

After having been separated for two years—from 1932 to 1934 Sartre was in Le Havre and Beauvoir in Marseilles—in October 1934 they found themselves for the first time since making their pact extremely close, geographically speaking, separated only by the mouth of the Seine River. Their adolescence was fading away, and they went on to their work as high school teachers of philosophy, work that Sartre hated but that captivated Beauvoir. Without children or social burdens, without any political purpose as of yet, their literary works ahead of them, they were relatively inexperienced in life, lacking the raw knowledge of reality that life brought to members of the working class or lawyers or wage earners. They did not question the privilege of scholars to relay knowledge from age to age without being troubled by the roar of the world.

Thinking back to that time of their lives almost thirty years later, Beauvoir confesses their remoteness in those days: "Cela nous faisait rire quand, dans leurs écrits et leurs propos, Jean Wahl ou Aron parlaient d'aller 'vers le concret'" [It made us laugh when Jean Wahl or Raymond Aron used to speak, in their writing or conversation, about "getting down to brass tacks"].[18] She refers to herself and Sartre as middle-class intellectuals whose life was characterized by its "dé-réalité" [lack of reality]. According to her,

> Nous avions un métier que nous exercions correctement mais il ne nous arrachait pas à l'univers des mots. Intellectuellement, nous étions sincères et appliqués; comme Sartre me l'a dit un jour, nous avions *un sens réel de la vérité* . . . ; mais cela n'impliquait aucunement que nous ayons *un sens vrai de la réalité.*
>
> [We had a profession, which we pursued in the correct manner, but which did not detach us from our own verbal universe. On an intellectual plane we were both honest and conscientious; as Sartre said to me one day, we had a genuine sense of the truth . . . ; though this was a step in the right direction, it did not in any way imply that we possessed *a true sense of reality.*][19]

Closed off from history, but open to happiness: nothing describes better Beauvoir's state of mind regarding her relationship with Sartre at that time than what she later wrote in 1939 confirming the permanence of her deep feelings toward Sartre as early as the days in Rouen: "I'm not afraid of anything. I am tangled up with Sartre once again, alone with him as in the days of Le Havre and Rouen before Kos. . . . So I'm happy."

One can wonder whether Sartre felt anguish in such close intimacy. In the fall of 1933, he accepted a position in Berlin to replace Raymond Aron, where he began to read Husserl's philosophy. On returning to Normandy, perhaps he felt the weight of its provincial boredom more profoundly. Beauvoir was locked in a love relationship with her student Olga Kosakiewicz, with whom Sartre would in turn fall in love. Sartre's relationship with Kosakiewicz was especially intense during the period from March 1935 to March 1937. In this case the triangle initiated by Sartre's feelings can be seen as a resistance to the provincial heaviness of the traditional family, especially stifling in Rouen, in a Normandy that, in those times, had remained almost unchanged since Maupassant or Barbey d'Aurevilly. The maturation of Sartre's thought during this time—seen in his new interest for Flaubert and no doubt stimulated by his study of Husserl's phenomenology—may have been another reaction to his deep-rooted hostility to the provincial environment. Although the links Sartre and Beauvoir formed with Kosakiewicz can be seen as a defense against the oppression they felt, they also can be seen as creating family ties of their own, obviously nontraditional ones, but with equivalent closeness and the same closure to the external world.

Like a family, a trio relationship shelters a collection of aspirations and desires, in this case a stubborn will to survive in accordance with its own rules despite all opposition and in resistance to the middle-class mentality from which the three had suffered. Beauvoir would later write about this mentality at the end of *Mémoires d'une jeune fille rangée,* the first volume of her memoirs, when she evokes the death of her friend Zaza Mabille: "Ensemble nous avions lutté contre le destin fangeux qui nous guettait et j'ai pensé longtemps que j'avais payé ma liberté de sa mort" [We had fought together against the revolting fate that had lain ahead of us, and for a long time I believed that I had paid for my own freedom with her death].[20] It was in that space of time from 1930 to 1934—that is to say, the passage from Marseilles, where she got her first teaching job, to Rouen, where she got the second one—that would sharpen her resolution never to let the middle-class mentality permeate her being. It is not an overstatement to say that the aversion it inspired in Sartre and Beauvoir would be the combustible center of their thought, especially in the political orientation to which they later turned. In these years, Beauvoir systematically cut herself off from the deeply rooted values of her original class, including social graces, education, taste, and down-to-earth common sense. Her first act upon arriving in Rouen, Deirdre Bair observes, was to settle in a mean room of the La Rochefoucauld Hotel, which had just one filthy bathroom that she used as little as possible. Many years later, Sylvie Le Bon, in spite of her desire to follow in Beauvoir's footsteps, would not be able to live in it. Today, at a time when French society has changed more in thirty years than during the previous centuries, especially in the middle class, it may be difficult, especially for a foreigner, to understand Beauvoir's rejection. When the trio takes refuge in its bubble, it may seem childish if the revolt that inhabits it is not perceived. The trio forms one body against what it rejects and in doing so experiences its own solidarity.

Olga Kosakiewicz, like Bianca Lamblin, was intelligent, vivacious, independent, and experiencing difficulties with her family, Russian in her case. There was also a slight gap between the two women's origins and the French culture that made them attractive. Their point of view was new and provocative, and their freshness was their trump card. When, in his *Carnets de guerre* (The war diaries of Jean-Paul Sartre), Sartre writes, "And then we fell, the Beaver and I, beneath the intoxicating spell of that naked, instant consciousness, which seemed only to feel, with violence and purity. I placed her so high then that, for the first time in my life, I felt myself humble and disarmed before someone, felt that I wanted to learn,"[21] he unveils the main appeal of the third person, which is the reverse of the couple, the pure emotion. The rare flower requires attention and care, it questions and wonders, and the object of such an interest does not want to surrender without being convinced. The talks, conversations, explanations are endless. Even if the will of the "royal couple," as Bost calls them, is in the air, the threesome wants to act as a democratic cell. But it no more belongs to nature than does democracy: both postulate reason, discussion, dialogue, and consensus, but these concepts are crossed by heavy pressures: the weight of the complicity of the couple. "Quite honestly, I did not witness everything that went on with them," said Colette Audry, "but I saw enough to know that it was an awful experience for Olga. They made her the invited one, the third party in their relationship, and she had to spend most of her time defending herself. The major complicity was between them, and they required that she bend to their wishes. The poor girl was too young to know how to defend herself really."[22] She could not withstand the power her guardians had over her. They made her feel as if life was no longer a dirty trick, but an elating adventure in which she did not have to look endlessly and alone for the answers: these flowed from the eloquent tongues of the people in whom she had the utmost confidence. On the other hand, if she did not fit in with the expectations of her protectors, she was smothered by the weight of their cohesion. Colette Audry observes:

> One more thing I must stress: one must not forget that her [Beauvoir's] influence on him was just as great as his on her; that a boy like Sartre (because he *was* just a boy then) who had such analytic power, both destructive and polemical, within himself was all the same taken by this girl—devoted, enraptured, tied, bound to her; that he, and I know it was he, insisted not only on establishing, but then also keeping her in, this famous contract with him. Theirs was a new kind of relationship, and I had never seen anything like it. I cannot describe what it was like to be present when those two were together. It was so intense that sometimes it made others who saw it sad not to have it.[23]

Olivier Todd remembers his first meeting with Simone de Beauvoir in these terms:

> [She] appeared decidedly more distant or reserved than Sartre during this first meeting, but I was struck by their matchless complicity. They seemed to think simultaneously even when they seemed to be mistaken. They were like some odd relay runners of ideas who did not need to pass the baton to continue the relay. They got in step, and followed one another in a way I have never seen any other couple in the world do. Those Siamese twins could be a little bit frightening. . . . Simone de Beauvoir was even able to finish Sartre's sentences and vice versa. There was even a kind

> of mimetism in their rasping voices. Sartre was more adventurous than she in his judgments. He almost always ended up dragging along the Beaver. She often kept silent in his presence, for he had a tendency to monopolize the conversation, with machismo. Why bother participating, in any case, since she recognized her own voice in his? Impressive. How touching was their way of addressing each other by "vous" in public right up until Sartre's death.[24]

Bianca Lamblin records the same perception on her side:

> At the beginning of my friendship with Simone de Beauvoir, I knew Sartre only from what she told me; I saw him through her eyes. But I was well aware that I did not know the most important thing, that is, how they influenced each other. Later, after I had met Sartre, I noticed that a like-mindedness strengthened their attachment, despite their very different natures. Since their beliefs about everyday life and their philosophical ideas matched, it was difficult to make a thorough analysis of their differences. They seemed to be a stone slab with two faces, a sort of Janus figure.[25]

As for Beauvoir herself, she speaks of the "twin sign on our foreheads." When she uses this phrase, she does not suspect how far it goes psychologically speaking, not because it evokes some kind of biological similarity, but because, as Ricardo Ainslie puts it, "Twinship is part of the psychological reality governing the twin's life, and thus, over time, it becomes part of the twin's personality organization."[26] Moreover, in my view, the concept of twinship is the only one allowing us to understand both incest and homosexuality—that is to say, the inclination of the same for the same—and simultaneously, the climate of tranquil amorality that bathes the trio relationship. "The commitment to tell each other everything," as Deirdre Bair notes, "which leads to an intensification of feelings and emotions," or as Bianca Lamblin suggests, "a certain contagion of feelings," should not be viewed as a perverted element of the dual relationship but as its kernel and emotional source: the need of the twin to share the experience of the other in the most intimate way, a way that intensified through Lacan's famous mirror stage.

We see clearly what a couple such as Beauvoir and Sartre, molded for five years by such a pact, gained from the experience: they were sheltered from the world around them, but also from maturity. They outsmarted the trap of the two-partner relationship by extending it to another one in order to get more flexibility for each of them and surely also to challenge the durability of their own link. In the process, the two subverted the student/professor relationship. Thus, in order to constitute a common field of experience, the third party was asked to lend herself to the voice of both of them. Both with Olga and Bianca, Sartre, who is the one who asked to be introduced into the love circle created by Beauvoir, gained a large advantage: he could taste "the seductive diversity" of the young women around him without the least cloud of culpability because, finally, the experiences with Olga and Bianca brought him closer to Beauvoir.

Apparently, Beauvoir was at times the least favored of the couple and of the threesome, but she knew, thanks to a patience directed against her natural impatience and a constant watchfulness, how to turn such a situation to her advantage. Through her personal attraction, she was involved in the power of fascination exercised by Sartre; besides, she kept a discreet and decisive control over the entire situation and its future. In this she did no more than what any intelligent woman linked to a man doomed to a bright future does instinctively. But her own experience also had something specific. Sartre once said that she was always ahead of her time, and it is true that the anguish of death in general gave her a sharp feeling of time passing that contributed to her maturity. On the other hand, she could cloister herself in her own world by a natural habit that was reinforced by her philosophical studies, standing apart in a way Sartre characterized, jokingly, as "schizophrenic." She transformed the challenge of being the necessarily watchful member of the threesome into a victory for herself. Beauvoir's loyalty to the pact with Sartre imposed a dependence on herself as well as on the others to welcome their closeness even if she was always ambivalent about it: the "guest" was at once friend, accomplice, potential foe—both close and inaccessible. It did not matter whether the guest was initially hers or Sartre's after his inclusion in their relationship since, in Beauvoir's eyes, the third presence tested the solidarity of the couple and after her passage reestablished it more solidly than ever.

"Il [the trio] était l'oeuvre de Sartre [The edifice as such was Sartre's work]," says Beauvoir in her memoirs: "on ne peut même pas dire qu'il l'eût bâti: il l'avait suscité, du seul fait qu'il s'était attaché à Olga. Quant à moi, j'eus beau tenter de m'en satisfaire, je ne m'y sentis jamais à l'aise. . . . Si j'envisageais le trio comme une entreprise de longue haleine, qui couvrirait des années, j'étais terrifiée" [though he had not, one may say, so much built it as called it into being, simply by virtue of his attachment to Olga. For my own part, though I vainly tried to achieve satisfaction from the relationship, I never felt at ease with it. . . . Whenever I thought of the trio as a long-term project, stretching ahead for years, I was frankly terrified].[27]

That statement is revealing at many levels. It shows first that because of Sartre's personality, both serious and charming, the triangle is also two-faced, both a serious and playful construction. It is the opposite of a fixed structure: it is a day-to-day improvisation, quick and appealing. At some point Lamblin says that it is an "acrobatic construction," referring surely to the dexterity of the performers, but some lines further she adds some recollection that has nothing to do with it: "So deep was my belief [in the trio] that one day in the spring of 1939, while strolling in Paris with the Beaver . . . I was struck by a sort of vision, a blinding intuition that overcame me: I imagined that my life was written in stone, that everything had been said and nothing important would ever happen to me again. This vision seized hold of me and frightened me. . . . I felt like a prisoner of the threesome. I immediately told the Beaver. This probably disturbed her deeply, for she said nothing."[28]

How can you be a prisoner of a threesome? You fall out of it, you are excluded, or you give it up, but whatever the case, you never come out of it undamaged, as in all high-risk games. At the end of her book, Lamblin tells us something we suspected from the beginning but that she did not learn before the process of psychoanalysis: she had confused the trio and the family triangle. In such conditions, because of Lamblin's personal problems (she lost her mother when she was a child), there was a deep misunderstanding on all sides of the triangle regarding its objective. Lamblin saw an unbearable dead future in an eternal family romance; in the minds of the older couple she occupied only a limited place in time.

The opportunity for breaking up the relationship came from the conjunction of two factors: Sartre's army mobilization and Bianca's new love for Bernard Lamblin. The attentive reader of *L'invitée* and especially of its end knows what the threesome meant to Beauvoir: there is always a time where you prefer yourself to the other, and it is preferable to know it as soon as possible. This point has to be put next to Beauvoir's statement that she never wanted to advocate this kind of relationship, and also with what Beauvoir writes to Sartre in February 1940 when Bianca pointed out to her the contrast between the passionate letter she had received from Sartre and the breakup letter she received from him just weeks later. Beauvoir's pain is indicated in her response to Sartre (quoted above): "I found it desperately unpleasant."

Between Bianca's (real) eviction from the trio and, later, the (fictional) murder of Xavière (the third person in *L'invitée,* which Beauvoir started during the summer of 1938 and finished in June 1941), there are all the layers of fiction and a large difference of intensity. Some thirty years later, Beauvoir refers to this, her first (published) book, defending its therapeutic value for her. In one of the most revealing texts she has ever written, she says:

> Et pourtant, dans la mesure où la littérature est une activité vivante, il m'était indispensable de m'arrêter à ce dénouement: il a eu pour moi une valeur cathartique. D'abord, en tuant Olga sur le papier, je liquidai les irritations, les rancunes que j'avais pu éprouver à son égard; je purifiai notre amitié de tous les mauvais souvenirs qui se mélangeaient aux bons. Surtout, en déliant Françoise, par un crime, de la dépendance où la tenait son amour pour Pierre, je retrouvai ma propre autonomie. Le paradoxe, c'est que je n'ai pas eu besoin pour la récupérer de commettre aucun geste inexpiable, mais seulement d'en raconter un dans un livre. Car, même si on est attenivement encouragé et conseillé, écrire est un acte dont on ne partage avec personne la responsabilité. Dans ce roman, je me livrais, je me risquais au point que par moments le passage de mon coeur aux mots me paraissait insurmontable. Mais cette victoire idéale, projetée dans l'imaginaire, n'aurait pas eu son poids de réalité: il me fallait aller au bout de mon fantasme, lui donner corps sans en rien atténuer, si je voulais conquérir pour mon compte la solitude où je précipitai Françoise. Et en effet, l'identification s'opéra. Relisant les pages finales, aujourd'hui figées, inertes, j'ai

peine à croire qu'en les rédigeant j'avais la gorge nouée comme si j'avais vraiment chargé mes épaules d'un assassinat. Pourtant ce fut ainsi. Stylo en main, je fis avec une sorte de terreur l'expérience de la séparation. Le meurtre de Xavière peut paraître la résolution hâtive et maladroite d'un drame que je ne savais pas terminer. Il a été au contraire le moteur et la raison d'être du roman tout entier.

[And yet, insofar as literature is a living activity, it was essential that I should end with this denouement, which possessed a cathartic quality for me personally. In the first place, by killing Olga on paper I purged every twinge of irritation and resentment I had previously felt toward her, and cleansed our friendship of all the unpleasant memories that lurked among those of a happier nature. But above all, by releasing Françoise, through the agency of a crime, from the dependent position in which her love for Pierre kept her, I regained my own personal autonomy. The paradoxical thing is that to do so did not require any unpardonable action on my part, but merely the description of such an action in a book. However attentive the encouragement and advice one receives, writing remains an act for which the responsibility cannot be shared with any other person. In this novel, I exposed myself so dangerously that at times the gap between my emotions and the words to express them seemed insurmountable. But such an abstract victory, projected onto an imaginary situation, would not, by itself, have carried sufficient weight of reality. If I was to overcome *on my own account* that solitary wilderness into which I had flung Françoise, I must work my fantasy through to the bitter end and not water my version of it down in any way. And in any event, the process of self-identification came off. Rereading the final pages, today so contrived and dead, I can hardly believe that when I wrote them my throat was as tight as though I had the burden of a real murder on my shoulders. Yet so it was; and sitting there, pen in hand, I felt a weird sort of terror as I set down Françoise's experience of mental isolation. Xavière's murder may look like the abrupt and clumsy conclusion of a drama I had no idea how to finish; but in fact it was the motive force and *raison d'être* behind the entire novel.][29]

What is striking is less the strength of the fantasy than the urgency of its rejection, or more appropriately, its expulsion. One finds the expulsion of the other from the situation itself, but also of the power of the twin, and that Beauvoir cannot abide: the constraints, the submission of reason, the daily negotiations, the childishness, the lack of maturity and responsibility, all the situations of dependency she loathes. In 1933, she had said to Colette Audry that she was interested in spirituality. In 1941, she expressed a violent fantasy of murder and took a new step of self-discovery. She was now completely in charge of her life. Eight years were necessary to build her maturity. On the day in June 1941 when Beauvoir finished her book, she had also drawn a line. By choosing herself in the relationship with Olga/Bianca, she insulated herself against Sartre and asserted her own strength. Surprisingly, we do not know anything about Sartre's reaction to Beauvoir's first published book, but no doubt he understood all its messages. From that time on, the experience of the triangular relationship was ended. After Kosakiewicz and Lamblin, there would be Wanda Kosakiewicz (Olga's sister) and Sartre and Nathalie Sorokine and Beauvoir—that is to say, the affairs with nonspouse participation. The truth is that there was just one trio (as Beauvoir told Deirdre Bair), the second one with Lamblin being torpedoed (as she did not tell Bair) in conditions that help us to understand both the failure of the first and the impossibility of now devising a third one. "Strangely, this man and this woman who did not want marriage have succeeded in forming a marriage," as the French columnist Françoise Giroud once put it. In the same way, by knotting together couples instead of producing children (Olga and Jacques-Laurent Bost, Lionel de Roulet and Hélène de Beauvoir, Natasha and Ivan Moffatt), they created their own family ("the holy existentialist family," to borrow the title of a 1947 book by Jean Kanapa, a former student of Sartre's) as complicated, entrenched, divided as any other, but one much more incestuous. What survived against all the odds, unsinkable in spite of the openness clause of the pact, was Beauvoir's relationship with Sartre.

By the end of the war, Beauvoir was fully aware of the existence of otherness. By understanding otherness she perceived dialectical connections in ways she had not thought of before. It is certain that neither her article about Sade, "Faut-il brûler Sade,"[30] nor *Le deuxième sexe* (The second sex), both weaving the threads of freedom and violence from one sex to another, would have been possible without the experience acquired during the years from 1934 to 1941.

After the war Beauvoir embarked on a new step in her sexual life. During the stage that ended with the war she was clearly attracted to younger women. To define her by this sexual tropism would be an error. Her long and passionate affair with Nelson Algren (1947–62) and the one with Claude Lanzmann that followed testify that heterosexuality marks the major part of her life. Whoever has read attentively the chapter of *Le deuxième sexe* devoted to "the lesbian" will have observed Beauvoir's firmness in stating and developing the idea that homosexuality is a choice. It is a choice that she flirted with but never made definitively. Her affairs with women were induced by the poverty of her sexual life with Sartre and her deep attachment for her adolescent friend Zaza Mabille. They appear, in the context of her entire sexual life cycle, as stopgap measures, a means to a heterosexual end. On this point I share the opinion expressed by Hazel Barnes and reported by Deirdre Bair that "women are what they think they are, and in this case, Simone de Beauvoir clearly did not consider herself as a lesbian."[31] This conclusion is supported by the intensity and the length of her affair with Algren; her admission to Lamblin that she preferred men; and the fact that she never lived with a woman for a long period of time, unlike Colette, who maintained a seven-year live-in relationship with a woman. Beauvoir's affairs with women were framed in a short time period, between 1934 and 1945. She had, one might suggest, a heterosexual preference that during that period took on a bisexual expression.

After the war, Lamblin and Beauvoir met again on Lamblin's initiative upon the latter's return to Paris in 1945. Although Lamblin does not seem to have recorded that reunion, we learn of it from a letter Beauvoir wrote to Sartre, who was traveling in the United States:

> Je suis secouée à cause de Louise Védrine. . . . Elle m'a remuée et pétrie de remords parce qu'elle est dans une terrible et profonde crise de neurasthénie—et que c'est notre faute, je crois, c'est le contrecoup très détourné mais profond de notre histoire avec elle. Elle est la seule personne à qui nous ayons vraiment fait du mal, mais nous lui en avons fait. . . . Elle pleure sans cesse, elle a pleuré trois fois pendant le dîner, elle pleure chez elle quand elle doit lire

> un livre ou aller à la cuisine pour manger. . . . Elle est terriblement malheureuse, lucide au possible sans rien tirer de sa lucidité. Elle avait de vrais airs de folle.
>
> [I'm upset about Bianca Bienenfeld. . . . She moved me—and filled me with remorse—because she's suffering from an intense and dreadful attack of neurasthenia, and it's our fault I think. It's the very indirect, but profound, aftershock of the business between her and us. She's the only person to whom we've really done harm, but we have harmed her. . . . She weeps all the time—she wept three times during the dinner, and she weeps at home when she has to read a book or go to the kitchen to eat. . . . She's terribly unhappy, and extremely lucid without her lucidity getting her anywhere. At times, she really looked quite mad.][32]

Lamblin connects the desire to see Beauvoir again to the beginning of an analysis with Dr. Pasche. Can we rule out the new celebrity of Sartre and Beauvoir as a decisive factor in that initiative? Lamblin does not tell us anything about it, but if we rely on Beauvoir's observation that for her value and social status coincide, how can we avoid thinking of that motivation? Why, moreover, would the search for the presence of influential friends of the past be viewed negatively, considering her state of insecurity? At least before the breakup, she had found support and protection from them. "My love for the Beaver during my early adulthood had been so deep that I naturally turned toward her during that difficult postwar period of my life," writes Lamblin in her book.[33] We can also tie this initiative to a piece of information provided by Lamblin at the beginning of her memoirs: between the ages of six and eight, because of her mother's health problems, she was separated from her parents and placed by her father in the care of another adult. Lamblin fell out of the nest twice. Paradoxically, she does not display grief in her book at the death of her husband in 1978, which by itself would not repeat the existential crisis experienced with Beauvoir and Sartre as a consequence of her separation from her parents.

In the potential power struggle between the one who is in possession of an answer and the one who is haunted by a question, to cross the line involves a risk. Yet, very often, one does it. When the transgression becomes public, the responsibility of the one who holds the power must be weighed more severely. Aware that Lamblin, as a Jewish woman, had narrowly escaped imprisonment or even death, Beauvoir, matured by the war and haunted by remorse, responded warmly to Lamblin's opening and proposed to her a new friendship "which I could count on but which would, of course, have none of the passion of the former relationship."[34] To avoid the errors of the past Lamblin presented her own conditions: first, Beauvoir was to take the initiative in making the appointments, and second, Lamblin made Beauvoir and Sartre promise they would not mention her name in their writings. So, for forty years, through a monthly lunch, as Lamblin writes, a new attachment substituted for the former one.[35] One can imagine that at these lunches the old disagreements surfaced: for example, the rejection of middle-class status that Beauvoir reasserted many times and that Lamblin never accepted, or arguments about the political positions embraced by Sartre, especially his strong support for the cause of Israel, given Lamblin's own sympathy with the Palestinian point of view.

As witnesses, we know how much Lamblin's suffering fueled her sharp criticism of the couple. Nevertheless, history shows that the relationship was of lifelong importance to both women. They nurtured this importance by discreetly forgiving and forgetting. After the renewal of their relationship neither mentioned the past, with one exception, when Beauvoir asked Lamblin what it had meant to her. Lamblin's answer showed that she had matured, was able to accept the past as a whole; she replied that all things considered, she had gotten the best and the worst from the couple and that the final result was mixed. In this way the two buried the past, to Beauvoir's relief. Lamblin does not tell us the precise date of this meeting.

It is interesting to note that Lamblin never told Beauvoir, or so she said, about her analysis with Lacan, the famous French psychoanalyst who died one year after Sartre and was well known to the couple. Neither does she inform the reader about the dates of that analysis. In light of Lamblin's reticence on this subject, and thinking of the Beauvoir I knew, I ended my reading of Lamblin's book haunted by one thing. How could the two renew their friendship and never talk about the past? How could Beauvoir, always so direct and to the point, have kept silent? Who compelled the other so long to silence? The one who curbed her natural impetuosity, honored Lamblin's request by never raising questions about the past, and kept in the closet the corpse of the dead love, or the one who preferred not to reveal anything about the presumed liberation that a successful analysis brought to her and those around her?

Notes

1. Lamblin, *Mémoires d'une jeune fille dérangée.*

2. Lamblin, *A Disgraceful Affair,* 17.

3. Ibid., 25.

4. Ibid., 89.

5. Ibid., 90.

6. Ibid., 59.

7. Tixier-Vignancour was a lawyer on the far right who uttered these words during a political debate in 1967 with d'Astier de la Vigerie, the journalist, writer, and early Gaullist.

8. Sartre, *Witness to My Life,* 190.

9. Ibid., 223.

10. Beauvoir, *Journal de guerre,* 203; quoted in *A Disgraceful Affair,* 64.

11. Beauvoir, *Lettres à Sartre,* 1:253; *Letters to Sartre,* 159–60.

12. Ibid., 1:254; 160.

13. Lamblin, *A Disgraceful Affair,* 65.

14. Beauvoir, *Lettres à Sartre,* 1:358; *Letters to Sartre,* 217.

15. Ibid., 1:388; 233.

16. Ibid., 2:80; 273.

17. Ibid., 2:92–93; 279.

18. Beauvoir, *La force de l'âge,* 371; *The Prime of Life,* 287–88.

19. Ibid., 371; 288.

20. *Mémoires d'une jeune fille rangée,* 359; *Memoirs of a Dutiful Daughter,* 382.

21. Sartre, *The War Diaries of Jean-Paul Sartre,* 78.

22. Qtd. in Bair, *Simone de Beauvoir,* 194.

23. Ibid., 183.

24. Olivier Todd, *Un fils rebelle,* 106; author's translation.

25. *A Disgraceful Affair,* 25.

26. Ainslie, *The Psychology of Twinship,* 66.

27. *La force de l'âge,* 262–63; *The Prime of Life,* 204.

28. Lamblin, *A Disgraceful Affair,* 41–42.

29. Beauvoir, *La force de l'âge,* 348–49; *The Prime of Life,* 270–71.

30. This article, originally published in *Les temps modernes* in 1951–52, is part of the collection *Privilèges* (1955).

31. Bair, *Simone de Beauvoir,* 512.

32. Beauvoir, *Lettres à Sartre,* 2:258–59; *Letters to Sartre* 389–90.

33. *A Disgraceful Affair,* 135.

34. Ibid., 133.

35. Ibid., 134. Those who have consulted Beauvoir's notebooks find that Lamblin's name does not appear on Beauvoir's calendar as often as she suggests.

3

Leçon de Philo/Lesson in Love

Simone de Beauvoir's Intellectual Passion and the Mobilization of Desire

MELANIE C. HAWTHORNE

FROM *Mémoires d'une jeune fille rangée* (Memoirs of a dutiful daughter) to *Tout compte fait* (All said and done) and *La cérémonie des adieux* (Adieux: A farewell to Sartre), Simone de Beauvoir appears to have touched on every aspect of her long and significant life in her autobiographical writing. Yet when asked by interviewer Alice Schwarzer in 1978, "Is there anything you did not write in your memoirs which you would say now, if you had to write them again," she elaborated on her affirmative answer as follows: "I would have liked to have given a frank and balanced account of my own sexuality. A truly sincere one, from a feminist point of view; I would like to tell women about my life in terms of my own sexuality because it is not just a personal matter but a political one too."[1] This tantalizing pronouncement hints that, despite her numerous publications on the subject, Beauvoir realized there remained things she had kept back from the public. When some of Beauvoir's work began appearing posthumously in 1990, it seemed that such a "frank" (though perhaps not "balanced") account of certain aspects of Beauvoir's sexuality might finally be available. The publication of Beauvoir's wartime diary and letters to Sartre, for example, seem retroactively to justify Elaine Marks's intuition of "a homosexual secret."[2]

Many readers of Beauvoir are by now familiar with the contents of her *Journal de guerre* (War diary) and *Lettres à Sartre* (Letters to Sartre) and the controversy they have generated. The main body of Beauvoir's wartime diary begins on 1 September 1939, when war is declared. The first six *carnets* give an almost continuous, day-by-day account of Beauvoir's experience of the "phony war," a period characterized by separation from her male companions Sartre and Bost. (The main narrative begins with Sartre's departure and ends just after his return—a temporary one, as it turned out.) One of the more startling revelations of both the letters and the diary is that in the fall of 1939, after Sartre had left to fight the so-called "phony war," Beauvoir was having affairs with at least two women.[3] The first was her student Nathalie (Natasha) Sorokine. This relationship would eventually lead to Beauvoir's being dismissed from teaching in 1943.[4] Until the publication of the letters and diary, it remained unclear if there was any substance to the complaints of Sorokine's parents that Beauvoir had "incited the corruption of a minor."[5] There was speculation regarding Beauvoir's involvement, but the most authoritative source Deirdre Bair was able to quote in her otherwise exhaustive 1990 biography was Nathalie's first husband, Ivan Moffatt, who relied only on "personal opinion" that the relationship had "lesbian undertones."[6]

Beauvoir's other female lover in the fall of 1939 was Bianca Lamblin (née Bienenfeld, and referred to throughout by the pseudonym "Louise Védrine"), another student from the lycée Molière, with whom Sartre had had a brief affair in the summer of 1939.[7] Lamblin was a Polish Jew with firsthand experience of Nazi persecution, and therefore after the outbreak of war kept a low profile and makes only intermittent appearances in Beauvoir's texts. In the period covered in the wartime diary, Lamblin lived part of the time away from Paris and made only brief visits to the capital when she stayed with Beauvoir.

Throughout the fall of 1939, Beauvoir's diary notes her meetings with these two women along with the other daily activities of her life. She recounts a visit by Védrine (Bienenfeld/Lamblin) from Thursday, 9 November, to Sunday, 12 November, for example. On Thursday, 22 November, she records, "Au lit Védrine se jette passionnément dans mes bras" [In bed Védrine throws herself passionately into my arms].[8] On Saturday morning "Je me réveille à 7h. 1/2, fatiguée après cette nuit de passion et d'alerte" [I wake at 7:30, tired from this night of passion and alarm] (141), and Saturday night is described as "Nuit pathétique—passionnée, écoeurante comme du foie gras, et pas de la meilleure qualité" [Pathetic night—passionate, sickening like foie gras, and not the best quality] (143). In her relationship with Sorokine, things progress rapidly from "On parle, on s'embrasse" [We talk, we hug] on Wednesday, 15 November 1939 (157), to "baisers" [kisses] by Saturday, 26 November (172), and eventually to a "complete" relationship noted on Thursday, 4 January 1940 (230). These events are not isolated incidents, as her entry for Saturday, 2 December, confirms: "*Comme chaque fois,* baisers, petite conversation tendre, baisers; puis on fait un peu de philo" [*As usual,* kisses, tender small talk, kisses; then we do a little philosophy] (179, emphasis added). "As usual," kisses and conversation alternate and serve as prelude to "un peu de philo." It is this pattern of interaction, the erotic juxtaposition of tender conversation with the discipline of philosophy, that I wish to examine here.

Until now, accounts of these relationships have placed Beauvoir in a passive role, the object of others' juvenile attractions. Deirdre Bair, for example, writes that Lamblin craved "Beauvoir's affection and approval," while Sorokine "adored Beauvoir and only tolerated Sartre with affectionate disdain."[9] Ivan Moffatt speculated that "Natasha had a crush on Simone de Beauvoir."[10] Claude Francis and Fernande Gontier describe Sorokine as a pathetically needy hanger-on who "clung" to Beauvoir.[11] In all cases, Beauvoir is presented as having submitted to these crushes rather than initiating them, and reciprocation is assumed to be minimal.[12] But Beauvoir was not one to be coerced, and she stated elsewhere that "quand j'ai eu d'autres relations qu'avec Sartre, c'est parce que ça me plaisait" [When I had relations with anyone besides Sartre, it was because I felt like it].[13] Based on such statements and on the evidence of the diary and letters, it is clear that these relationships were willed by Beauvoir, not merely endured. To be sure, the wartime diary confirms that Beauvoir often found the attentions of Sorokine and Védrine too demanding and importunate, but it also gives Beauvoir a more active role in the development of these relationships, as her journal entry for Wednesday, 22 November, illustrates. After lecturing Sorokine for an hour on "substance," Sorokine begins to show signs of agitation and impatience: "'Après ça, on n'aura plus de temps' dit-elle mystérieusement; on s'arrête et je ne sais plus quelle habile manoeuvre (ah oui!

j'ai été rendre les 10f. à Wanda) nous amène tout naturellement sur le lit" ["After that, we won't have enough time," she said mysteriously; we stop and some clever maneuver I've forgotten (oh yes! I went to return the 10 francs to Wanda) led us quite naturally to the bed] (166). After thus finding an excuse to move to the bed, Beauvoir blurts out "une énorme grossièreté" [some huge vulgarity] that makes even her blush but that leads, five minutes later, to "la séance de baisers" [the kissing session]. Similarly, it is Beauvoir who takes the initiative in making the relationship "complete," explaining, "si je posais la question, *c'est ce que je voulais*" [If I raised the question, *it's because I wanted to*] (230, emphasis added).

In light of such posthumous revelations, Beauvoir's equivocation on the issue of sexuality could easily be construed as an outright lie. Asked point-blank by Schwarzer in 1982 if she had ever had a sexual relationship with a woman, Beauvoir answered "no," which seems in direct opposition to the evidence now available.[14] A similar denial already appears to be at work in the wartime diary itself. When Sorokine asks Beauvoir in December 1939 if she has had "physical relations" (197), she answers "Yes, with Sartre." Could Beauvoir possibly have forgotten that just three days earlier (10 December), she had confided to her diary an account of another visit by Védrine, ending with the words "on a un bout de nuit passionnée où je suis un peu prise, corps et coeur" [we had a bit of a passionate night where I was a little taken, in body and heart] (193)?[15] True, Beauvoir went on to qualify her 1982 denial to Schwarzer by adding, "I have had some very important friendships with women, of course, some very close relationships, sometimes close in a physical sense. But they never aroused erotic passion on my part." Read in the light of the wartime diary, this quibbling is at best a prevarication: the question was not whether she had experienced erotic passion, but whether the relationship was sexual. The evidence of the diary itself suggests that these relationships did not come close to the intensity that Beauvoir enjoyed in her relationships with Sartre and Bost, but it is hard to read the diary without concluding both that the relationships with Sorokine and Védrine were sexual and that they at times aroused erotic passion.

Whether Beauvoir would consider the picture of her sexual activity that emerges from these documents a "frank and balanced account" remains impossible to know. The details suggest that Beauvoir was less than frank in what she did reveal about herself during her lifetime, and fuel the anger and sense of betrayal many readers feel in reaction to these recent publications. For a person who flouted every other convention, who never shrank from challenging society on every other issue, who even claimed to have done illegal things that she in fact had not done (for example, claiming to have had an abortion in order to provoke public discussion of the issue), Beauvoir's inability or unwillingness to confront this aspect of her life seems the most egregious example of bad faith.[16]

Several responses have already been offered to these revelations. Existentialist philosophy maintains that a person's life cannot be summarized until after death, but in Beauvoir's case, it seems, even death is not the last chapter. On the one hand, critics have attempted to confront and situate Beauvoir's affairs. Margaret Simons proposes to incorporate what we now know by using Adrienne Rich's lesbian continuum to account for Beauvoir's complicated sexuality, while Alice Jardine describes Beauvoir as "historically heterosexual" as a way of allowing for differences in dimensions other than the historical.[17] On the other hand, there also has been simple denial of the need to offer any response, as in Catharine Savage Brosman's declaration that "although Beauvoir wrote that homosexual feeling exists in masked form in nearly all women, this assertion is suspect in general and almost surely does not reflect her own tendencies."[18] There is also the possibility of claiming that Beauvoir was lying or acting in bad faith. I want to offer a different response, one that does not privilege the wartime diary and letters to Sartre by treating them as a form of truth that supersedes previous "truths," but instead treats them as posthumous fictional works that connect Beauvoir to a larger fictional tradition.

One problem in dealing with Beauvoir's affairs with women is that Beauvoir herself seems never to have labeled them as lesbian; but the categories of sexual behavior and identity that Beauvoir perceived are to some extent idiosyncratic, as illustrated by her writings on the subject. Thus, the category "lesbian" certainly existed for Beauvoir, as the chapter on the topic in *Le deuxième sexe* (The second sex) illustrates, but the discussion gives the label a fairly precise meaning. Beauvoir opens the chapter by citing the popular stereotype: "On se représente volontiers la lesbienne coiffée d'un feutre sec, le cheveu court, et cravaté; sa virilité serait une anomalie traduisant un déséquilibre hormonal" [We commonly think of the lesbian as a woman wearing a plain felt hat, short hair, and a necktie; her mannish appearance would seem to indicate some abnormality of the hormones].[19] Although Beauvoir announces that she will challenge this stereotype and show that nothing could be further from the truth, she proceeds to explain why lesbians appear to play butch-femme roles,[20] why "les femmes entre elles sont impitoyables" [women are pitiless toward each other] (2:188; 420), why "la lesbienne aime souvent boire sec, fumer du gros tabac, parler un langage rude, s'imposer des exercices violents" [the lesbian often likes to drink hard liquor, smoke strong tobacco, use rough language, take violent exercise] (2:190; 422), and finally addresses the question of "si c'est par goût ou par réaction de défense qu'elle s'habille si souvent d'une manière masculine" [whether the lesbian commonly dresses in mannish fashion by preference or as a defense reaction] (2:190; 422). Beauvoir thus constructs the lesbian as pathologically masculine, and it is clear that her own relationships with Sorokine and Védrine did not appear to her to match this model.

Nor did she identify with the nascent homosexual movement in France, which came under attack in the 1930s and suffered severe repression under the Vichy régime of World War II. Although homosexual acts were still legal during the period described in the wartime journal, they were made illegal in 1942 (shortly before Beauvoir's dismissal from teaching). Pétain's new law, which recriminalized homosexuality for the first time since 1791, prescribed a prison sentence for "corruption de la jeunesse"[21] (precisely the charge brought by Sorokine's mother). Beauvoir could not have been unaware of the passage of this new law and its legal implications for her, especially in light of the complaints lodged against her, but given the perceived primacy of her relationship with Sartre, she seems to have maintained a distinction between homosexual acts and a homosexual identity, between what Foucault called a "temporary aberration" and a "species."

If Beauvoir did not identify with the categories of the lesbian or homosexual, were there other ways of describing her situation? In the journal and letters, Beauvoir refers to homosexuals as "piège."[22] This, Sylvie Le Bon de Beauvoir states in a footnote, is the idiosyncratic slang word borrowed by Sartre and Beauvoir from their friend Mme. Morel: "Elle appelait 'pièges à loups' les homosexuels des deux sexes" [She referred to homosexuals of both sexes as "wolf traps"].[23] But Beauvoir does not use this word to describe her relationships with Lamblin and Sorokine. Indeed, when Beauvoir applies it to her own actions it tends to be precisely when she is *not* in a "piège" situation. For example, in her letters to Sartre, she describes an incident in which she is comforting her friend Gégé and finds herself falling into a "piège" role: "Gégé s'est sauvée et s'est jetée sur un lit en sanglotant: je me suis jetée à côté d'elle et je suis devenue tellement piège et habituée à ces situations que je l'ai cajolée avec de tendres 'ma petite fille, ma chérie,' pour un peu j'aurais dit 'mon amour,' ça m'a fait rire" [Gégé rushed off to fling herself sobbing on a bed. I flung myself down beside her and have become such a piège, and so used to these situations, that I petted her with tender little whispers of "There now, dear" and "There now, kid," and came within an ace of saying "My darling"—it was hilarious].[24] It is clear from Beauvoir's account that this is one occasion when she found herself lying on the bed with another woman in which she felt that sexuality was *not* at issue. She assumes the label "piège" ("I . . . have *become* such a piège"), but it is in order to distance herself from this identity, to point out that it was merely a role she caught herself falling into, but ultimately avoided. The incident draws attention to the fact that Beauvoir was conscious of being somehow inauthentic, not herself, and sets itself apart from the descriptions of her encounters with Sorokine and Lamblin, as her impulse to laugh makes clear.

These readings suggest that Beauvoir would not have identified with any of the labels that contemporary readers might apply to her relationships with women. Beauvoir did not define herself as homosexual or even bisexual,[25] nor did she perceive that her behavior fit her own slang categories (such as "piège").

The difficulty in interpretation is compounded by the tendency to assume that the writings in the journal and letters are somehow more "authentic" than other, explicitly fictional, texts. It is this tendency I wish to argue against now. A more productive way of understanding Beauvoir's affairs with women, I believe, is to place them in a tradition of writing about the *gynaeceum,* but in order to do this, it is necessary to read the letters and diaries as constructing narratives that borrow from fictional genres.

Beauvoir left as many as five distinct versions of events, and it is tempting to see these successive layers as increasingly "true" redactions, from most to least fictionalized—that is, the least fictionalized would be the most true. To take one example, the period 1939–40 is recorded explicitly in two narratives: the wartime diary and Beauvoir's letters to Sartre. These two similar yet slightly different accounts cover more or less the same ground, and appear to constitute a raw, unmediated—and therefore the "truest"—record of day-to-day events. At a third level, Beauvoir's personal experience also forms the basis of other nonfictional work, such as *Le deuxième sexe.* One example will suffice to illustrate the way the same incident migrates from the most "raw" to a more "processed" form of nonfictional representation. Early in the chapter on "The Lesbian" in *Le deuxième sexe,* Beauvoir refers to hermaphroditism, defending her assertion that "l'hermaphrodite . . . a souvent une sexualité féminine" [the hermaphrodite . . . may display a feminine sexuality] with the observation "j'en ai connu une" [I myself knew one such] (2:170–71; 404). She then proceeds to describe the situation of the hermaphrodite described on page 110 of the wartime diary. Both versions would be considered "true," though one is more structured and processed than the other. At the same time, while *Le deuxième sexe* is generally classified as a nonfictional (i.e., "true") work, upon publication it was (mis)read as an autobiographical text.[26] Even so, in its level of abstraction and claim to "objectivity" it remains distinct from Beauvoir's published autobiography, which announced itself as self-referential (though still "true"). The raw material of the diary and letters is also re-presented (processed) in the autobiography, a more personal and interpretive genre than a supposedly scientific and philosophical work such as *Le deuxième sexe,* yet still, supposedly, nonfictional. Here, then, are four layers of the same narrative: two (the diary and letters) assumed to be the raw form of two more (a philosophical work and a published autobiography) that are generally understood to be more structured versions of the truth. While autobiography is supposedly anchored in truth, however, there is increasing recognition of the fact that with benefit of hindsight and in order to shape the overall themes of intellectual development, some license may be taken in the representation of that truth.[27] At the same time, autobiography is still viewed as distinct from fiction, which generally makes no claims to be representing specific truths (only general ones about, say, life and the human condition). Yet in the case of Beauvoir's work, material deemed to have autobiographical origins also formed the basis of her novels, which thus become yet another layer of representation helping to blur the boundary between truth and fiction. Novels such as *L'invitée* (She came to stay) were quickly recognized as romans à clef and subjected to decoding in the pursuit of the "reality" on which they were based.

From the diary and letters, then, to the level of what is labeled as fiction, there is a perception of a hierarchy of authenticity, with the diary and letters somehow being the closest to "reality." But precisely because Beauvoir wrote multiple versions of the same event, it is possible to see how even the most "authentic" experiences are narrativized. The diary and letters, for example, purport to represent the same events; even so, there are slight modifications in certain letters when compared to the diary, and Margaret Simons speculates that it is because Beauvoir was already shaping certain interpretations.[28] In the case of the autobiography, it is probably unnecessary to dwell here on the fact that the apparent authenticity of this genre is belied by the knowledge we now possess of how thoroughly Beauvoir's life was censored, edited and modified in the composition process. Nevertheless I will offer one example. A rhetorical flourish that marks the fictional status of the autobiography is Beauvoir's use of the authorial preface to create verisimilitude. Like gothic and fantastic novels that begin with accounts of how the "editor" (i.e., author) came to find "the following narrative" among papers in an attic, a library, or a writing box, Beauvoir's authorial prefaces offer the reader reassurances that what follows is the truth, the whole truth, and nothing but the truth. Thus, in the last sentence of the preface to *La force des choses* (Force of circumstance), Beauvoir states, "je répète que jamais je n'ai délibérément triché" [I repeat that I have never intentionally distorted the truth], using the confession of previous errors ("beaucoup de menues erreurs et deux ou trois sérieuses" [many small errors and two or three serious ones])[29] as what Roland Barthes would call a "vaccination"—the confession of a smaller deception to inoculate against the need to confess to a larger one. The fake editorial preface was also a rhetorical device Beauvoir would have read in the editors' note at the beginning of *Nausea* (first published in 1938), where Sartre wrote, "These notebooks were found among the papers of Antoine Roquentin. They are published without alteration,"[30] a patently conventional invocation of authenticity.

Since such estimates of authenticity rest on convention, however, there is increasing acceptance of the paradox that autobiography is the most fictional of genres. From here it is but a step to accepting that diaries and letters, too, can be read as novels, and perhaps are even conceived as such (albeit unconsciously) by their authors.

When Beauvoir's *Journal de guerre* is treated as a novel, one of its most striking patterns is the way Beauvoir represents her relationships with Sorokine and Lamblin as pedagogical encounters. All the women Beauvoir seems to have been involved with were at one time or another her students: Olga, Bianca, and Nathalie. Not only were the relationships conceived in classrooms (those of the lycées where Beauvoir taught), they continued to be structured around a pedagogical situation, as the case of Sorokine illustrates clearly. Her intimacies with Beauvoir take place outside the formal classroom and are intertwined with tutorials on philosophy. I cite again from the diary: "As usual, kisses, tender small talk, kisses; then we do a little philosophy" (179). Elsewhere, Beauvoir describes giving lectures on substance and on Descartes (166, 172), and the tutorials even took place in bed: "on doit travailler mais on commence par des étreintes, et quand je veux travailler elle me retient dans ses bras; . . . On finit, très tard, par prendre Kant, mais sans quitter le lit où on est étendues" [we must work but we begin with holding each other, and when I want to work she holds me back in her arms; . . . We finish, much later, by taking up Kant, but without leaving the bed where we are spread out] (196). Thus kisses, conversation, and Kant become the structuring syntagmatic elements of these relationships. With various paradigmatic substitutions (now Kant, now Descartes; first "étreintes," then "baisers"), each encounter stages the mobilization of desire through a pedagogical encounter.

This repeated structure situates Beauvoir's diary in a broader tradition of fiction by European (mostly women) writers who represent same-sex eroticism in intergenerational, pedagogical experiences. As Elaine Marks has noted, "the gynaeceum, ruled by the seductive or seducing teacher has become, since the eighteenth century, the preferred locus for most fictions about women loving women."[31] I want to refer to this tradition of representation as one of pedophilia, meaning by that term to evoke the elements of age difference and of pedagogy that form part of its core definition, though not meaning to imply (as current usage often does) that the child involved is necessarily pre-adolescent. In all the cases I am about to examine, the younger person (the "pupil") is of an age at which heterosexual feelings (if not always activity) might be expected and understood as normal. Moreover the partner (the "teacher") is not necessarily much older in years, but is set apart by her social role as educator.

The tradition of same-sex love in school settings (sometimes of a pedophile nature, sometimes between equals) has received less extensive treatment in the case of French women than in the case of anglophone women or French men.[32] Here, then, I shall sketch out some of its manifestations with a view to suggesting several things in the process. My first aim is to demonstrate the persistence of this tradition (and indeed the very "traditionalness" of it). Second, I want to highlight not merely the same-sex elements of these encounters, but the way difference is frequently eroticized (differences of generation, social status, or power, for example).[33] Finally, I want to show how easily Beauvoir's *Journal de guerre,* when read as a novel, fits into this larger context of pedophile writing. This overview will lead to a discussion of what it might mean (both for biography and for queer studies) to think of Beauvoir as a pedophile.

What Marks refers to as the gynaeceum has a long and noble history in France, but although, as she notes, one can cite examples as far back as the eighteenth century, one must wait for the Third Republic for the experience of schooling to become a common topos for girls (as pupils) and women (as teachers). Education for girls in France was formalized in the last decades of the nineteenth century. At the same time, the works of Sappho—the Greek schoolmistress with a soft spot for her pupils who gave her name to female same-sex love—were being rediscovered and reinterpreted, as well as imitated (for example in Pierre Louÿs's *Chansons de Bilitis* of 1895), during what Joan DeJean calls "the most active decade of Sapphic production in the entire French tradition." Louÿs, according to DeJean, has the honor of "making Sappho, for the first time in fiction, the absolute female counterpart of the older man who is the erotic teacher in *pederastia.*"[34]

From the end of the nineteenth century to the present day, there is an unbroken pattern of the classroom as the site of erotic same-sex encounters. Sometimes these encounters are between pupils, but not infrequently the eroticism is further charged by the power and age difference that makes the teacher-pupil relationship the focal point. The difference in age between teachers and pupils may be slight if measured only in chronological years, but the perceived difference in status between the adolescent and the (even young) adult makes such relationships seem intergenerational. This perceived age imbalance is echoed by the power differential due to the social perceptions of the relatively powerless status of the pupil as compared to the authority accorded to the teacher.

Sometimes this power difference takes the form of mild sadomasochism, as in one of the first and most well-known examples of the eroticized gynaeceum, Colette's Claudine series. *Claudine à l'école* (Claudine at school), first published in 1900 (not long before Beauvoir's birth in 1908), introduced the character of Claudine, born in 1884, just two years after the Loi Camille Sée made secondary lay education mandatory for girls in France. In this novel, the primacy of the relationship between the adolescent Claudine and the schoolteacher with the disciplinary name of Mademoiselle Sergent is mediated by their girardian rivalry for a third person, Aimée ("Beloved") Lanthenay. A sadomasochistic element, meanwhile, is displaced onto Claudine's relationship with a fellow student, Luce, but connected to the primary love triangle by the fact that Luce is Aimée's sister. Luce seeks Claudine's attention and is rewarded by slaps and pinches. The sadomasochism becomes more explicit as the series evolves: in the sequel *Claudine à Paris* (1901; Claudine in Paris), Claudine meets up with Luce in Paris after a period of separation. Luce greets Claudine with an affectionate hug, to which Claudine responds, "Luce! Do you want a slap?" Luce, "with an ineffable expression of happy slavery," answers, "Oh yes! *Do* beat me a little!"[35]

Claudine was one of only two heroines the young Beauvoir recognized as having any relation to her own experience, at least according to her memoirs: "à part *Claudine* et *Mademoiselle Dax* de Farrère, les héroïnes—niaises jeunes filles ou femmes du monde futiles—m'intéressaient peu" [except for Claudine and Farrère's Mademoiselle Dax, the heroines—inane young girls or frivolous women of the world—had very little interest for me].[36] *Mademoiselle Dax* concerns the sexual awakening (and eventual downfall) of its eponymous heroine, a girl raised in a sheltered, conventional bourgeois family not unlike Beauvoir's. Alice Dax finds herself drawn to a couple she meets on vacation in Switzerland, a fiercely independent, feminist novelist named Carmen de Retz (author of *Les filles de Loth* [The daughters of Lot]) and a young diplomat, Bertrand Fougères. While Carmen de Retz is in some ways Alice Dax's rival for Fougères, there is also the suggestion that the male figure serves merely to mediate the relationship between the two women in another girardian triangulation of desire. This possibility is underscored by the way Alice Dax describes her wish to be loved the way she was in school: "when I was ten, just before my first communion, I was sent to a boarding school for six months. . . . And there, my schoolmates loved me, my teachers loved me . . . a very good, tender kind of love . . . people played with me, people kissed me. . . . There, that is how I would like to be loved still."[37] Although her adult sexual orientation appears to be heterosexual, then, the experience of same-sex pedagogical formation clearly played an important though misperceived role in shaping her erotic expectations.

At about the same time that the fictional Claudine was supposedly in school (late 1890s), another, nonfictional, school drama was unfolding. The account of it was not unlike Beauvoir's work, being based on autobiographical experience, although as the author states: "Its truth has been filtered, transposed, and, maybe, superficially altered, as is inevitably the case with all autobiographies."[38] It was written in English and not published until 1949, but was based on experiences in France during the late nineteenth century, which is why I include it here as part of the French tradition. This was the underground classic *Olivia*. The author, Dorothy Strachey Bussy (Lytton Strachey's sister, André Gide's translator, and wife of the French painter Simon Bussy), had attended a girls' school near Fontainebleau called Les Ruches.[39] In *Olivia* (the name was that of a younger sister who died in infancy but the Shakespearean connotations have not gone unnoticed), "Julie T." is a thinly veiled portrait of the headmistress of Les Ruches, Marie Souvestre, while "Cara M." represents her assistant Mademoiselle Dussand. Olivia recounts the rivalry between the two mistresses and how she quickly fell into the camp of Miss Julie.[40] She experiences a moment of epiphany when listening to Miss Julie recite Racine: "I have often wondered what share Racine had in lighting the flame that began to burn in my heart that night, or what share proximity." Olivia proceeds to describe her reaction to the erotic pedagogy: "It suddenly dawned upon me that this was beauty—great beauty—a thing I had read of and heard of without understanding, a thing I had passed by perhaps a hundred times with careless, unseeing eyes."[41] In this account, it becomes indeed impossible to determine if the "this" in "this was beauty" refers to Racine's *Andromaque,* Miss Julie herself, or some fusion of the two. Later, Olivia is content to sit and read poetry on the floor while Miss Julie works nearby, again finding an erotic charge in the pedagogical situation.[42] Although Olivia is "intoxicated" by Miss Julie and her "brilliant speech," she discovers that a relationship with her is not painless: "Sharp and pointed, [her brilliant speech] would sometimes transfix a victim cruelly. No one was safe, and if one laughed with her, one was liable the next minute to be pierced oneself with a shaft of irony."[43] The metaphors of piercing are clear reminders of the frequent association between sadomasochism and the discipline of the gynaeceum. "Olivia," like other authors, stresses the pleasure of such interactions.

Although the drama of *Olivia* purportedly took place in France in the late nineteenth century and the novel was published mid-century (1949), Bussy actually began writing it in 1933. That same year, Sartre left France to study in Berlin. Also that year, a novel appeared based on a film (which in turn was based on a play) that had premiered amidst critical acclaim in Berlin on 27 November 1931. The film, *Mädchen in Uniform,* was based on a play by Christa Winsloe.[44] It tells the story of Manuela, a student in a Prussian school who, like most of the other students, falls in love with one of the teachers, Fräulein von Bernburg.

Although German in origin, both film and author play a role in the French female pedophile tradition. The film—with subtitles by the expert in schoolgirl literature, Colette[45]—was shown in France to great acclaim, while the author of the play, Winsloe, became a refugee in France. In 1938, Winsloe's works were forbidden in Germany, so she packed her bags and moved to Paris, where she remained until 1939. After that, she moved to Cagnes, just outside Nice, and lived there until she was found dead in mysterious circumstances: on 10 June 1944, Winsloe and her friend Simone Gentet were shot in the woods by five Frenchmen; it has never been clearly established why.[46]

Mädchen in Uniform (in all its incarnations as play, film, and novel) continues the eroticization of the pedagogical situation with the elements already noted. Like the Claudine novels and *Olivia,* the events portrayed take place in the late nineteenth century. The discipline of the school is harsh (the food is insufficient, the heating minimal, and everything is summed up by the adjective "Prussian"), but the suffering is offset by certain indulgences, most notably the tradition that the beloved Elizabeth von Bernburg kisses each student good night. This ritual is not so different from the daily habit of Madame Jules Favre, the formidable first headmistress of the equally spartan Ecole de Sèvres: "Every evening, at 8:30, in her private apartment, the door of her study was open to those pupils who wanted (and that was almost the whole School) an intimate and respectful goodnight where, filing one by one, each pupil received, along with a handshake, a word and a smile which seemed to sum up their day." [47]

The climax of *Mädchen in Uniform* comes during the annual school play (a French play, no less: Voltaire's *Zaire*). As in *Olivia,* where the carnivalesque atmosphere of the Mardi Gras fancy-dress ball frees the students from their usual inhibitions, playing a role transforms Manuela.[48] Manuela's classmate Ilse is removed from the lead role at the last minute. Besides leaving the way open for Manuela to shine, this incident has the additional narrative advantage that it allows the sadomasochistic side of Fräulein von Bernburg to emerge. She uses emotional blackmail to persuade Ilse to accept her punishment, but in such a way that it makes accepting punishment seem like a pleasure. (Is it only coincidence that areas of study are referred to as "disciplines"?) Drunk both with her success in the play and on the grog served afterward, Manuela declares her love for von Bernburg, idealizing it as "the love that passeth all understanding."

As *Mädchen in Uniform* was establishing its cult following and Beauvoir was establishing her own following as a teacher in Rouen (around the time she met Olga, a student with whom she would have an affair), a now forgotten writer, Jeanne Galzy, changed publishers. In 1934, Galzy's first novel with her new publisher, Gallimard (soon to be Beauvoir's publisher, too), appeared. Although neglected today, Galzy was a fairly well-known writer in the mid-1930s and had won several literary prizes: the Prix Fémina in 1923, the Prix d'Académie in 1928, and the Prix Brentano's in 1931. Her latest novel, *Jeunes filles en serre chaude* (Girls in a hothouse), surely would have caught Beauvoir's attention: the hothouse referred to was the Ecole normale supérieure de Sèvres, the institution shaped by Madame Jules Favre that Beauvoir herself had so wanted to attend.[49] Deirdre Bair's biography is revealing on this subject: Beauvoir read an article in a magazine about "a woman who had been one of the first to take a university degree in philosophy and who was now successfully teaching the subject. It seemed the ideal solution, especially since she [Beauvoir] had been considering a teaching career ever since reading the article about Sèvres. The photo accompanying the article enticed her even further: it showed a mature woman, the philosopher, seated at her desk surrounded by books and papers, while her 'niece,' whom she had adopted and of whom she was very fond, hovered nearby."[50] It would seem that Sèvres, with its reputation for intense relationships (at least partially known to Beauvoir's parents, who would not hear of sending their daughter there), is what fired the imagination of Beauvoir. To what extent this desire was due to the photo of the philosopher and her adopted "niece" (a destiny Beauvoir was to realize in her own adoption of Sylvie Le Bon), "of whom she was very fond," must remain a matter of speculation, but the anecdote seems richly suggestive.

Jeanne Galzy herself was a product of Sèvres, where she had had some of the same experiences as her heroine Isabelle; but in what must by now seem a familiar rhetorical move, Galzy denies in an *avertissement* (warning) to her readers on the first page of *Jeunes filles en serre chaude* that hers is a roman à clef. Hélène de Monferrand sums up the novel thus: "Isabelle falls in love with the English *répétitrice,* Miss Benz, a fascinating young woman with whom all the pupils are more or less in love. But this is not *Olivia,* and Isabelle and Miss Benz sleep together."[51]

In *Jeunes filles en serre chaude,* as in other novels described here, the eroticism of the relationship is permeated by the pedophile elements of intergenerational love and the pedagogic context. Some of Galzy's descriptions of highly charged instructional moments anticipate the way Beauvoir would structure the record of her encounters with students in her diary five years later. Some interactions between Isabelle and Miss Gladys Benz, for example, take place in Miss Benz's room against the backdrop of tutorials:

> —Aren't you working, child?
>
> Gladys pointed to the page she had begun, on the table beside her. Isabelle picked up her pen once again, tried to interest herself in Paul-Louis Courrier. The draft pages piled up in disorder. But her mind could scarcely recall the lines already written, give them some meaning. A suffocating happiness beset her. Gladys was there. Her beautiful transparent arm was stretched out next to the open book.[52]

Jeunes filles en serre chaude is told from the point of view of the pupil Isabelle, but if Miss Benz had left a record of her version of these moments, they might well have resembled some of the passages of Beauvoir's diary. Isabelle is aware of her loss of concentration caused by the "suffocating happiness" of the teacher's presence. Gladys Benz, on the other hand, might have been thinking, in Beauvoir's words, "Elle est charmante, souvent avide et nerveuse, mais si plaisante dans la tendresse. Mais je ne sais que faire et je suis emmerdée" [She is charming, often avid and nervous, but so pleasing when it comes to tenderness. But I don't know what to do and I'm tired of it].[53]

So far I have presented examples of pedophile writing that might have influenced Beauvoir, shaped the way she perceived of herself as both a pupil and a teacher, but I want to stress that this tradition does not end there. On the contrary, it was extended in the postwar period by one of Beauvoir's own protégées (one who seems to have had her own version of a schoolgirl crush on Beauvoir), Violette Leduc. Leduc's *Thérèse et Isabelle* (Thérèse and Isabelle; also made into a film)[54] concerns schoolgirl peers and may at first appear to be an exception to the intergenerational pedophilia of the girls-school setting, but it should not be forgotten that this novella was not intended for separate publication but formed part of a larger work. It originally served as the prologue to *Ravages* (Ravages),[55] a novel subsequently reworked in *La bâtarde* (La batarde; also sometimes translated as *La Batarde: An Autobiography*), thus producing the same kind of textual layering noted in Beauvoir's work.[56] Both *Ravages* and *La bâtarde* depict significant same-sex relationships with intergenerational and pedagogical elements, from early crushes on the *pions* to the more sustained relationships with the teachers Cécile (in *Ravages*) and Hermione (in *La bâtarde*). It is well known that Beauvoir helped launch Leduc's career, but it is less well known why Beauvoir continued to tolerate this sometimes importunate and politically suspect hanger-on. The publication of Beauvoir's diary suggests that the two may have had more in common than was previously evident.

Other postwar novels that introduced lesbian themes also did so by invoking pedophile contexts, such as Françoise Mallet-Joris's *Le rempart des Béguines* (1951; The illusionist). The first-person narrator of this novel, Hélène Noris, is fifteen when the story begins. When she meets her father's thirty-five-year-old mistress, Tamara Soulerr, she is immediately attracted to her. Hélène, who finds school unstimulating and pretends to be a poor student, suddenly feels educationally motivated by Tamara's presence: "I experienced the same happiness I had often had in the library, sitting between the roaring stove and the shelves full of books, but with a greater intensity. I suddenly felt *good.* I loved my father, I wanted to be first in my class, I resolved to keep my exercise books in impeccable order, I resolved all sorts of things."[57] The first time they kiss they are in Tamara's apartment on the Rempart des Béguines, a disreputable neighborhood but a suggestive address: Béguines were a Belgian conventual order of nuns, a model of female community in which some scholars have seen lesbian possibilities. On this occasion, Hélène comes to Tamara's apartment directly from school, so that bedroom and classroom are juxtaposed: "[Tamara] had sat down on the bed. Now she cast off her leather slippers and stretched herself out between the sheets. I felt perfectly ridiculous standing there in front of her, encumbered with my coat and brief case—I had just come from school—and I flushed with anger" (46). In undressing and joining Tamara in the bed, it is literally the signs of her schoolgirl status that Hélène must divest herself of in order to enjoy the pleasure of Tamara's first kiss. The kiss is followed by a command to make conversation, an order Hélène finds so intimidating, she bursts into tears, a "delightful pain" (51) for Hélène, who likes to cry.

After the two women begin a sexual relationship Hélène's performance as a student begins to improve dramatically: "Triumph of immorality! My marks in class . . . noticeably improved. Formerly deplorably low, they rose to such an extent that it could be foreseen that this year, for the first time, I would not be obliged to repeat my examinations" (59). Thus, although Tamara is not strictly speaking a teacher, the relationship is marked by pedagogical formation. It is also inflected by an element of sadomasochism. At the end of the novel, when Tamara marries Hélène's father, Hélène realizes that all the things she had loved about Tamara—her poverty, her "virile energy," and her cruelty—were illusions (242). The sequel, *La chambre rouge* (The red room), makes Hélène and Tamara rivals for the same man, but one does not need to be Freud to understand that their mutual hatred is another form of love.

Another, less well known postwar novel also describes the intensity of schoolgirl crushes and their potentially destructive effects. The author, Eveline Mahyère (whose mother was a schoolteacher), committed suicide in July 1957, and it is tempting to see her posthumously published novel *Je jure de m'éblouir* (1958; I will not serve) as a thinly disguised autobiography. The heroine, Sylvie, is preparing to take her baccalaureate exams, but has fallen in love with one of her teachers, Julienne Blessner, at her convent school. Julienne, aware of Sylvie's crush, encourages her to sublimate her love into academic achievement ("if you love me . . . you will pull yourself together and make the effort to work and to pass your exams"),[58] but when Julienne announces that she is becoming a novice and won't see Sylvie again, the disappointment proves unbearable and Sylvie winds up in the hospital.

The female pedophile novel continues to be a vibrant genre in the present day. Recently, Hélène de Monferrand reinvigorated the female intergenerational pedagogical tradition in two novels that use two very personal genres (letters and diaries, an echo of Beauvoir's posthumous works) to present the loves of Héloïse and Suzanne. *Les amies d'Héloïse* (The friends of Heloise), published in 1990 (the same year as Beauvoir's letters and diary), uses the epistolary form to tell the story of Héloïse and her relationship with one of her schoolteachers, Suzanne. The novel nods in passing to its predecessors by including a Prussian schoolgirl character named Manuela. The sequel, *Journal de Suzanne* (1991; Suzanne's diary), tells part of the previous novel from Suzanne's point of view, using a diary to fill in Suzanne's past. It also uses flashback to describe Suzanne's experiences during the Occupation when she and her lover Madeleine were deported, thereby retroactively making Suzanne a contemporary of Beauvoir, a witness to the Occupation and the disruption of women's relationships that often went unacknowledged. The two novels together offer the same kind of layered re-presentation of the same events noted in Beauvoir's work. The success and recognition these two novels have enjoyed—*Les amies d'Héloïse* received the prize for the best first novel from the Académie Goncourt—suggest that the topos of the gynaeceum remains an important filter of sexual experience.[59]

In her third novel, *Les enfants d'Héloïse* (1997; The children of Héloïse), Monferrand continues the epic, focusing on the children of her heroine Héloïse: the twins Suzanne and Mélanie and their elder brother, Anne (traditionally a boy's name, and Héloïse is very traditional). A chain of associations is set up when a classmate enlists Mélanie's help to finish Simone de Beauvoir's *Mémoires d'une jeune fille rangée,* which she has been forbidden to read. Though ignorant of Beauvoir's work, Mélanie responds with empathy, comparing her friend's disappointment to her own when she was not allowed to read *Claudine à l'école* (thereby establishing for the reader a parallel between Beauvoir and Colette).[60] On the other hand, Mélanie is allowed to read Zola, and it is here, in *Nana,* that she finds troubling allusions to the kind of feelings she has for her classmates in her all-girls boarding school, feelings that are confirmed when her sister, Suzanne, buys her a secondhand copy of a novel by Jeanne Galzy, *La cavalière.* The tradition of schoolgirl literature from Colette to Galzy is thus evoked as echo to the emerging desires of a young heroine grappling with the meaning of schoolgirl crushes. In the process, Beauvoir's name becomes attached to the enumeration as, in some ways, its point of departure.

I don't mean to suggest such continuous tradition is unique to French literature. Indeed, some of the examples I have discussed have been drawn from other national literatures (such as English and German), and I could have cited numerous others.[61] To see the continued relevance of the genre, one has only to look to the work of contemporary authors such as Jeanette Winterson, whose *Oranges Are Not the Only Fruit* (widely interpreted as autobiographical despite the author's disclaimers) bears many points of comparison with other novels discussed here. Like *Mädchen in Uniform,* it is perhaps better known as a (made-for-television) film, but the novel contains one scene in particular that was not included in the film.[62] It concerns the relationship between Jeanette and her teacher, Miss Jewsbury. In the film, Miss Jewsbury is just an understanding friend, but the relationship is developed more explicitly in the novel. After an unpleasant scene in church in which Jeanette's lover renounces her, Jeanette is taken home by Miss Jewsbury, who comforts her: "And she began to stroke my head and shoulders. I turned over so that she could reach my back. Her hand crept lower and lower. She bent over me; I could feel her breath on my neck. Quite suddenly I turned and kissed her. We made love and I hated it and hated it, but would not stop."[63] The experience is both desired and hated by Jeanette, just as Beauvoir describes her ambivalent relationships that are "écoeurant" [sickening] yet actively pursued.

Perhaps it is easier today to recognize the pedophile elements of these novels because some have begun explicitly to theorize the desire(s) at work in the classroom.[64] "*All* pedagogy comes under the sign of sexuality," writes Juliet Flower MacCannell.[65] "When is a scene of instruction *not* a scene of seduction?" asks Diana Fuss rhetorically.[66] Marjorie Garber explores "the erotic center of the attraction" that is "somewhere between wanting to *be* the teacher and wanting to *have* him or her."[67] Jane Gallop speculates that "if schools decide to prohibit not only sex but 'amorous relations' between teacher and student, the 'consensual amorous relation' that will be banned from our campuses might just be teaching itself."[68]

Sometimes this theoretically bold and innovative writing addresses the erotics of the classroom without confronting the fact that the student-teacher attraction may be of a same-sex kind, or even in resolutely heterosexual terms. Thus, in her introduction to a 1995 collection of essays, editor Jane Gallop focuses on teaching as "impersonation," and as a number of the essays suggest, part of what is impersonated is a sexual being. Gallop writes about the teacher's desire to please the student as a reversal of the more widely recognized but diffuse desire of the student to please the teacher, but this desire remains gender-nonspecific here and is not exclusively nor even necessarily sexual.[69] Jane Tompkins, too, describes teaching as a form of erotic activity, but in stereotypically heterosexual dating terms: "Sometimes the feelings I have toward my students are romantic. It's like being in love. . . . It's the roller-coaster of love—up one day and down the next—no two classes the same. How soon will we be going steady? Will our love be true? Do you love me like I love you?"[70] By invoking, even self-consciously, the heterosexual—and slightly nostalgic—pop culture vocabulary of "going steady" and "true love," and by focusing on romantic feelings rather than sexual desire, Tompkins manages to make such teacher-student relationships seem less threatening while still preserving an intense emotional charge. It's as though acknowledging the role of sexual desire in pedagogy already breaks so many taboos about the assumed purity of the student-teacher bond that adding the possibility of same-sex eroticism to the mix, however platonically, cannot be contemplated in certain types of discourse. As Garber reminds us, "there need not (necessarily) be any *sex* between teachers and students for there to be lots of *eroticism*,"[71] but contemplating even eroticism makes many people nervous when it is *homo*-eroticism.

At other times, however, the same-sex aspects of the relationship are foregrounded. In Joseph Litvak's essay "Discipline, Spectacle, and Melancholia in and around the Gay Studies Classroom," the homoerotic element of the desire to please is explored further from a gay male perspective. Litvak writes about "the pedagogue as pederast," but the pederast in this case is gendered as a "flamboyantly lovesick, stagestruck Gay Man."[72] When the focus is on the homoerotics of female institutions, it is once again Elaine Marks who comes closest to describing the affect of the gynaeceum when recollecting her own experience of being taught by Germaine Brée.[73] Citing examples from Marceline Desbordes-Valmore, Colette's Claudine, and Roland Barthes, Marks describes school "as an erotic space of pleasure" and meditates on the seductiveness of the French forms of address "Madame, Mademoiselle, and Monsieur." The French teacher in particular is a "deep reservoir for desire, pleasure, and memory in the classroom," but it is "Madame" in particular that, for her, represents the word in French that has "the strongest poetic and affective charge."[74]

In summary, then, it would be all too easy to draw simplistic biographical conclusions from the evidence of the *Journal de guerre* and *Lettres à Sartre* and decide that Beauvoir was a lesbian or bisexual with a case of bad faith. But, to borrow a line from Woody Allen, Beauvoir was homosexual "only according to the dictionary definition,"[75] and the uselessness of dictionary definitions is becoming increasingly apparent as work on the history of sexuality, social construction, and queer theory challenges the received paradigms. To apply such a dictionary definition in the case of Beauvoir is to accept that the categories of sexual behavior can be reduced to a binary opposition having to do only with the sexual sameness or difference of one's partner. If there is anything useful for queer studies about resisting the interpretation that Beauvoir was simply acting in bad faith when she denied having had sexual relationships with "women," it is that her attempts to record her experience challenge such simple categorization. If instead we take Beauvoir at her word, perhaps it entails understanding what it might mean for her to have had sexual relationships not with "women" but with "(female) students." Reflecting on her relationships in a letter to Nelson Algren, Beauvoir wrote:

> If I were a man, maybe I should be a very wicked one, because I surely should enjoy to make love to young girls and having them love me, and then indeed I should drop them because they are often very silly, too childish and become quickly tedious. When I

> was a teacher, they often fell in love with me and sometimes I enjoyed it a bit and even three or four times I really cared a little for it, and I happened to behave *very* badly; there were long stories because if pleasant but not important for me, it was important for the girls during at least some time and I had to manage them very carefully. . . . I should not be interested any more in such business.[76]

When she was a teacher, in other words, Beauvoir found it hard to resist such pedophilic engagements, but in 1948 she no longer finds such adventures tempting. Is it the passage of time, maturity, or the sexual fulfillment offered by Algren that has brought about this change? Or is it also that she is no longer a teacher? Is it merely coincidence that after she was fired from teaching, relationships with girls no longer held any attraction for her? After all, if Beauvoir was no longer a teacher, girls were no longer students or pupils to her, and a certain kind of pedophilia was closed off. A reading of Beauvoir's work suggests that her relationships with women were not merely homosexual (or bisexual or lesbian or "piège"). Beauvoir describes intergenerational, sexual relations between women in which the distribution of roles is not based simply on sex (man-woman/woman-woman), nor on gender (butch-femme), but on a less well recognized distribution of erotic roles: teacher-pupil. Beauvoir's relationships were not with just any women, but with younger women who subsequently became members of what the group called "the family." Sartre and Beauvoir were the parents and their protégé(e)s were implicitly their children. Beauvoir verges on recognizing a connection between her experience as a teacher and her homoerotic experience in the confession to Algren, but stops short of making the link that today seems more legible. When Jane Gallop says (ironically and provocatively) "graduate students are my sexual preference," she might be giving voice to a version of Beauvoir's desires.[77] So little is known about female pedophilia that it is hard to generalize from Beauvoir's case. Discussion of female experiences of pedophilia and pederasty is limited, even in clinical literature.[78] Moreover, these terms invoke only the age difference aspect of the relationship and do not include the pedagogical and occasionally sadomasochistic elements that accompany the staging of such relationships in the classroom. In her letter to Algren, Beauvoir seems to be struggling to articulate a kind of eroticism that lacks a taxonomy, something that includes a homoerotic element but that cuts across traditional boundaries of hetero- and homo-, an eroticism predicated on sameness of sex but difference of status and knowledge. Queer studies, which challenges simple binary taxonomies, makes it possible to think of "students" as a sexual preference.

In the instances I have alluded to in Beauvoir's diary, discipline in its many forms causes different people to learn different things, and who is learning what becomes an important distinction. The students—Olga, Natasha, Bianca—may go off and write about Descartes, but Beauvoir goes off and writes about them. Beauvoir's summary of the typical encounter—"on fait un peu de philo"—captures the complicated relationship between pedagogy and desire now being theorized more explicitly. "Philo" is a common French abbreviation for "philosophy," but given the etymology of "philosophy" (love of knowledge), a lesson in philo is also a lesson in love, a lesson that combines Kant and kisses. In her *Journal de guerre,* Beauvoir illustrates how difficult it is to separate the love of the teacher and the love of the subject matter. The subject matter—love of (the) discipline itself, as it were—may come to replace the teacher as the object of desire, but before such displacement occurs, the love that is activated may be first and foremost for the teacher herself. People have long reacted to Beauvoir as an intellectual and a passionate one, but thanks to the publication of the *Journal de guerre,* we know more about Beauvoir's intellectual passions.

Notes

1. Schwarzer, *After "The Second Sex,"* 84.
2. Marks, "Transgressing the (In)cont(in)ent Boundaries," 184.
3. Beauvoir's affair with Olga occurred before the period covered in the wartime diary. Olga continued to figure prominently in Beauvoir's life, but not as a sexual partner.
4. Bair, *Simone de Beauvoir,* 278–79. A fuller account is given in Joseph, *Une si douce Occupation,* 197–222. See also Galster, "Simone de Beauvoir face à l'Occupation allemande."
5. Thus, Deirdre Bair chooses her words carefully and leaves the question open. See for example *Simone de Beauvoir,* 640, note 1.
6. Bair, *Simone de Beauvoir,* 237.

7. Ibid., 214. Bair was the first person to break the secret of "Védrine's" identity, which had remained undisclosed until the publication of her biography. Following the revelation, Bianca Lamblin added her own autobiographical testimony of her relationship with Sartre and Beauvoir in *Mémoires d'une jeune fille dérangée* (A disgraceful affair).

8. *Journal de guerre,* 139, my translation. All further references to the diary will be given in the text, and translations are my own.

9. Bair, *Simone de Beauvoir,* 214.

10. Ibid., 237.

11. Francis and Gontier, *Les écrits de Simone de Beauvoir,* 197. See also their *Simone de Beauvoir.*

12. See also Catharine Savage Brosman, who, even after the publication of Beauvoir's letters to Sartre, maintained that Beauvoir "appears to have lent herself passively to the caresses of a series of admiring schoolgirls who had passionate crushes on her, including Olga. These same documents make it amply clear, however, that she did not initiate the contacts and that she had no taste for them" (*Simone de Beauvoir Revisited,* 27).

13. Dayan and Ribowska, *Simone de Beauvoir,* 74.

14. Schwarzer, *After "The Second Sex,"* 112.

15. At times, the relationships were even more closely spaced. As Gilbert Joseph reports, "son caractère passionné . . . la rendait capable dans la même journée d'aimer avec la même sincérité Bianca, puis Nathalie et de se rendre le soir dans un autre hôtel avec Bost. Ce qui ne l'empêchait pas d'écrire des lettres aimantes à Sartre à l'issue de ces parties de plaisir" (*Une si douce Occupation,* 110).

16. In the interview quoted at the beginning of this article, the interviewer, Alice Schwarzer, comments that people want to deny women's passions, but that Beauvoir "never bowed to these expectations" (*After "The Second Sex,"* 84). Beauvoir agreed, contrasting herself to the image of an old lady who has repressed her desires all her life and really "lets rip" when she gets old. "I on the other hand," continued Beauvoir, "have always spoken my mind as far as I have been able. I have always followed my desires and my impulses; in other words, I didn't suppress anything, so that I have no need to get even with my past now" (84). The evidence of the war diary suggests that, on the contrary, Beauvoir suppressed plenty. It is not surprising, then, that Beauvoir did have a need to get even: the posthumous publication of the diary appears to be just such a settling of scores with the past.

17. Simons, "Lesbian Connections," 136–61; Jardine, "Death Sentences," 121.

18. Brosman, *Simone de Beauvoir Revisited,* 27.

19. Beauvoir, *Le deuxième sexe* 2:170; *The Second Sex,* 404. Further references are given in the text.

20. The English translation here leaves a lot to be desired. Parshley translates "un couple bi-sexué" (2:186), for example, as "a bisexual couple" (418).

21. Aldrich, "Homosexuality in France," 6.

22. The word is translated (e.g. by Simons) as "homosexual," but I believe that the

distinction Beauvoir evidently wished to preserve between homosexuality as generally understood and its meaning for the "famille" of Sartre, Beauvoir, and their intimates should be preserved.

23. Beauvoir, *Journal de guerre,* 23.

24. Beauvoir, *Lettres à Sartre* 1:91; *Letters to Sartre,* 43. For a discussion of the different treatment of this scene in the *Journal de guerre,* see Simons, "Lesbian Connections," 144.

25. Gilbert Joseph does not hesitate to characterize Beauvoir in such rigid terms (see, for example, *Une si douce Occupation,* 109), but this is characteristic of his book as a whole, which paints moral issues in black or white terms.

26. I am thinking, for example, of Mauriac's reaction, recorded by Beauvoir in *La force des choses:* "Il écrivit à un des collaborateurs des *Temps modernes:* 'J'ai tout appris sur le vagin de votre patronne'" [He wrote to one of the contributors to *Les temps modernes:* "Your employer's vagina has no secrets from me"] (*La force des choses,* 205; *Force of Circumstance,* 187).

27. In an unpublished talk given at Columbia University in 1985, for example, Dominique Desanti set out to address the "degree of truth" in the different versions of events in Beauvoir's life as represented in her work. Although the published documents then available did not include the wartime diary and letters, Desanti concluded that sometimes "the fictional truth is more truthful than the one expressed in the memoirs" (quoted in McPherson, *Incriminations,* 35).

28. Simons notes, for example, that in a letter to Sartre "Beauvoir did not express the same jealous possessiveness toward Sartre that she reveals in her journal" ("Lesbian Connections," 154). However, one should beware of concluding that Beauvoir wished to keep information from Sartre, since she showed him her journal whenever they saw each other (for example, when Sartre came to Paris on leave). At most, Beauvoir may have wanted to delay certain knowledge.

29. Beauvoir, *La force des choses,* 10; *Force of Circumstance,* vii. Perhaps not so coincidentally, "deux ou trois" would seem to be the number of female lovers Beauvoir had somehow neglected to mention before. In deciding whether or not to continue her autobiography, she had been advised, "Attendez de pouvoir dire tout: des lacunes, des silences, ça dénature la vérité" [Wait until you can say everything: lacunae, silences distort the truth](7; v).

30. Sartre, *Nausea,* 6.

31. Marks, "Lesbian Intertextuality," 357.

32. In the case of anglophone women, there have been a number of studies. Martha Vicinus, for example, examines English boarding-school friendships from a historical perspective in "Distance and Desire." The topic has recently received literary treatment by Terry Castle, who suggests that the world of school and adolescence is one of "two basic mimetic contexts in which, in realistic writing, plots of lesbian desire are most likely to flourish" (*The Apparitional Lesbian,* 85). Marjorie Garber blends reality and fiction in *Vice Versa,* her study of bisexuality. In her chapter on "Erotic Education"

Garber notes that "the classroom is one place where same-sex desire is often opened for the adolescent lover" (336). For discussion of the tradition of pedophilia in gay male French fiction, see Robinson, *Scandal in the Ink.* In discussions of representations of same-sex love, the pedophile element often seems to receive more comment in male, rather than female, contexts. In one exception, an article from 1965 (i.e., before the 1970s lesbian-feminist emphasis on equality in sexual relationships), Marion Zimmer Bradley maintains a distinction between the "novel of adult lesbianism" and the "novel of feminine Greek love" ("Feminine Equivalents of Greek Love in Modern Fiction").

33. This is one of the ways my treatment of these novels will differ from other discussions of the same texts. Thus Diana Fuss's reading of *Olivia* (see "Sexual Contagions" in *Identification Papers*) uses Bussy's novel to examine the meaning of "identification" in Freud. Although "sameness" (an element of identification) always also implies difference, Fuss's focus is on how characters in the novel come to identify (see sameness) with others.

34. DeJean, *Fictions of Sappho,* 276.

35. Colette, *The Complete Claudine* (New York: Avenel Books, 1984), 300–301.

36. Beauvoir, *Mémoires d'une jeune fille rangée,* 111; *Memoirs of a Dutiful Daughter,* 116.

37. Farrère, *Mademoiselle Dax,* 10, my translation.

38. Bussy, *Olivia,* 8.

39. The author's name was given as simply "Olivia." Since its original publication in 1949 the novel has been reprinted by Arno Press (New York, 1975) and by Penguin/Virago Press (New York, 1987), with an afterword by Susannah Clapp. Quotations from the novel in this chapter refer to the Arno edition. *Olivia* also was made into a film starring Simone Simon.

40. Dorothy Bussy herself later taught at Allenswood, the school in London where Marie Souvestre was head and Eleanor Roosevelt a favorite pupil. See Blanche Wiesen Cook, *Eleanor Roosevelt,* especially chapter 5, "Allenswood and Marie Souvestre" (102–24).

41. Bussy, *Olivia,* 29.

42. Ibid., 74.

43. Ibid., 36.

44. Both film and play (*Gestern und Heute*) had originally been conceived as a novel, although the novel, *Das Mädchen Manuela,* was published only later. It was translated (by Agnes Neill Scott) into *The Child Manuela* in English, first published by Farrar and Rinehart of New York in 1933, and reprinted by Arno Press of New York in 1975. Winsloe co-wrote the screenplay of the film, which was directed by Léontine Sagan and starred Herta Thiele (Manuela), Dorothea Wieck (Frau von Bernburg), and "one hundred young boarding-school girls."

45. Colette adapted the French text for *Jeunes filles en uniforme* (1932), distributed in France by Gaumont-Franco-Film-Aubert. See Virmaux, *Colette at the Movies,* 210.

46. See Claudia Schoppmann, *Im Fluchtgepäck die Sprache.*

47. Louise Belugou, *Le cinquantenaire de l'Ecole de Sèvres, 1881–1931,* quoted in Mayeur, *L'enseignement secondaire des jeunes filles,* 118, my translation. See also Margadant, *Madame le Professeur.*

48. As Terry Castle has noted, "scenes of plays and costume parties are a staple in novels having to do with girls' schools—and usually betoken a moment at which lesbian undercurrents in the fiction come to a crest." Castle goes on to cite examples from the anglophone tradition—Brigid Brophy's *King of a Rainy Country* (1956) and Christine Crow's *Miss X, or the Wolf Woman* (1990)—and to trace these scenes back to Brontë's *Villette* (*The Apparitional Lesbian,* 43).

49. Galzy was not the first to use the Ecole de Sèvres as the setting of a novel. See also *Les Sévriennes* by Gabrielle Reval (1900), for example, and Waelti-Walters, *Feminist Novelists of the Belle Epoque.*

50. Bair, *Simone de Beauvoir,* 92–93.

51. Monferrand, "Campagne pour faire rééditer Jeanne Galzy," 15, my translation.

52. Galzy, *Jeunes filles en serre chaude,* 172, my translation.

53. Beauvoir, *Journal de guerre,* 84.

54. *Thérèse et Isabelle* (1968), produced and directed by Radley Metzger, with screenplay by Jesse Vogel, and starring Essy Persson and Anna Gael.

55. Courtivron, *Violette Leduc,* 21–22.

56. Ibid.

57. Mallet-Joris, *The Illusionist,* 36. Further references will be given in the text.

58. Mahyère, *I Will Not Serve,* 59. The translation is by Antonia White, author of her own schoolgirl novel, *Frost in May,* as well as translator of Colette.

59. See for example Jaeggy, *Les années bienheureuses du châtiment.*

60. Monferrand, *Les enfants d'Heloïse,* 325.

61. In German, for example, see Anna Elisabet Weirauch's *Der Skorpion,* first published in 1919 (Berlin: Askanischer Verlag) and recently republished (Maroldsweisach: Feministischer Buchverlaf, 1992), and translated into English as *The Scorpion* by Whittaker Chambers, first published in 1932, revised 1948. In English, see Margaret Ferguson, *The Sign of the Ram* (London: Hale, 1943; Philadelphia: Blakiston, 1945), and Pamela Moore, *Chocolates for Breakfast* (New York: Rinehart, 1956). Terry Castle notes further examples: Clemence Dane's *Regiment of Women,* Antonia White's *Frost in May,* Lillian Hellman's *The Children's Hour,* Muriel Spark's *The Prime of Miss Jean Brodie,* and Catharine Stimpson's *Class Notes* (*The Apparitional Lesbian,* 85). See also Fuss, *Identification Papers,* 110.

62. *Oranges Are Not the Only Fruit* was adapted by Winterson for a BBC production starring Geraldine McEwan and Charlotte Coleman and directed by Beeban Kidron in 1989. For a discussion of what got left out of the film, as well as Winterson's responses to the tendency to read both novel and film as autobiographical, see her "Introduction in Four Acts" to the script *Oranges Are Not the Only Fruit* (London: Pandora, 1990).

63. Winterson, *Oranges Are Not the Only Fruit,* 106.

64. See, for example, Barreca and Morse, eds., *The Erotics of Instruction;* Gallop, *Pedagogy* and *Feminist Accused of Sexual Harassment;* Haggerty and Zimmerman, *Professions of Desire;* Morton and Zavarzadeh, *Theory/Pedagogy/Politics.*

65. MacCannell, "Resistance to Sexual Theory," in Morton and Zavarzadeh, *Theory/Pedagogy/Politics,* 66.

66. Fuss, *Identification Papers,* 126.

67. Garber, *Vice Versa,* 325.

68. Gallop, *Feminist Accused of Sexual Harassment,* 57.

69. Gallop, *Pedagogy,* 3. Gallop recognizes that the erotic and the sexual are not always the same and that some discussions of the erotics of the classroom are more concerned with infantile sexuality and the relation to the mother at a psychoanalytic level than with adult forms of sexual expression. In *Feminist Accused of Sexual Harassment,* on the other hand, the experience that triggered the work is explicitly same-sex.

70. Tompkins, *A Life in School,* 144–45.

71. Garber, *Vice Versa,* 325.

72. Litvak, "Discipline, Spectacle, and Melancholia," in Gallop, *Pedagogy,* 19. See also some of the essays in Haggerty and Zimmerman, *Professions of Desire.*

73. Marks, "Memory, Desire, and Pleasure in the Classroom." See also Marks, "It Is a Question of What I Find Exciting."

74. On the American invention of French teachers, see Litvak, "Pedagogy and Sexuality," in Haggerty and Zimmerman, *Professions of Desire.*

75. The character Kleinman (played by Allen) responds to the claim of his friend (played by Mia Farrow) that she is not a prostitute simply because she slept with a man for money by saying that she is only a prostitute in the dictionary definition (in Allen's film *Shadows and Fog,* 1992).

76. Beauvoir, *A Transatlantic Love Affair,* 135–36 (22 January 1948).

77. Gallop, *Feminist Accused of Sexual Harassment,* 86. It is interesting to note how in this book Gallop attributes a foundational role in her feminist development to Beauvoir; see 2–4.

78. For an exception, see the special "women's issue" of *Paidika.*

4

Sensuality and Brutality

Contradictions in Simone de Beauvoir's Writings about Sexuality

ÅSA MOBERG

FROM her first completed literary work, *Quand prime le spirituel* (When things of the spirit come first), Simone de Beauvoir's fiction has explored female experiences of love and sexuality in unusual detail. Sexuality described by women tends to mirror male expectations of what women ought to feel rather than their actual experiences. *Quand prime le spirituel* was completed in 1937 but not published until 1979, as a service to "ceux de mes lecteurs qui me sont vraiment attachés: c'est, somme toute, sous une forme un peu maladroite [a clumsy form], un roman d'apprentissage où s'ébauchent beaucoup des thèmes que j'ai repris par la suite" (viii).[1] It was refused by Gallimard and Grasset. In retrospect what seems even more important is that Sartre did not like it.

In her foreword to the 1979 edition, Beauvoir is full of understanding for the refusals. The text falls between two categories: it is neither a proper novel nor a collection of short stories. It has five leading characters, all women. Each has one section devoted to her, but they also appear in each other's stories. These are called formal flaws (see Beauvoir's comment about "clumsy form," above). The unconventional form, however, could just as well be regarded as an interesting innovation. The book is, in fact, better structured than some of Beauvoir's later novels. The reader is never left on her own with questions about what has happened, to whom, and when, which is often the case in Beauvoir's other novels, where experiments in chronology and literary perspective at times slip out of control.

Reading *Quand prime le spirituel* with a 1990s feminist perspective, it is difficult to avoid the suspicion that the main weakness in those stories of five women's lives (and one death, an early literary representation of Zaza's death) is the fact that men play such a small role. They are not independent human beings; they are portrayed only in relation to women and not at all in a flattering way. (The small part men play is much like the role male writers usually reserve for women in their literary work. But for Beauvoir men do exist, contrary to the frequent practice of male writers, who can allow themselves to write as if women did not exist at all.)

In 1937, the Parisian literary world apparently was not ready for a completely feminine literary perspective that included explicit sex scenes: a detailed description of young Marcelle's wedding night with Denis Charval; several stories about how Marcelle's younger sister Marguerite tries to break out of her protected bourgeois family by pretending to be a prostitute in Parisian bars (convincing nobody, but exposing herself to sexual harassment by strangers); and a description of an unsuccessful lesbian seduction. This is to my knowledge the only fictional piece by Beauvoir about lesbian sex, and it is as chilly and "unsexy" as all other accounts of erotic experiences in the book.

Quand prime le spirituel is a story, or five stories, about how innocent girls meet the world outside of the home, including encounters with adult sexuality. The atmosphere surrounding sexual encounters in these stories can hardly explain why anyone would engage in such activities of their own free will, much less through desire. Brutality and sensuality are intertwined to such a degree that pleasure has to be forced upon the young bride Marcelle by the "commanding hands" of her husband on their wedding night:

> Denis la serra contre lui et elle sentit la chaleur, la tendre élasticité d'un crops nu qui se collait au sien; contre son ventre tressaillait une chair mystérieuse, palpitante et dure; mais plus que par ce contact animal, Marcelle était troublée par les mains habiles qui la caressaient; ces mains n'étaient pas seulement sur la peau un doux

frôlement: elles étaient douées de conscience et de volonté; indiscrètes, impérieuses, elles imposaient le plaisir, c'était leur tyrannie qui faisait défaillir Marcelle de volupté.

Elle souleva les paupières; le visage de Denis lui apparut, changé par le désir, avide, presque méconnaissable; il semblait capable de la battre, de la torturer; cette vue remplit Marcelle d'une jouissance si aiguë qu'elle se mit à gémir. "Je suis à sa merci," se dit-elle et elle sombra dans une extase où se mêlaient la honte, la crainte et la joie. Elle gémissait si fort que Denis dut lui fermer la bouche de sa main; elle baisa cette main; elle aurait voulu crier à Denis qu'elle était sa chose, son esclave, et des larmes coulèrent sur ses joues. Soudain il pénétra en elle; sans qu'elle éprouvât exactement du plaisir, ce viol de sa chair la plus secrète la fit suffoquer de gratitude et d'humilité; elle acceptait avec une soumission passionnée chacun des coups que Denis lui portait, et comme pour rendre cette possession plus entière elle laissa sa conscience glisser dans la nuit.

Quand elle sortait de sa torpeur, Denis avait repris son visage ordinaire et souriait; alors, gênée, elle tira les draps jusqu'à son menton. Elle voulait parler et ne trouva rien à dire. "Tu es heureuse?" murmura-t-il. "Mais oui," dit-elle avec un petit rire. En cet instant, elle le haït violemment; elle pensa avec colère qu'elle avait gémi dans ses bras et qu'il avait deviné la profondeur de son trouble. Elle rougit de honte et cette fois sa confusion ne se doublait d'aucun plaisir.

[Denis drew her close and she felt the warmth, the tender suppleness of a naked body against her own: and a mysterious, quivering, hard flesh throbbed against her belly. But even more than by this animal contact, Marcelle was stirred by the skilful hands that fondled her; it was not only a delightful stroking of her skin, for these hands had an awareness and a will of their own; they were shameless and masterful, they compelled the coming of her pleasure; and it was their tyranny that made Marcelle faint with sensual delight.

She opened her eyes; Denis' face appeared before her, changed with desire, intensely eager, almost unrecognizable: he looked capable of beating her, torturing her, and the sight filled Marcelle with so piercing a pleasure that she began to groan. "I'm at his mercy," she said to herself and she was engulfed by an ecstasy in which shame and fear and joy were all intermingled. She groaned so loudly that Denis had to put his hand over her mouth: she kissed the hand—she would have liked to call out to Denis that she was his thing, his slave: and tears ran down her cheeks. All at once he penetrated her: she did not exactly feel pleasure, but this violation of her most secret flesh made her gasp with gratitude and humility. She took every one of Denis's piercing thrusts with passionate submission, and to make his possession of her the more complete she let her consciousness glide away into the night.

When she woke up Denis' face had its usual look once more, and he was smiling; this embarrassed her and she pulled the sheet up to her chin. She would have liked to speak, but she found nothing to say. "Happy?" he murmured. "Of course," she said with a little laugh. In that instant she utterly hated him: angrily she remembered that she had groaned in his arms and that he had known how very deeply she was moved. She blushed for shame and this time there was no pleasure mingled with her confusion.][2]

The submission is taken one step further. When the bride says what her groom wants to hear—"I adore you"—he takes it as her acceptance of whatever sexual desire he may have. He turns her body around and asks her to kneel over:

> "Reste ainsi, chuchota-t-il, c'est plus agréable." Elle frémit, un homme, doué de conscience, lui proposait une immonde complicité; délibérément, il la pliait dans cette posture ridicule, il en savourait l'ignominie. "A quatre pattes, comme les bêtes," pensa-t-elle; cette idée l'affola; il lui fallait tendre tous ses muscles pour maintenir son corps dans cette attitude avilissante, elle était semblable à ces victimes que le bourreau oblige à danser sous le fouet. "Il jouit de moi, il jouit de moi," se dit-elle dans un paroxysme de volupté. Quand Denis se retira d'elle, elle retomba sur le lit pantelante, presque évanouie.

> ["Stay like that," he whispered. "It's more fun." She trembled: a man, a being endowed with a conscience, wanted her to join him in an unclean act. He was bending her into this ridiculous position and relishing its ignominy. "On all fours, like animals," she thought: the idea made her head spin and he [*sic*] had to tense all his [*sic*] muscles to keep her in this degrading posture—she was like one of those victims the executioners force to dance under the whip. "He's enjoying me, he's enjoying me," she said to herself in a paroxysm of sensual delight. When Denis drew away she fell gasping on the bed, almost fainting.] [3]

The wedding night ends with the bride in tears, turned to the wall, unable to face her husband. The next day, they travel to Mont-Saint-Michel, another disappointment: "une fois de plus elle éprouva que la vie est toujours en deçà des rêves" [Once more she perceived that life always fell short of dreams].[4]

Life never meets your expectations. Not in sex, not in travel. This has very little to do with the general romantic dream of what a first sexual encounter should be like.

Having worked for seven years in the 1980s as an advice columnist on love and sex for young girls in the Swedish weekly *Vecko-Revyn,* I was surprised to discover a passage about a young woman's first sexual experience that so openly recognizes how repelling the situation can be. Shock and questioning, or denial by the young woman of her own reactions, seem to be common to this day. If you don't respond the way women do in books you have read or movies you have seen, you normally lack the confidence to trust your own experience.

In Beauvoir's description of Marcelle's wedding night, it's interesting to see how she deals with this problem: she is strong enough to insist on remembering and describing the brutal side of intercourse. She concedes to convention by trying to make this brutality an erotic experience for the bride who, were it not for her own excited exclamations, would be regarded by the reader as a victim. (The French word *trouble* [excitement] is not synonymous with the English word "trouble" [problem], which would otherwise seem appropriate to describe Marcelle's situation.)

In *Det kallas kärlek* (It's called love), an interesting Swedish social-psychological study of "woman's subordination and man's superordination among young, equal couples," the English summary ends with a list of "new social mechanisms." One has to do with how a couple describes their mutual reality: "Finally, the woman expresses an *uncertainty about her own conception of reality.* In different situations she turns to the man and allows him to determine whether what she feels is real. It is the man who stands for reality and thus is given the opportunity to interpret their shared reality."[5]

When Beauvoir wrote *Quand prime le spirituel* the people who judged it were men: Jean-Paul Sartre, who was (or had already ceased to be?) her lover, and the editors at Gallimard and Grasset.

My own experience has led me to the conclusion that nothing is so sensitive for men making literary decisions as male erotic vanity. My first novel was never submitted to a publisher; it was put away on a shelf by the man I was living with. He had decided that no one ought to read it, since it could reveal to the world that I had had an affair with another man. I had a choice, of course: I could have had the book published, but it would have ruined the relationship, and I wanted the relationship.

I recently wrote a book on Beauvoir and her influence on my life,[6] and to my surprise all the men who read the manuscript and gave me good advice were preoccupied with the same issue: I must not be too hard on the man with whom I shared twenty-four years. I now seem to be getting in touch with all the anger toward him that I could not express when he was part of my life. He died in 1988, leaving me a widow at the age of forty-one.

I thought I had been gentle in my description of him, of how he wanted to rule my life and my career (a successful one; he did a good job), but I encountered a sort of collective male protectiveness: could you please cut this or that out, it is too private, or too detailed, or whatever. Men who did not even know him felt personally hurt, so I ended by cutting a few things, deciding to rewrite them later, as fiction.

Fiction has this great advantage: you can tell the truth. Nowhere is this more obvious than in the writing of Simone de Beauvoir. Her memoirs, with their adjustment to the demands of "fact," end up being her most fictive work. Her novels, where she was free to write as she wished, tell a truth.

Her love for Sartre is never described erotically, not even in a few lines. The closest she gets is in a letter to Nelson Algren dated Sunday, 8 August

1948: "He was my first lover, nobody had even kissed me before. We spent a long time together and I told you already how I care for him, but it was rather deep friendship than love; love was not very successful. Chiefly because he does not care much for sexual life. He is a warm, lively man everywhere, but not in bed."[7] The lack of information about the erotic side of Beauvoir's love for Sartre marks a sharp contrast to many other love affairs she had throughout her life. It seems that even those with women, denied by Beauvoir during her lifetime, are now known and documented.[8]

Writing about sex is the most difficult thing a writer can do, according to my experience. It takes courage to go anywhere beyond prevailing clichés. You have to be prepared for questions and attacks, even though much of the criticism will never be brought into the open. Most people are scared of even discussing sex. Whatever standpoint you take, you have to reveal something about yourself, and you risk making involuntary revelations out of ignorance or prejudice.

To give such an unconventional picture of a sexual encounter as Beauvoir does in *Quand prime le spirituel* means taking a brave literary stance. The writer must have some kind of personal experience to lean on when meeting objections, in this case a dismissal from a male literary establishment that would feel unanimously ill at ease: this is not what a bride feels on her wedding night! (A correct objection from the male point of view, since no bride is likely to have made this kind of complaint in real life.)

The character of Denis Charval is based on Beauvoir's cousin Jacques, but according to her *Mémoires d'une jeune fille rangée* (Memoirs of a dutiful daughter) the relation between young Simone and her cousin was one without sex.

I am not saying that everything she (or any other writer) produces has to have a background in personal experiences. But having read some thousand pages of various books and articles by Beauvoir, I believe that in her case the autobiographical base is solidly established. This does not seem to be contested by anyone any longer, now that the writer is dead and does not have to do so herself in order to protect her private life. If there is a real-life person behind Denis Charval as lover, who could he be except Sartre? This also makes sense regarded the other way around: if Sartre was such an insensitive lover, the erotic part of the relation could never be openly described by a woman who wanted to maintain a close relationship with him, and it was never described by Simone de Beauvoir.

The opposite can be seen in *Les mandarins* (The mandarins), where the real-life Nelson Algren is openly connected to the wonderful literary lover Lewis Brogan: "Not Exactly Our Story, but . . ."[9]

If a man is described as a marvelous lover in literature, a woman writer obviously has less to contend with. The real-life man is not likely to be hurt, even if the readers believe they can identify him. I don't think Beauvoir would have made Algren so easily recognizable if she had suspected that his feelings would be hurt. Maybe the fact that they *were* hurt proves that men don't want be recognized as fictional lovers, even if they are idolized.

The intensity of the sexual passion between Anne Dubreuilh and Lewis Brogan in *Les mandarins* is great, but you look in vain for physical details in the description. The atmosphere is one where sensuality reigns. Maybe tenderness cannot survive the kind of detailed reporting of physical sensations that makes the description of brutality so poignant. The following scene of mutual desire, even in all its beauty, makes me think of the old kiss and hug "and afterwards they smoked a cigarette" stuff. The two lovers-to-be find themselves in Brogan's apartment and Anne dives into bed, where a slightly embarrassed Brogan finds her when he comes with the clean sheets he had planned to put on the bed before they used it:

> Il restait sur le pas de la porte tout embarrassé de son fardeau pompeux. "Je suis très bien," dis-je en tirant jusqu'à mon menton le drap tiède dans lequel il avait dormi, la nuit dernière. Il s'est éloigné, il est revenu.
>
> —Anne!
>
> Il s'était abattu sur moi et son accent m'a bouleversée. Pour la première fois, je dis son nom: "Lewis!"
>
> —Anne! Je suis si heureux!
>
> Il était nu, j'étais nue, et je n'éprouvais aucune gêne; son regard ne pouvait pas me blesser; il ne me jugeait pas, il ne me préférait rien. Des cheveux aux orteils, ses mains m'apprenaient par coeur. De nouveau je dis: "J'aime vos mains."
>
> —Vous les aimez?
>
> —Toute la soirée je me suis demandé si je les sentirais sur mon corps.
>
> —Vous les sentirez toute la nuit, dit-il.

Soudain, il n'était plus ni gauche ni modeste. Son désir me transfigurait. Moi qui depuis si longtemps n'avait plus de goût, plus de forme, je possédais de nouveau des seins, un ventre, un sexe, une chair; j'étais nourrissante comme le pain, odorante comme la terre. C'était si miraculeux que je n'ai pas pensé à mesurer mon temps ni mon plaisir; je sais seulement que lorsque nous nous sommes endormis on entendait le faible pépiement de l'aube.

Une odeur de café m'a réveillée; j'ouvris les yeux et je souris en voyant sur une chaise voisine ma robe de lainage bleu dans les bras d'un veston gris.

[He remained standing in the doorway, embarrassed by his ceremonious burden. "I'm very comfortable," I said, pulling the warm sheet up to my chin, that sheet in which he had slept the night before. He moved away, came back again.

"Anne!"

The way he said it moved me deeply. He threw himself on me and for the first time I spoke his name. "Lewis!"

"Anne! I'm so happy!"

He was naked, I was naked, and I felt no constraint; he couldn't hurt me by looking at me, for he didn't judge me, didn't compare me. From head to toe, his hands were learning my body by heart. Again I said: "I like your hands."

"Do you like them?"

"All evening I've been wondering if I'd feel them on my body."

"You'll feel them all night long," he said.

Suddenly, he was no longer either awkward or modest. His desire transformed me. I who for so long a time had been without taste, without form, again possessed breasts, a belly, a sex, flesh; I was as nourishing as bread, as fragrant as earth. It was so miraculous that I didn't think of measuring my time or my pleasure; I know only that before we fell asleep I could hear the gentle chirpings of dawn.

The smell of coffee awakened me. I opened my eyes and smiled when I saw my blue woolen dress in the arms of a gray jacket on a chair next to the bed.][10]

In *Les mandarins,* sensuality and brutality show up in different sexual situations. Much of the atmosphere of Marcelle's wedding night is replayed in the description of Anne Dubreuilh's night with Victor Scriassine at the beginning of the 1954 novel, including the moments of violence:

> —Ah! tu ne veux pas! disait-il. Tu ne veux pas! Tête de mule! Il me frappa légèrement au menton; j'étais trop lasse pour m'évader dans la colère; je me mis à trembler. Un poing qui s'abat; mille poings. . . . "La violence est partout," pensai-je; je tremblais et des larmes se mirent à couler.
>
> ["You don't want to!" he was saying. "You don't want to! Stubborn mule!" He struck me lightly on the chin; I was too weary to escape into anger. I began to tremble. A beating fist, thousands of fists. . . . "Violence is everywhere," I thought. I trembled and tears began running down my cheeks.][11]

In *Le deuxième sexe* (The second sex) there are frequent references to the violent character of male sexuality: "C'est par le vagin que la femme est pénétrée et fécondée; il ne devient un centre érotique que par l'intervention du mâle et celle-ci constitue toujours une sorte de viol" [Woman is penetrated and fecundated by way of the vagina, which becomes an erotic center only through the intervention of the male, and this always constitutes a kind of violation].[12] The following lines in *Le deuxième sexe* seem to be more or less a theoretical summary of what Beauvoir wanted to describe with Marcelle's wedding night in *Quand prime le spirituel,* at the time still unpublished:

> Ces étreintes analogues à celles de la lutte alors qu'elle n'a jamais lutté la terrorisent. Elle s'abandonnait aux caresses d'un fiancé, d'un camarade, d'un collègue, d'un homme civilisé et courtois: mais il a pris un aspect étranger, égoïste et têtu; elle n'a plus de recours contre cet inconnu. Il n'est pas rare que la première expérience de la jeune fille soit un véritable viol et que l'homme se montre odieusement brutal.
>
> [These embraces, so much like a hand-to-hand tussle, frighten her, for she has never tussled. She is used to the caresses of a fiancé,

a comrade, a colleague, a civilized and polite man; but now he takes on a peculiar aspect, egoistical and headstrong; she is without recourse against this stranger. It is not uncommon for the young girl's first experience to be a real rape and for the man to act in an odiously brutal manner.]

A few lines further down:

> D'ailleurs, l'homme fût-il déférent et courtois, la première pénétration est toujours un viol. Parce qu'elle souhaite des caresses sur ses lèvres, ses seins, que, peut-être, elle convoite entre ses cuisses une jouissance connue ou pressentie, voilà qu'un sexe mâle déchire la jeune fille et s'introduit dans des régions où il n'était pas appelé.
>
> [Furthermore, however deferential and polite the man may be, the first penetration is always a violation. Because she desires caresses on lips or breasts, or even longs for a known or imagined pleasure more specifically sexual, what happens is that a man's sex organ tears the young girl and penetrates into regions where it has not been desired.]

In the Swedish translation, the rest of the paragraph is cut out. H. M. Parshley remains true to the French original, which continues:

> On a souvent décrit la pénible surprise d'une vierge pâmée dans les bras d'un mari ou d'un amant, qui croit toucher enfin à l'accomplissement de ses rêves voluptueux et qui sent au secret de son sexe une douleur imprévue; les rêves s'évanouissent, le trouble se dissipe, et l'amour prend la figure d'une opération chirurgicale.
>
> [Many writers have described the painful surprise of a virgin, lying enchanted in the arms of lover or husband, who believes she is at last to fulfill her voluptuous dreams and who feels an unexpected pain in her secret sexual parts; her dreams vanish, her excitement fades, and love assumes the aspect of a surgical operation.] (2:144; 382–83)

The perception of intercourse as resembling a surgical operation is repeated several times in *Le deuxième sexe.* So is the question of light and dark. The demand for light made by the man is part of the violence he inflicts on the woman, who needs darkness to protect herself in this embarrassing and humiliating situation:

> L'amant est plus redoutable encore qu'un regard: c'est un juge; il va la révéler à elle-même dans sa vérité; même éprise passionnément de son image, toute jeune fille au moment du verdict masculin doute de soi; et c'est pourquoi elle réclame l'obscurité, elle se cache dans les draps.
>
> [Her lover is still more redoubtable than a look: he is a judge. He is to reveal her to herself in very truth; though passionately enchanted with her own reflection, every young girl feels uncertain of herself at the moment of the masculine verdict; and so she wants the light out, she hides under the bedclothes.] (2:142; 381)

All young women in this situation feel the imperfection of their bodies strongly, states Beauvoir. Some may fear "quelque malformation secrète," some secret deformation. (It is a fear much stronger to this day than I would have thought before reading the mail from young women to the advice column I wrote. A common dream of Swedish teenage girls was one of plastic surgery to the labia minora or majora to make the genitals "normal," although I'm not sure where they could have encountered an image of normality for this part of the body.) "Même si elles ne connaissent pas ces obsessions, elles s'effraient à l'idée que certaines régions de leur corps qui n'existaient ni pour elles, ni pour personne, qui n'existaient absolument pas, vont soudain émerger à la lumière." "Girls without these obsessions are often alarmed at the idea that certain actually nonexistent parts of the body will suddenly become visible," says the Parshley English translation (2:142; 382). The French original talks of those nonexistent parts of the body "qui vont soudain émerger à la lumière," which will suddenly emerge into the light. Women's fear of light is a recurrent theme in Beauvoir's writings about sexuality, for example, in *Quand prime le spirituel, Le deuxième sexe,* and Anne's night with Scriassine in *Les mandarins.*

I could cite endless quotes from *Le deuxième sexe* to strengthen the point Beauvoir makes: intercourse between woman and man is a rather brutal affair, more surgical than sexual. For tenderness, women had better turn to each other.

The fact that tenderness is not at all a striking aspect of Beauvoir's notes on her relations with Olga Kosakiewicz, Bianca Lamblin, and Nathalie Sorokine, as related in the *Journal de guerre* (War diary) and *Lettres à Sartre* (Letters to Sartre), is another matter, a lesbian side of the brutality-sensuality contradiction that I'm not going to explore here. The chilly atmosphere reaches a freezing point in the seduction scene between Marie-Ange and Marguerite in *Quand prime le spirituel* (204–6).

Any discussion of *Le deuxième sexe* is complicated by the fact that translators and publishers in different countries have had great difficulties handling the almost one thousand pages of the original. The Swedish version, published in 1973, covers about half. "L'initiation sexuelle" is cut from forty to twenty-five pages. In part 2, the sections "La lesbienne," "La vie de société," and "Prostituées et hétaïres" are left out altogether, as well as the sections in part 3 called "Justifications: La narcissiste, l'amoureuse, la mystique."[13]

It would not be correct to say that the text has been altogether misrepresented in Swedish, but it is mutilated and has lost some of its edge. In "L'initiation sexuelle" some of Beauvoir's reasoning about sex and violence has been lost:

> Pour l'amant, l'acte amoureux est donc conquête et victoire. Si, chez un autre homme, l'érection apparaît souvent comme une dérisoire parodie de l'acte volontaire, chacun cependant la considère en son propre cas avec quelque vanité. Le vocabulaire érotique des mâles s'inspire du vocabulaire militaire: l'amant a la fougue d'un soldat, son sexe se bande comme un arc, quand il éjacule il "décharge," c'est une mitrailleuse, un canon; il parle d'attaque, d'assaut, de victoire. Il y a dans son rut on ne sait quel goût d'héroïsme.
>
> [So for the lover the act of love is conquest, victory. If erection is often regarded in another man as a comic parody on voluntary action, each one none the less views it in himself with a touch of

> vanity. The erotic vocabulary of males is drawn from military terminology: the lover has the mettle of a soldier, his organ is tense like a bow, to ejaculate is to "go off"; he speaks of attack, assault, victory. In his sex excitement there is a certain flavor of heroism.] [14]

Another example of truncation in the Swedish translation is a passage where love between women is compared to love between a woman and a man. Girls have the same longing as boys, Beauvoir writes, for things that are soft and tender. The following lines are not translated into Swedish:

> Elle n'a pas de goût pour les étoffes rugueuses, les graviers, les rocailles, les saveurs âpres, les odeurs acides; c'est la chair maternelle qu'elle a d'abord comme ses frères caressée et chérie; dans son narcissisme, dans ses expériences homosexuelles diffuses ou précises elle se posait comme un sujet et elle cherchait la possession d'un corps féminin. Quand elle affronte le mâle, elle a dans la paume de ses mains, sur ses lèvres, l'envie de caresser activement une proie. Mais l'homme avec ses muscles durs, sa peau râpeuse et souvent velue, son odeur rude, ses traits grossièrement taillés ne lui paraît pas désirable.
>
> [She has no liking for rough fabrics, gravel, rockwork, bitter flavors, acid odors; what she, like her brothers, first caressed and cherished was her mother's flesh. In her narcissism, in her homosexual experiences, whether diffuse or definite, she acts as subject and seeks possession of a feminine body.] [15]

The Swedish translation starts as the text continues: "When she confronts the male, she feels in her hands and her lips the desire to caress a prey actively. But crude man, with his hard muscles, his rough and often hairy skin, his strong odor, his coarse features, does not appeal to her as desirable"—you can almost feel the editors cry "enough is enough!," and the end of this sentence is not translated into Swedish—"he even seems repulsive."

Of course it is possible that this repulsion is theoretical and has nothing to do with Beauvoir's personal experiences. But is it likely? I find it hard to believe that heterosexual intercourse would be described in such a consistently negative way if she had had experiences that were completely different. The repulsion here is not something that is inspired by men in general; it comes from men whom she has gone to bed with. It probably comes from one man, Sartre. It seems likely that he would communicate this negative feeling about his physical appearance, since this was how he experienced his own body.

In *La cérémonie des adieux* (Adieux: A farewell to Sartre) Beauvoir interviews Sartre about his concept of his body and his sexuality. You get the impression that he engaged in sexual acts for formal reasons, because it was expected of a man, rather than for pleasure:

> Il faudrait dire que ce qui dominait, c'était la tendresse active de la main qui caresse; mais la réciprocité était la chose que je sentais le moins; le fait que l'autre personne pouvait également avoir du plaisir à sentir mon corps. . . . Il y avait une coupure entre ce que la personne pouvait prendre, et donner en face de moi, parce que cette coupure existait chez moi. Alors, comme j'étais convenablement sexué, je bandais rapidement, facilement; je faisais l'amour souvent, mais sans un très grand plaisir. Juste un petit plaisir à la fin, mais assez médiocre.
>
> [One ought to say that the dominant aspect was the caressing hand's active tenderness, but reciprocity was the thing I felt least—the fact that the other person might also have pleasure in feeling my body. . . . There was a gap between what the other could take and give in relation to me, since that gap existed in me. So as I was reasonably well equipped sexually my erection was quick and easy, and I often made love, but without very great pleasure. Just a little pleasure at the end, but pretty feeble.] [16]

The demand to have intercourse comes not from within, but from outside:

> Ça me paraissait obligatoire, et c'est pour ça que dans mes rapports avec une femme, il fallait que ça se termine comme ça . . . Mais ça venait de la représentation d'autrui, de ce qu'on lit dans les livres, ce qu'on me disait. Mais ça n'était pas mon désir à moi. J'aurais très bien été dans un lit, nu avec une femme nue, à la caresser, l'embrasser, mais sans aller jusqu'à l'acte sexuel.

> [The act seemed to me required and that was why, in my relations with women, things had to end that way. . . . But this came from other people's ideas, from what was read in books, from what one was told. It wasn't my personal desire. I should have been quite happy naked in bed with a naked woman, caressing and kissing her, but without going as far as the sexual act.][17]

If a man does not feel at ease in his own body, he cannot imagine that anyone else could take pleasure in it. Instead of pleasure there is a void around him for his partners to fill with their versions of "représentation d'autrui." We are all socialized to know what to expect in a sexual situation, or at least we believe we are until we find ourselves in circumstances where there is no connection between expectations and reality.

For a man who takes so little pleasure in making love to women, the situation has to have another purpose in order to make sense at all. Why repeatedly engage in a kind of behavior that you do not like? It seems likely that this emptiness, this lack of sexual pleasure, is filled with attempts of conquest, and that Sartre's personal problems as a sexual being explain many of the negative views Beauvoir expresses on heterosexuality in general.

If intercourse is a question of conquest and victory for the man, the affair between Anne Dubreuilh and Victor Scriassine in *Les mandarins* is a typical case of how a male-female relationship develops, from the first introduction to bed. Here the man is usually referred to by his last name. To me there is an intuitive association with a scream, to someone who is in pain or who inflicts pain, maybe because the first part of "Scriassine" is pronounced exactly like the Swedish word for scream, *skri,* or for that matter like the English "scream." It contains the French word for scream, *cri.*

Scriassine's first name—Victor—is hardly a coincidence. For a man who is portrayed as engaging in lovemaking as an act of conquest, it fits almost too well. Of course, in his victory he loses everything he wants to win. This is Beauvoir at her best, describing life's inevitable contradictions that dominate everything, sex included.

Victor Scriassine wants to seduce Anne Dubreuilh, and by the next morning he may think he has succeeded in doing so. But he sets out in such an impersonal and clumsy way that he loses over and over again, from the initial sexual excitement he inspires in her to the victory of giving her an orgasm. She pretends in order to get it over with—to my knowledge the first faked orgasm in the history of literature.

It is clear to the reader that Anne submits to this humiliating game due to a feeling of sympathy, if not pity, for the lonely writer. During the process of male victory, even this initial female sympathy is lost.

I have read from this part of *Les mandarins* in Sweden several times when speaking publicly about Beauvoir. The audience typically consists of 90 to 95 percent women, and the response is overwhelming. This 1954 description of a woman trying to get through an erotic encounter without hurting the fragile male ego by showing how repulsed she is obviously has relevance for Swedish women of all ages today.

Scriassine meets Anne at a party. He is impressed by her intelligence and compliments it in a way that is insulting to her sex:

> "Vous n'êtes vraiment pas sotte. En général je n'aime pas les femmes intelligentes: peut-être parce qu'elles ne sont pas assez intelligentes; alors elles veulent se donner des preuves, elles parlent tout le temps et elles ne comprennent rien. Ce qui m'a frappé la première fois que je vous ai vue, c'est votre manière de vous taire."
>
> ["You're not so dumb, you know. Generally, I dislike intelligent women, maybe because they're not intelligent enough. They always want to prove to themselves, and to everyone else, how terribly smart they are. So all they do is talk and never understand anything. What struck me the first time I saw you was that way you have of keeping quiet."][18]

No doubt this is the dream of many intellectual men: a woman who knows how to keep quiet in an intelligent way. There is a mutual attraction, much to Anne's surprise. She accepts Scriassine's invitation. They have a drink together, and the conversation closes in on the decisive, seductive phrase, which in this case will be recognized by the faithful Beauvoir reader from *L'invitée* (She came to stay), where Françoise uses it when seducing Gerbert.

> Un instant ils se toisèrent comme deux ennemis. Françoise fit le vide en elle et les mots franchirent enfin ses lèvres.

—Je riais en me demandant quelle tête vous feriez, vous qui n'aimez pas les complications, si je vous proposais de coucher avec moi.

[For a moment they surveyed each other like two enemies. Françoise became completely numb, but the words finally crossed her lips.

"I was smiling—wondering how you would look—you who loathe complications—if I suggested your sleeping with me."][19]

The use of this phrase in *Les mandarins* marks an interesting gender switch compared to what appears to be "the original." Toril Moi has pointed to the real-life source, which is found in *Lettres à Sartre,* where Beauvoir describes her seduction of Bost.[20]

In *Les mandarins* a general discussion follows as to why a woman who is perceived as emancipated has to go to bed with just anybody. Then Scriassine looks seriously at Anne and says: "Si un homme pour qui vous auriez quelque sympathie vous proposait de but en blanc de passer la nuit avec lui, le feriez-vous?" ["If a man, a man for whom you might have a little liking, asked you straight out to spend the night with him, would you do it?"]. That depends, says Anne Dubreuilh, "on him, on me, on the circumstances."[21] When Scriassine drives the conversation to a quick "yes," the attraction that Anne first felt suddenly vanishes. They don't have anything left to talk about. Anne is thirty-nine years old, but you get the feeling that she ends up in bed with this man because she does not know how to avoid it without hurting his feelings. He says:

—Montons dans ma chambre.

—Tout de suite?

—Pourquoi non? Vous voyez bien que nous ne trouvons plus rien à nous dire.

["Let's go up to my room."

"Right away?"

"Why not? It's obvious we have nothing more to say to each other."]

Half a page later they are in bed and Scriassine has managed to destroy the emerging erotic atmosphere several times over. If this man had any sensitivity for other people, he would keep his mouth shut. But alas, he talks:

> "On dirait que la jeune fille est intimidée. Nous ne ferons pas de mal à la jeune fille; nous la déflorerons, mais sans lui faire du mal." Ces mots qui ne s'adressaient pas à moi m'éveillèrent durement. Je n'étais pas venue ici pour jouer à la pucelle violée, ni à aucun autre jeu.
>
> ["The little girl seems frightened. But we won't hurt the little girl; we'll deflower her, but painlessly." Those words, which hardly had anything to do with me, rudely brought me out of my dream. I hadn't come here to play at being the ravished maiden, nor at any other game.] (73; 81)

When the atmosphere is back to a more erotic level, he talks again, asking in a matter-of-fact way if Anne uses any contraceptive:

> "Faut-il que je fasse attention? —Si c'est possible. —Tu n'es pas bouchée?" La question était si brutale que j'eus un haut-le-corps: "Non, dis-je. —Ah! pourquoi?" C'était difficile de repartir; de nouveau je me recueillis sous ses mains, je rassemblai le silence, je me collai à sa peau et je dévorai sa chaleur par tous mes pores: mes os, mes muscles fondaient à ce feu et la paix s'enroulait autour de moi en soyeuses spirales quand il dit impérieusement: "Ouvre les yeux."
>
> ["Do I have to be careful?"
>
> "If you can."
>
> "You mean you're not wearing anything?"
>
> The question was so brutal it made me start.
>
> "No," I replied.
>
> "Why not? Why aren't you?" he asked angrily.
>
> It was difficult to begin again. Once more I gathered myself together under his hands, welcomed the silence, clung to his body and absorbed his warmth through my every pore. My bones, my flesh melted in that fire; a feeling of serenity wrapped itself around

> me in silky spirals. And then he said commandingly, "Open your eyes."] (73; 81–82)

This is a lover who not only wants everything to be visible, but wants it described as well. He talks all the time. Anne closes her eyes after having obeyed and looked once. Disaster is close at hand when he once again commands her to look:

> "Regarde." Je secouai faiblement la tête: ce qui se passait là-bas me concernait si peu que si j'avais regardé, je me serais fait l'effet d'un voyeur. Il dit: "Tu as honte! la jeune fille a honte!" Ce triomphe l'occupa un moment puis de nouveau il parla: "Dis-moi ce que tu sens? dis-le-moi." Je restai muette. Je devinais une présence en moi, sans vraiment la sentir, comme on s'étonne de l'acier du dentiste dans une gencive engourdie. "As-tu du plaisir? Je veux que tu aies du plaisir." Sa voix s'irritait, elle exigeait des comptes. "Tu n'en as pas? ça ne fait rien: la nuit est longue." La nuit serait trop courte, l'éternité trop courte: la partie était perdue, je le savais. Je me demandais comment en finir: on est bien désarmée quand on se trouve la nuit seule, nue, dans des bras ennemis.
>
> ["Look!" I feebly shook my head; what was happening down there concerned me so little that had I looked I would have felt like a Peeping Tom. "You're ashamed!" he said. "The little girl's ashamed!" He lingered over that triumph for a moment and then began muttering again. "Tell me what you feel?" he said. "Tell me." I remained mute. Inside me, I sensed a presence without really feeling it, as you sense a dentist's steel tool against a swollen gum. "Do you like it? I want you to like it." His voice sounded vexed, demanded an accounting. "You don't? That's all right—the night is long." But the night would be all too short, eternity itself too short. The game was lost, I knew it and wondered only how to finish with it. When you find yourself at night, alone and naked, in enemy arms, you're completely defenseless.] (74; 82)

Those lines strike me as an incredibly accurate description of the war between men and women, a daily battle that takes place everywhere, including in bed. Scriassine wants his woman of thirty-nine to play the role of a young virgin. He commands her to enjoy the show he stages, he strikes her when she does not show the right amount of excitement, and he finally ends by pleading for a last sacrifice to his male vanity: a mutual orgasm. "Tu veux? tu me diras: C'est maintenant. . . ." ["All right? When you're ready, say 'now.'"]

The situation becomes so ridiculous that Anne, despite her anger, ends up feeling sorry for him.

> Voilà ce qu'ils ont trouvé: la synchronisation! comme si ça prouvait quelque chose; comme si ça pouvait tenir lieu d'entente. Même si nous jouissons ensemble, en serions-nous moins séparés? Je sais bien que mon plaisir n'a pas d'écho dans son coeur, et si j'attends le sien avec impatience, c'est seulement pour être délivrée. Cependant j'étais vaincue: j'acceptai de soupirer, de geindre; pas très adroitement, j'imagine, puisqu'il me demanda:
>
> —Tu n'as pas joui?
>
> —Si, je t'assure.
>
> ["That's all they've ever discovered—synchronization!" As if it proved anything, as if it could take the place of simple understanding! Even if it did happen at the same instant, would we be any less apart? I knew my pleasure found no echo in his heart, and if I impatiently awaited his it was only to be done with. And yet I had been subdued, was willing to sigh, to moan. But not very convincingly, I imagine, for he asked me, "Didn't it happen to you?"
>
> "Yes, believe me."] (75; 83)

Comparing this to Marcelle's wedding night in *Quand prime le spirituel,* the most striking difference is the writer's refusal to concede to male convention. This may be erotic behavior that a man imagines to be sexy, but the woman is carried away by desire only for a few brief moments. Every time he instructs her, he turns her off a bit more, until she is finally cooled down so much that she fakes an orgasm just to put an end to the sad situation.

The man and the woman who meet each other in Scriassine's hotel room are not human beings exploring each other's lust and desire; they are playing roles according to a script determined by circumstances, by society, by expectations.

Who has described such a way of handling erotic situations? Sartre is one, as quoted above. Arthur Koestler is often mentioned as the person on whom Victor Scriassine may be based, and Beauvoir writes about having spent a night with him in a letter to Nelson Algren (30 September 1947).[22] However, there are several reasons to suspect that the personality of Scriassine is a literary construction and not a description of Koestler's habits as a seducer, a suspicion that is both contested and confirmed by the picture given in David Cesarani's *Arthur Koestler: The Homeless Mind.*[23] In this fascinating biography Cesarani presents Scriassine as a picture of Koestler: "Nothing Koestler wrote about himself, or anyone else for that matter, is as perceptive as this fictionalised portrayal" (277–78). But in the biography you also can find several indications that Victor Scriassine is not identical to Koestler, the most important being that compared to Scriassine, Koestler emerges as a much more violent man.[24] He even raped his friends' wives, one of whom says that the way he went about it indicated that it was part of a pattern. "He was a hell of a raper," says Richard Crossman, a prominent leader of the Labor Party.[25] I believe that the real-life lover behind Victor Scriassine is Sartre, though concealed in an elegant way. Nobody would suspect it to be him because everybody knows that, whatever role he played in Beauvoir's life, he was not a casual lover dismissed after a deplorable one-night stand.

On the other hand, there are obvious resemblances between Denis Charval and Victor Scriassine, such as their insensitive way of trying to force pleasure upon a woman and their disrespect for her sexual integrity, including demands of lights on, clothes off, and eyes open.

If you compare the atmosphere, and even some details, with the account of Sartre as seducer given by Bianca Lamblin in *A Disgraceful Affair,* it is hard to avoid the impression that these stories are about the same man. Sartre exerted much effort courting Lamblin, Beauvoir's student and lover ("Louise Védrine" in the memoirs), in 1939. When he starts talking about consummating the relationship, she sees no reason to refuse. He takes her to the hotel where both he and Beauvoir are living. As they approach the building, he says: "The hotel chamber-maid will really be surprised, because I already took a girl's virginity yesterday."[26]

Sartre clearly has an obsession with virgins. The formal procedure of "seducing a virgin" is more important than what the virgin of the day may feel. He has to state his conquest even before it is made. The only reason a victory is still possible after such an opening is, of course, that virgins don't know anything about what intercourse should or could be like if there were to be any sexual pleasure in it for them.

It starts badly, you might say, and Lamblin says so too: "I'll never understand why I didn't react to such boorishness, nor why Sartre saw fit to say what he did." The seduction continues in the same disastrous psychological climate:

> When we got to his room, Sartre undressed almost completely and stood by the sink to wash his feet, raising first one leg, then the other. I was intimidated. When I asked him to draw the curtains a bit to shut out some of the light, he refused flatly, saying that what we were going to do should be done in broad daylight. I hid behind the curtain of a closet to undress; I felt overwhelmed and intimidated to be naked in front of a man for the first time. . . . I was distressed and did not understand why he was not his usual gentle self; it was as if he wanted to brutalize something in me (but also in himself) and was driven by a destructive impulse, rather than the natural desire to initiate pleasure and physical intimacy. (42–43)

Lamblin explains Sartre's rudeness as being connected with his view of himself as ugly. Once he started to talk, nobody thought of his looks, but he seems to have been obsessed by his own ugliness to an extent that made him completely bewildered in situations where communication required more than words: "His body was useful only insofar as it had a mouth capable of uttering truth, flattery and lies." Lamblin continues: "I was completely on edge, terribly stiff. There was no affection to ease the situation, no truly spontaneous gesture. It seemed as if the man was following some sort of prewritten, prelearned program. It was as though he were a doctor preparing for an operation, and I had only to let myself be taken" (44). Reading this I give a start at the comparison to a surgical operation, so frequent in *Le deuxième sexe*.[27] I also remember Anne Dubreuilh in bed with Victor Scriassine: "I sensed a presence without really feeling it, as you sense a dentist's steel tool against a swollen gum."[28]

There is something odd here: surgeon and dentist—these are words I have never seen or heard elsewhere to describe a man making love to a woman. Neither have any such associations occurred in my own life. I can remember times when sex was dull or painful, even when it was emotionally disastrous, but never a situation that made me think of surgeons or dentists.

This must correspond to an atmosphere of impersonal, formal chill surrounding intercourse. My guess is that this was a special kind of coldness that came from Sartre and that Beauvoir transformed into literature, whereas Lamblin describes it as having really happened.

The first time Sartre tried to consummate his relationship with Lamblin, he did not succeed, despite great efforts that obviously included preparations by Beauvoir, here referred to by her nickname, "the Beaver": "Then, like a science professor, Sartre began lecturing me about the anatomy and physics of lovemaking. He was surprised that, given my contact with the Beaver, I was not better informed. In the days that followed, he achieved his goal, but I began a period of frigidity that lasted throughout our entire relationship."[29] When Anne Dubreuilh says "yes" to Scriassine's invitation to spend the night with him, the reaction is: "—Ah! Voilà une bonne réponse, dit-il d'une voix encourageante de médecin ou de professeur" ["Ah! now there's a good answer," he said in the encouraging voice of a doctor or professor].[30] Both Anne and Lamblin seem to have met a man who tries to handle his insecurity by posing as a teacher. If Lamblin felt this coldness with Sartre, it is possible, of course, that it emanated from her. She seems to refute such an objection by pointing to the warmth in her relations with Beauvoir. Despite emotional complications within the trio, Beauvoir and Lamblin continued their relationship: "Little by little, we renewed our physical intimacy, which I found very pleasing and captivating. Unlike Sartre, the Beaver had a comforting ability to let herself go."[31]

Beauvoir's warmth seemed real, notes Lamblin, who wrote her book more or less as a response to the negative picture of this relationship presented to the public in 1990 in Beauvoir's *Lettres à Sartre* and *Journal de guerre* and Deirdre Bair's revelation of the identity of Louise Védrine.[32]

Lamblin searched Beauvoir's memoirs for an account of the erotic relationship with Sartre and found nothing. Reading her *A Disgraceful Affair* it is difficult not to feel sympathy for her: why all those detailed reports about herself and others (often false), she writes, and not a word about Sartre as lover?

> Her silence can no longer be attributed to delicate reserve; maybe there was just not much to tell. I'm sure that the fairly hot-blooded Beaver was deeply disappointed in her first physical relations to Sartre.
>
> Several years after their mutual pact of 1929, Sartre already preferred to seek out new experiences with other women or girls, instead of with the Beaver. When I knew Simone de Beauvoir, she and Sartre were no longer having sex with each other. One day much later, she herself hinted at her disappointment when, surprisingly, we were talking about the past. I told her that Sartre was a very poor lover: far from contradicting me, as I had expected, she agreed immediately, saying that he was not very skilled in that domain.[33]

With the past still weighing too heavily to confront, the two women left the subject at that. Lamblin contemplates the difference between Beauvoir's feelings for Sartre and for Nelson Algren: "Simone de Beauvoir knew her first truly sensual love with Nelson Algren, her American lover. He gave her a new awareness of herself. The contrast between their relationship and her purely intellectual relationship with Sartre is fascinating. This makes it even more amazing that she decides to leave Algren, who was very much in love with her, in order to remain with Sartre."[34] Lamblin adds a footnote here: "Nelson Algren inspired that character of Lewis Brogan in Simone de Beauvoir's novel *The Mandarins*." I don't know if this means that Lamblin regards the novel as testimony to events in Beauvoir's life, or if the novel confirms things Beauvoir had told her personally (the English translation is somewhat less precise than the French).

The French word *l'amour* as Lamblin uses it (for example in her reference to Sartre as science professor) refers to the physical side of love (it is translated as "lovemaking"). Love in a mental, spiritual sense is what Beauvoir must have known with Sartre. I would suggest an answer to Lamblin's question about why Beauvoir renounced her passion with Algren and turned back to Sartre. Beauvoir explained it as being a consequence of their famous pact, but I think she followed a pattern from her own family, described in *Une mort très douce* (A very easy death). Even after her father's death, her mother refused to admit that he had made her anything but happy:

> Après la mort de papa, tante Germaine suggérant qu'il n'avait pas été un mari idéal, elle l'a violemment rabrouée: "Il m'a toujours rendue très heureuse." Et, certainement, elle n'avait jamais cessé de se l'affirmer. Tout de même, cet optimisme de commande ne suffisait pas à combler son avidité.
>
> [When, after my father's death, Aunt Germaine hinted that he had not been an ideal husband, Maman snubbed her fiercely. "He always made me very happy." And certainly that was what she always told herself. Still, this forced optimism was not enough to satisfy her hunger.][35]

All this despite the fact that Georges Bertrand de Beauvoir never concealed having mistresses, keeping their photos in his office and forcing his wife to socialize with them when their husbands were among the guests invited to the Beauvoir home. Simone de Beauvoir clearly saw that her mother was not happy, despite her "optimisme de commande." She wrote with great compassion about her mother's difficult situation, deprived as she was of any opportunity to develop her own talents. And she showed equal understanding for her father:

> Je ne blâme pas mon père. On sait assez que chez l'homme l'habitude tue le désir. Maman avait perdu sa première fraicheur et lui sa fougue. Pour la réveiller, il recourait aux professionnelles du café de Versailles ou aux pensionnaires de Sphinx. Je l'ai vu plus d'une fois, entre mes quinze et mes vingt ans, rentrer à huit heures du matin, sentant l'alcool et racontant d'un air embarrassé des histoires de bridge ou de poker. Maman l'accueillait sans drame; elle le croyait peut-être, tant elle était entraînée à fuir les vérités gênantes. Mais elle ne s'accommodait pas de son indifférence. Que le mariage bourgeois soit une institution contre nature, son cas suffirait à m'en convaincre.
>
> [I do not blame my father. It is tolerably well known that in men habit kills desire. Maman had lost her first freshness and he his ardour. In order to arouse it he turned to the professionals of the café de Versailles, or the young ladies of the Sphinx. More than once, between the age of fifteen and twenty, I saw him coming home at eight in the morning, smelling of drink, and telling

> confused tales of bridge or poker. Maman made no scenes: perhaps she believed him, so trained was she at running away from awkward truths. But she could not happily adapt herself to his indifference. Her case alone would be enough to convince me that bourgeois marriage is an unnatural institution].[36]

If you grow up with parents who have this kind of relationship, you absorb a particular image of what is natural between men and women. You know that in men, habit kills desire.

This is not a law of nature, although Beauvoir seemed to think so. She was a role model for me: a woman who was visible, controversial, childless, and yet connected to a man—a trait that in my eyes (as a Swedish teenager in the early '60s) convinced me that, despite her deviancies, she was a normal woman. I wanted to be like her. I wanted a long-term relationship with a man but I didn't want marriage. And I met the man of my life at the age of sixteen and remained unmarried to him until the day of his death twenty-four years later.

He was in no way like Sartre. He was a man who stood behind me at every step of my career as a journalist and writer, but he wanted to remain invisible. As for love and sex, he was vehemently monogamous, which was unusual in the 1960s. We did not share sexual passion and I often longed for something different, although I rarely did anything about this longing.

When I was struck by the resemblance between the Beauvoir-Sartre relationship and that of her parents, I asked my father how the relationship between him and my mother had been during my childhood. Their marriage had convinced me that bourgeois marriage had nothing to offer me. They divorced shortly after I left home at the age of seventeen. My mother died of leukemia in 1986. My father answered my question by describing himself as "constitutionally monogamous," whereas my mother, according to him, always longed for something and someone else.

One resemblance between my mother and Beauvoir's mother, Françoise, is that they both had resolutely optimistic and happy personalities. I have written a short story about my difficult relation to my mother; translated into English, the title would be "The Happiest Person in the World."[37]

Maybe this determination to be happy is inherited by daughters of such mothers. Beauvoir describes herself as a person with an unusual aptitude for happiness. I remember writing love letters to a man who was in love with me but preferred to stay with another woman "because she is unhappy and I have to try to make her happy." I told him that he was a fool: you cannot make anyone else happy. He ought to choose me, since I would be happy with or without him. I wrote this during a period when I spent half my days in tears, a widow for one year, and terribly unhappy that my new love preferred another woman. It seems ridiculous in retrospect.

In the first novel I wrote twenty-five years ago—and never published—the main character, a young woman, explains to a man she loves that she does not believe in happiness. This was an insight I seem to have lost later on. I have often thought about this when reading *Le deuxième sexe,* where happiness is an issue that comes up again and again.

Happiness, judging by how Beauvoir describes it, is not something that takes place between lovers, a man and a woman, as I was brought up to believe. Happiness is a mother-daughter issue: either you are happy, subconsciously, because you pleased your mother, having made the choice (of a man) that she endorsed, or you are happy because you defied your mother, having made a choice that she was against.

The latter alternative is something I recognize from my own life. The question that remains is: how could someone who saw this mechanism as clearly as Beauvoir did still be proud of her own aptitude for happiness? Having an aptitude for happiness can't mean anything but surrendering to an ideal: a wish to be happy whatever happens to you. This seems like the essence of the female cliché, happiness being every woman's utopian goal in life, whereas men don't have to bother: they can devote themselves to socialism or capitalism or any other worldly or worthy cause.

Beauvoir's father was not happy, but her mother was. Sartre was not happy, but Beauvoir was. The conception that their relationship broke with tradition is a misunderstanding. They were very much a traditional double-standard couple in sexual matters. The shocking side of their relationship is the emotional one.

Intellectually they formed a completely new constellation: a lifelong relationship between a man and a woman where both openly admitted their dependence on the other. Thus they both became traitors to their own sex; no woman, especially one fighting for independence for her sex, should be so dependent on a man. And no man should be so dependent on a woman.

Men could have a life built on support by wives, mistresses, secretaries, and daughters; indeed, most great men have. But Sartre's most radical act was that he openly admitted that Beauvoir read everything he wrote, and that he always changed his texts according to her advice: "It's difficult to say what one owes a person. In one way, you could say I owe her everything. . . . When I show her a piece of writing, which I always do, and she offers critiques, at first I get angry and call her all sorts of names. Then, I always accept them." He later continues: "When I met Simone de Beauvoir, I thought I had the best relations I could have with anyone. . . . In fact, I've never really talked about my theories to anyone besides her."[38] Beauvoir spent her life in the same situation as her mother, tied to a man who satisfied his sexual needs—assuming they could be satisfied at all—with a variety of other women. But Sartre was different from her father in one respect: he was never indifferent. He gave her credit for her intellectual contributions to his life, something that to this day is rare in a man.

In an article in the German feminist magazine *Emma,* Alice Schwarzer, the German feminist and friend of Beauvoir, writes: "The 'free love' between Beauvoir and Sartre, model to an entire postwar generation, had its very own conditions and therefore cannot be imitated. Between the two of them sexuality—often dynamite in love affairs—never played an important role. Sartre was a lousy lover and made no secret of that (Beauvoir once called him 'frigid' in public). But intellectually, literarily, and politically they shared one heartbeat: here two persons had met, whose work and life could never have reached such dimensions without the other."[39]

Beauvoir perhaps described the relationship herself, in the last pages of *Le deuxième sexe:*

> Entre les sexes naîtront de nouvelles relations charnelles et affectives dont nous n'avons pas idée: déjà sont apparues entre hommes et femmes des amitiés, des rivalités, des complicités, des camaraderies, chastes ou sexuelles, que les siècles révolus n'auraient su inventer.
>
> [New relations of flesh and sentiment of which we have no conception will arise between the sexes; already, indeed, there

> have appeared between men and women friendships, rivalries, complicities, comradeships—chaste or sensual—which past centuries could not have conceived.][40]

Maybe there will come a time less obsessed with sex, when it will become obvious that the Beauvoir-Sartre relationship was a "heterosexual best friendship," so unusual that most people cannot imagine the existence of such a thing. If Sartre had not been such a poor lover, this kind of friendship may never have survived. The relative ease with which Beauvoir could regard his other women must have been related to the fact that sex with him was not a fantastic thing to lose. Yet there was pain in this loss. If you want to read about that, I suggest *L'invitée.* There is hardly a word about sex, certainly not between the leading characters, Françoise and Pierre, but you can feel an anger, many sizes too big for the conflict in the novel.

Notes

1. Only the original French is quoted here since the "author's preface" to the translation (1982, by Patrick O'Brian) is totally different from the text that appears at the beginning of the French edition. The publication of this book was part of Claude Francis and Fernande Gontier's effort to give the public access to unpublished writings of Simone de Beauvoir. This unpublished first novel was considered too long to be part of their collection *Les écrits de Simone de Beauvoir.*

2. Beauvoir, *Quand prime le spirituel,* 28–29; *When Things of the Spirit Come First,* 32–33.

3. Ibid., 30; 34. Note that O'Brian's translation makes Denis the one who maintains the position.

4. Ibid., 31; 35.

5. Carin Holmberg, *Det kallas kärlek: En socialpsykologisk studie om kvinnors underordning och mäns överordning bland unga jämställda par* (It's called love: A social psychological study of the woman's subordination and the man's superordination among young, equal couples) (Göteborg: Anamma förlag, 1993), 209. For the English summary, see 203–9.

6. Moberg, *Simone och jag.*

7. Beauvoir, *A Transatlantic Love Affair,* 208.

8. During my studies for *Simone och jag,* when reading in Francis and Gontier's *Les écrits de Simone de Beauvoir* the list of people to whom her books are dedicated, I noticed that all of her lovers have books dedicated to them (Sartre has two). This includes the women, as if she wanted to give those relationships a literary recognition for posterity.

In an interview in January 1996, I asked Claude Lanzmann if these were all Beauvoir's love affairs, or if there were others, unknown to the public. "She only had known love affairs," he said, adding that she did not have many lovers and that he doubted that her relationships with women were "complete sexual relations." Not all her books have dedications, and the ones that she made are not always indicated in translations. The following books are dedicated to lovers: *L'invitée* (1943): To Olga; *Le sang des autres* (1945): To Nathalie Sorokine; *Tous les hommes sont mortels* (1946): To Jean-Paul Sartre; *Pour une morale de l'ambiguïté* (1947): To Bianca; *Le deuxième sexe* (1949): To Jacques Bost; *Les mandarins* (1954): To Nelson Algren; *La force de l'âge* (1960): To Jean-Paul Sartre; *Les belles images* (1966): To Claude Lanzmann; *Tout compte fait* (1972): To Sylvie. The complete list of dedications also includes *Pyrrhus et Cinéas* (1944): A cette dame; *Les bouches inutiles* (1945): A ma mère; *L'Amérique au jour le jour* (1948): A Ellen et Richard Wright; *Une mort très douce* (1964): A ma soeur. You can also include the less personal: *La cérémonie des adieux* (1981): A ceux qui ont aimé Sartre, l'aiment, l'aimeront.

9. Bair, *Simone de Beauvoir.* This is the title of the chapter about *The Mandarins* and the Algren-Beauvoir story.

10. Beauvoir, *Les mandarins,* 318–19; *The Mandarins,* 341.

11. Ibid., 75; 83.

12. Beauvoir, *Le deuxième sexe,* 2:131; *The Second Sex,* 372 (further references to this work and to its English translation will be given in the text). The French word *viol* has only one translation in my French-Swedish dictionary: "rape." In the English-Swedish dictionary, however, the word "violation" has a wide range of meanings, "rape" being only one of them, listed after several less severe kinds of abusive behavior. It seems as though H. M. Parshley has tried to make Beauvoir's statement less categorical in his translation.

13. The third section of part 1 is also missing, with its critical review of Montherlant, D. H. Lawrence, Claudel, Breton, and Stendhal. *The Second Sex* (Det andra könet [Stockholm: Gebers, 1973]) was translated into Swedish "following the French paperback version of 1968," and "published in an abridged version with the consent of the writer," according to information in the book. But Claude Lanzmann found it unlikely that Beauvoir would have given her consent to this (personal interview with the author, January 1996). Seeing *how* it's abridged, I find it impossible to believe that Beauvoir could have given her consent.

14. Beauvoir, *Le deuxième sexe,* 2:134; *The Second Sex,* 375.

15. Ibid., 2:136–37; 377.

16. Beauvoir, *La cérémonie des adieux,* 400; *Adieux,* 314.

17. Ibid., 400; 314. The English translation, *Adieux: A Farewell to Sartre* by Patrick O'Brian, has been improved with a useful index missing in the French original. However, you look in vain for words like "sex" or "love," even though that would have made this piece easier to identify. (The closest you get is "contingency, of the body: 315–16.")

18. Beauvoir, *Les mandarins,* 70; *The Mandarins,* 78.

19. Beauvoir, *L'invitée,* 458; *She Came to Stay,* 368.

20. Moi, *Simone de Beauvoir,* 140–41. "Enfin j'ai ri bêtement en le regardant, et il m'a dit: 'Pourquoi riez-vous?' et j'ai dit: 'Je me demande la tête que vous feriez si je vous proposais de coucher avec moi' et il a dit: 'Je pensais que vous pensiez que j'avais envie de vous embrasser sans oser le faire.' Ensuite nous avons encore pataugé un quart d'heure, avant qu'il se décidât à m'embrasser" (*Lettres à Sartre,* 27 July 1938 [62–63]).

21. Beauvoir, *Les mandarins,* 72; *The Mandarins,* 80. Further references to this novel and to its English translation will be given in the text.

22. Beauvoir, *A Transatlantic Love Affair,* 69.

23. Cesarani states the date for the famous one-night stand by quoting Koestler's Paris diary, the entry for the evening of 23 October 1946: "With Simone and Sartre, slept there" (*Arthur Koestler,* 277).

24. Cesarani states over and over in the more than six hundred pages that Koestler could not listen to others, yet still quotes Anne as appreciating Scriassine for being "a very good listener." Moreover, nothing in the information given about Koestler's remarkably active sex life indicates any similarity to Scriassine's obsession with the virginal state.

25. See Cesarani, *Arthur Koestler,* 400–401.

26. Lamblin, *A Disgraceful Affair,* 42. Further references will be given in the text.

27. During the work of translating *The Second Sex* into Swedish (the first complete version in Swedish is expected from Norstedts in 2000 or 2001), I have been struck by the number of "surgeon" references in the text. For example, Beauvoir records this child's fantasy: "'Quand on veut un enfant,' disait une petite fille, 'on va chez le médecin; on se déshabille, on se bande les yeux, parce qu'il ne faut pas regarder; le médecin attache les parents l'un à l'autre et il aide pour que tout marche bien'; elle avait changé l'acte amoureux en une opération chirurgicale, sans doute peu plaisante, mais aussi honorable qu'une séance chez le dentiste" ["When a child is wanted, the parents go to the doctor's office; they undress, they blindfold themselves because they mustn't look; then the doctor attaches them together and sees to it that all goes well"; she had transformed the act of love into a surgical operation, unpleasant, no doubt, but as correct as a session with the dentist] (*Le deuxième sexe,* 2:51; *The Second Sex,* 301). A bit later in the chapter about childhood, when the girl's crisis of adolescence with its physical and psychological problems is described in detail, Beauvoir comments on Helene Deutsch's description of how young Nancy thought removal of the appendix would cure her: "Ce désir d'une opération—et en particulier de l'ablation de l'appendice—se rencontre souvent à cet âge; les jeunes filles expriment ainsi leur peur du viol, de la grossesse, de l'accouchement. Elles sentent dans leur ventre d'obscures menaces et elles espèrent que le chirurgien les sauvera de ce danger inconnu qui les guette" [This desire for an operation—especially the removal of the appendix—is often met with at that young age; young girls express in this way their fantasies of rape, pregnancy, and childbirth. They feel vague threats inside them, and they hope that the surgeon will save them from this unknown danger that lies in wait for them] (ibid., 2:69–70; 318).

28. Beauvoir, *The Mandarins,* 82.

29. Lamblin, *A Disgraceful Affair,* 45.

30. Beauvoir, *Les mandarins,* 73; *The Mandarins,* 80.

31. Lamblin, *A Disgraceful Affair,* 46.

32. Lamblin takes it for granted that Beauvoir wanted to keep her from talking to Bair and therefore made up false details about her life. Is it not as likely that Beauvoir wanted to keep her identity hidden and did not even mention to Bair how important it was not to reveal it?

33. Lamblin, *A Disgraceful Affair,* 29.

34. Ibid., 30.

35. Beauvoir, *Une mort très douce,* 57; *A Very Easy Death,* 38.

36. Ibid., 54–55; 36.

37. "Världens lyckligaste människa," published in the anthology *Mamma är död* (Mother is dead [Stockholm: Alfabeta, 1993]).

38. Francis and Gontier, *Les écrits de Simone de Beauvoir,* 20–21, editor's translation.

39. Schwarzer, "Beauvoir und die Frauen," author's translation.

40. Beauvoir, *Le deuxième sexe,* 575; *The Second Sex,* 730.

5

Simone de Beauvoir and Nelson Algren

Self-Creation, Self-Contradiction, and the Exotic, Erotic Feminist Other

BARBARA KLAW

Ecrire embaume le passé, mais cela le laisse un peu figé comme une momie [Writing embalms the past but that leaves it a bit stiff like a mummy].

Simone de Beauvoir, in Josée Dayan and Malka Ribowska, *Simone de Beauvoir: Un film*

TOWARD the end of her life Simone de Beauvoir implied that if she were to rewrite her memoirs, she would give a frank and balanced account of her own sexuality because it would influence the behavior of other women: "I would like to tell women about my life in terms of my own sexuality . . . it is not just a personal matter but a political one too."[1] The posthumous publication of her letters and journal shows how widely her publicly constructed and private selves diverged. Whereas in her autobiography Beauvoir depicted herself as the perfectly rational, moral, emancipated, and politically involved female engaged in a freely chosen, lifelong, primarily monogamous sexual and emotional relationship with Jean-Paul Sartre, her letters and journals show her to be to be very human, with failings, caprices, contradictions, and a complicated sexuality. Not only did she have many male and female lovers with whom she was both physically and sentimentally involved while she maintained her relationship with Sartre, but she was intensely emotional, illogical, and not always willing to acknowledge her feelings in public or take responsibility for her actions. Many readers mistakenly embraced her as a heroic ideal because of the focus in her autobiography on the perfect feminist, their own need for a role model, and their tendency to conflate Beauvoir the author constructing a written or verbalized public self and Beauvoir the person.[2] Her letters to Sartre from 1930 to 1963 and her war diary, published posthumously in 1990, suggest, in keeping with traditional images of the female role in a couple, that she indulged in certain behaviors primarily to compensate for Sartre's absence or to amuse him. This is why many readers were shocked when these letters and journals appeared. It is worth remembering, however, that Beauvoir wrote these letters and her supposedly private war diary primarily for Sartre's reading pleasure, and that this undoubtedly influenced her self-construction. In contrast, Beauvoir's unpublished letters and diaries and her most recently published letters add two important dimensions that imply that she used Sartre and his behavior as excuses that allowed her to reject the traditionally feminine role in a societally acceptable way and to explore other situations and relationships without having to commit to them. First, in her unpublished diaries written between the ages of eighteen and twenty-two, it is clear that she struggles with her self-image and gender construction even before knowing Sartre. Second, in her letters to Nelson Algren, the American novelist who became her lover, she creates a traditional feminine identity as an ideal wife who cares primarily for him and who suffers from intense emotional and physical longing when he is not around. In these letters, Sartre is still her best friend but often appears to be a convenient excuse for Beauvoir (the feminist involved in a nontraditional heterosexual relationship) to travel frequently and fuel her own work and fame.

Beauvoir's published and unpublished journals and letters more openly portray the conflicted self hidden beneath the personality created for the world, but still offer only another version of her. Her rendition of her relationship with Nelson Algren in her autobiographical volume *La force des choses* (Force of circumstance) offers a particularly acute example of the contradictions involved in the sexual self-portrait that she bequeathed to the world during her lifetime: in an attempt to embalm the past, she focuses on an ideal image of herself and events, but also betrays confusion about gender roles and her relation to them. In this construction Algren becomes a means of expressing a traditionally acceptable range of sexual desires and animal passions when Beauvoir could not write about other feelings and experiences. Just as the undertaker's care of a corpse transforms it into a more beautiful dead object and attempts to hide its reality, so too Beauvoir's uncertainty results in a mummified self-portrait in her autobiography that unrealistically freezes her image into one of ideal feminism and tones down the strength of her eroticism and exoticism. It is only in reading between the lines of her letters, diaries, and autobiography that one perceives a three-dimensional picture of Beauvoir, one that reveals her struggle to explore her sexuality within the constraints of patriarchy, the dominant ideology's system of stereotypes and gender hierarchy that prescribes the ways in which women and men should think, act, and interact together. Such an interpretation suggests that the dominant ideology's view of appropriate behaviors for men and women caused her to intellectualize, mythologize, and often embalm the expression of her sexuality and the pursuit of her desires in the autobiographical construction of her relationship with Algren.[3]

Although Beauvoir stated that she was little interested in applying her philosophical analyses to herself,[4] her writings indicate that she was obsessed by her self-image. Author of several volumes of autobiographical works—*Mémoires d'une jeune fille rangée* (Memoirs of a dutiful daughter), *La force de l'âge* (The prime of life), *La force des choses, Tout compte fait* (All said and done), *Une mort très douce* (A very easy death), *La cérémonie des adieux* (Adieux: A farewell to Sartre)—innumerable letters and journals, as well as novels such as *L'invitée* (She came to stay), *Le sang des autres* (The blood of others), *Tous les hommes sont mortels* (All men are mortal), *Les mandarins* (The mandarins), and *Les belles images* (Les belles images) that question the meaning of self and existence, Beauvoir gives the impression of someone self-consciously or at least subconsciously anxious to create a self that would show her as a woman who had simultaneously profited and escaped from societal notions of gender construction. Her theoretical ideas about autobiography also show her awareness of the difference between reality and the presentation of one's life. She wanted, in re-creating herself, to invent a universal woman who would influence the largest number of other women: "le 'je' que j'utilise est un 'je' qui a une portée générale, il concerne un très grand nombre de femmes" [the *I* that I use is an *I* that is far reaching, it stands for a great number of women].[5] She admits that she, like all autobiographers, distorts reality in order to produce a certain message: "Dans l'autobiographie, je saisis la facticité du réel, sa contingence; mais alors je risque de me perdre en détails oiseux, de manquer le sens du vécu; décrire un vécu privé de sens, ce n'est rien dire. . . . Il faut choisir. Jamais une oeuvre ne pourra donner à la fois le sens et la réalité" [In autobiography, I seize the artificiality of the real and its contingence; but then I risk losing myself in idle details, missing the meaning of that experienced; to describe an experience stripped of its meaning is not to say anything. . . . One has to choose. Never will a work be able to produce meaning and reality simultaneously].[6] Beauvoir's 1926 unpublished diary is somewhat less exalted and clearly states her desire to please those who surround her and to play whatever role her public desires: "j'aime assez ceux qui m'entourent pour leur paraître telle qu'ils me désirent" [I like those around me enough to give the impression of being what they desire me to be] (19 August). Her *Journal de guerre* (War diary) of 1939–40 implies that she packages herself to appeal to her audience, but does not know what character to assume for a large crowd: "je ne sais pas en face d'un grand nombre quelle attitude prendre, ça n'est plus appelé par les besoins de l'adaptation; et je n'aime pas me penser en fonction d'eux" [When I am faced with many people I do not know how to present myself, there is no longer a need to adapt myself, and I don't like to think of myself as a function of them].[7] The many contradictions in *La force des choses* could be read as an effort to create a political self that will move women toward emancipation and that thus prefers structured meaning to reality, but which still tries to capture the largest readership. To please the traditional, Beauvoir is femininely erotic, overcome by her passions, and too weak to control her emotions.[8] She attenuates her more rational, independent, and feminist moments with her attempts to embrace exoticism: for Algren she periodically abandons her language and country to adopt his. In short, Beauvoir becomes a textual chameleon, an ever changing Other who, in depicting herself as erotic, exotic, and feminist, can be all things to all readers. Just as the embalming of a corpse beautifies death, prolongs the image of life for others, and causes the mourners to reflect on their relationship to the deceased, so too *La force des choses* resuscitates and embellishes Beauvoir's past as she contemplates her relationship to the body of her experiences. In *La force des choses,* she alternately stresses then denies her sexual feelings for Algren; her portraits of female sexuality in unpublished diaries and letters, earlier volumes of autobiography, and *Le deuxième sexe* (The second sex) offer theoretical and personal reasons for this vacillation.

Simone de Beauvoir met Nelson Algren, the prizewinning author of *The Man with the Golden Arm, A Walk on the Wild Side,* and numerous other publications that depict the Chicago slums and the negative side of the American dream, in Chicago on 21 February 1947. Their meeting was the start of a love affair that lasted officially for four years. During that time she spent two weeks in 1947 vacationing in Chicago with him, where he introduced her to the seedier sides of the city, and two months in 1948 first cruising down the Mississippi on a paddleboat and then touring Yucatan, Guatemala, and Mexico with him. Although at the end of this time Algren asked Beauvoir to marry him, she refused, but hoped to continue their relationship as lovers. In June 1949 Algren visited her in Paris, and from there they traveled to Italy, Tunisia, Algeria, and Morocco. She spent two months at his summer home on Lake Michigan in 1950; and it was during her last month at this home, in October 1951, that she learned of his plans to remarry his ex-wife. She subsequently decided to stay until the end of her vacation with him and continue their relationship on a platonic basis. The year 1952 brought the beginning of her six-year love affair with her co-worker Claude Lanzmann, a journalist and political activist and the eventual director of the celebrated film *Shoah.*[9] Beauvoir and Lanzmann separated at the end of 1958. In the spring of 1960 Algren came back to Paris to visit Beauvoir. Their amicable relationship ended when the translation of *La force des choses,* which re-creates their relationship in a very unflattering light for Algren, appeared in 1965.

In this third volume of her autobiography, Beauvoir's portrayal of their relationship as a couple foregrounds her erudition, her linguistic and cultural versatility, her independence, and her generosity in occasionally giving up her satisfying Parisian life to participate in Algren's lackluster American world, and this creates an exotic American side of her. She defines Algren, like many of the significant others in her autobiography, predominantly by his foreign attributes, his poverty, and his inability to be more like her. Algren is exotic because he lives in the United States, a country foreign to France. Whereas she readily becomes exotic in both French and American culture—she is French, and that allows her to seem exotic in America, and she develops an American side that permits her to escape boring aspects of her life in France—he is incapable of similar transformation. He leads a solitary and empty life in America without her and makes little effort to understand her homeland. Although Beauvoir writes that she accepts much of the blame for the failure of their relationship, many paragraphs focus on her plenitude and his lack:

> Mais il y avait entre nous une grande différence. Je parlais sa langue, je connaissais assez bien la littérature et l'histoire de son pays, je lisais les livres qu'il aimait, ceux qu'il écrivait; près de lui je m'oubliais, j'entrais dans son univers. Il ignorait à peu près tout du mien . . . les auteurs français en général le touchaient peu. D'autre part, j'étais infiniment mieux lotie à Paris que lui à Chicago; il souffrait de la dure solitude américaine. Maintenant que j'existais, ce vide autour de lui se confondait avec mon absence, et il m'en voulait.
>
> [But there was a great difference between us. I spoke his language, I knew his country's literature and history rather well, I read the books that he liked and those that he was writing. When I was near him, I entered into his universe. He was ignorant of almost everything in mine. . . . French authors in general held little interest for him. What's more I was infinitely better off in Paris than he in Chicago; he suffered from the harsh loneliness of America. Now that I was part of his life, this emptiness around him was confused with my absence and he held it against me.] [10]

She portrays him as even more exotic by stressing not only his foreignness to France as an American, but also his difference from other Americans who conform to the status quo and care foremost about money. He, unlike many Americans, chooses to live simply. It is his unusual poverty, not his personality, his physique, or his intellect, that she fondly remembers:

> Dans le train de Los Angeles, je lus un de ses livres et je pensai à lui; il vivait dans une baraque, sans salle de bains ni frigidaire, au bord d'une allée où fumaient des poubelles et où tournoyaient de vieux journaux; cette pauvreté m'avait rafraîchie, car je supportais mal l'épaisse odeur de dollars qu'on respirait dans les grands hôtels et dans les restaurants élégants.
>
> [In the Los Angeles train, I read one of his books and I thought about him; he lived in a shanty without a refrigerator or a place to bathe, on the edge of an alley where trash cans smoked and old newspapers blew about; this poverty had refreshed me for I could barely stand the thick odor of dollars that one breathed in the big hotels and the elegant restaurants.] [11]

In retaliation, although he could not read the original French, Algren immediately wrote several uncomplimentary reviews of the translation of *La force des choses* that included the following comments: "I've been in whorehouses all over the world and the woman there always closes the door. . . . But this woman flung the door open and called in the public and the Press"; "Mme de Beauvoir's early determination 'to write sacrificial essays in which the author strips himself bare without excuses' she has since employed with such earnestness and skill that practically everybody has now been sacrificed excepting herself"; "Her insistence upon aggrandizing a casual affection twenty years dead into a passion of classic dimension is employed to support her contention [about freedom]." [12] From then on, Algren cut off all contact with Beauvoir.

Readers of Beauvoir or Algren have also offered their versions of the relationship, but to date none has examined the link between Beauvoir's portrayal of herself and Algren and her recorded theories and experiences involving gender construction.[13] Traditional interpretations of Beauvoir's published fictional and autobiographical works view them as literal portraits of the events, feelings, and people in her life, as opposed to recognizing both Beauvoir and Algren as constructs, and offer explanations based on these supposed facts.[14] There is a tendency not to raise the question of Beauvoir's writing as a creative process that informs memory despite her comments that stress that writing both alters and guarantees a certain remembering of events: "Quant à la mémoire du passé, alors, il arrive une drôle de chose: c'est que lorsqu'on a trop raconté ou trop écrit les choses, on ne se rappelle plus les événements eux-mêmes. . . . Ecrire embaume le passé, mais cela le laisse un peu figé comme une momie" [So, as for memory of the past, a funny thing happens: when one has too often told or written about things one can no longer remember the events themselves. . . . Writing embalms the past but that leaves it a bit stiff like a mummy].[15] In *La force des choses,* Beauvoir's use of discord and transformation operates as an illustration of the process necessary for creating a feminist, thoroughly emancipated female self or the unique gender alluded to in Beauvoir's essay: *Le deuxième sexe* contends, famously, "On ne naît pas femme: on le devient. . . . c'est l'ensemble de la civilisation qui élabore ce produit intermédiaire entre le mâle et le castrat qu'on qualifie de féminin" [One is not born, one becomes a woman. . . . it is the entirety of civilization that develops this product halfway between the male and the eunuch that is labeled as feminine].[16] As Judith Butler reformulates this hypothesis, gender is no longer causally dependent upon biological sex and each sex permits a number of different genders that blend the current meanings of masculine and feminine.[17]

There are, however, contradictions in Beauvoir's theoretical stance that culture and not biology dictates sex roles, and this further complicates interpretations of her theories or self-portrait. Beauvoir discusses two female types who are not the same but who are similarly belittled by society. The totally dependent *amoureuse* (woman in love) is not at all the same thing as the *femme qui couche* (the woman who sleeps around), who acts freely on her sexual desires, but the ruling class of Beauvoir's society tended to discount any woman who had sexual relationships, and this opinion seemingly engendered part of the conflict evident in *La force des choses.* If a woman (Beauvoir, for instance) was sexually active with no serious thought of marriage, she was considered a whore. On the contrary, if she was involved in a serious monogamous relationship, she lost her identity to her man because society assumed that anything valuable she accomplished was in imitation of him. *Le deuxième sexe* contends that the emancipated woman actively seeks sexual satisfaction but must guard against becoming too attached to those who give her sexual pleasure. According to *Le deuxième sexe,* for a woman, having sexual relations with another person always implies a form of service imposed by a master, which evokes the image of slavery: "on a toujours admis que le lit était pour la femme un 'service,' dont le mâle la remercie par des cadeaux ou en assurant son entretien: mais servir, c'est se donner un maître; il n'y a dans ce rapport aucune réciprocité" [It has always been acknowledged that going to bed was for the woman "a service" for which the male thanks her with gifts or financial support, but to serve means to give oneself a master; there is in this relationship no reciprocity].[18] In *La force de l'âge,* Beauvoir comments that her first adult attempts at writing fiction were meant as self-purging illustrations of the dangers of forgetting that she was responsible for herself and of depending too much on another person.[19] Her unpublished diaries from 1926 through 1930 confirm that this was a constant concern for her during adolescence and early adulthood. Each new relationship, including those with her cousin Jacques, the future philosopher Merleau-Ponty, and her married classmate Maheu, evoked similar opposing desires for unity and separation. As Bair points out, not only her best female friend, Zaza, and Sartre, but also Algren caused Beauvoir for a short while to drop her other friends so as to cater to her beloved's needs and to devote herself entirely to him or her. Furthermore, according to Bair, she enjoyed such subservient behavior.[20] Both *La force de l'âge* and *Le deuxième sexe* suggest that Beauvoir worried about being considered a contemptuous sexual or emotional object with no ideas of her own, and that for her own self-respect she felt she should fight to show the ambiguity of the human condition, but neither her autobiography nor her theory reveal if Beauvoir's self-construction was more a denial of biology or culture. Nevertheless, it is in the erotic experience that one discovers this ambiguity, that of being simultaneously body and mind, subject and other.[21] Because woman already sees herself as an object, she must work at finding dignity as a transcending subject while acknowledging her physicality. If a woman successfully combines this erotic and exotic experience with her freedom and does not forget that her partner is also subject, object, and constantly changing, she becomes an ideal feminist.[22] Man, in contrast, dupes himself that he is primarily an acting subject, thus hesitating to see himself as other, as body, and thus ignoring half of his existence. Due to this situation, Beauvoir concludes, "La femme a d'elle-même une expérience plus authentique" [Woman has a more authentic experience of herself].[23]

In light of these theories, Beauvoir's autobiographical portrait in *La force des choses* could be read as her attempt to blur gender boundaries in her recorded self, to become the ideal feminist, and to work out her confusion concerning whether slavelike passion was biologically or culturally dictated. As part of this process, she unconsciously contradicted the very feminist self that she was inventing with autoportraits of a stereotypically sexually wanton and mysteriously exotic persona who, in rewriting her life, limits her partner's freedom. There is a constant tension between her desire to experience total otherness in the erotic experience, as the woman who cannot control her passions, who lives only for her man, who becomes an enigmatic and desired (exotic) object, and her need to deny her objectivity by constantly reaffirming her thinking subjectivity. Overall, Beauvoir teases readers with an erotic body that cannot completely unveil itself due to her indecision and her related tendency to resuscitate her partners as equally enshrouded and mummified objects of art. It seems that Beauvoir, as the writer of *La force des choses,* attempts to come to terms with her own erotic feelings, which, in the terms of her philosophy, make her more authentic but which also correspond poorly to her image of the independent woman seeking pleasure like a man. As if to reexperience and to understand her animality, she sporadically unveils her bodily passions, which in accordance with her principles lend a certain depth and sincerity to her public portrait, but reason and the desire to prove that women and men are equal and should have the same societal rights cause her to deny the importance of her sexual longing for Algren. Her autobiographical illustration of equality results in a self-portrait that adopts many traditionally masculine traits and behaviors. The historically feminine, in contrast, is erotic and exotic; it manifests itself as the Other that Beauvoir invariably negates with lengthy explanations. Yet she never clearly articulates how eroticism, exoticism, and these more masculine qualities ideally mesh in herself.

Beauvoir's conflict can be partly explained by her experiences. As mentioned earlier, *Le deuxième sexe* shows that the body is not a natural fact but a historical idea and that one is not born but rather becomes a woman. Beauvoir's 1927 diary indicates that she was very much a product of her Catholic upbringing: "c'est parce que le catholicisme parle trop à mon coeur que ma raison s'en défie: traditions, hérédité, souvenirs me porteraient à donner mon adhésion à cela" [It is because Catholicism speaks too well to my heart that my mind distrusts it: traditions, heredity, memories encourage me to believe in this religion] (17 July 1927). She had a penchant for refusing pleasure: "je sens bien que je n'appuie sur aucune raison morale mon refus du plaisir; simplement je ne *peux* pas m'y livrer" [I am well aware that I am not basing my refusal of pleasure on any moral reason, I simply cannot give myself over to it] (23 October 1926). Martyrdom pleased her: "Je suis telle que dans la souffrance, la punition ou l'effort je trouve ma joie" [I am made such that in suffering, punishment, and effort, I find my joy] (5 November 1926). Catholic ideologies on marriage and earthly life informed her discourse: "Peut-être qu'un jour je me marierai. . . . En tout cas, c'est le plus grand bonheur que je puisse rencontrer dans cette vie" [Maybe one day I will marry. . . . In any case, it is the greatest happiness that I could encounter in this life] (21 August 1926). She did not want the public to know during her lifetime of her desire for women, and she therefore denied having homosexual tendencies.[24] Her education and society had taught her that the verbalization of her sexual desires would be simultaneously rewarded and punished. The reward was that society would show its admiration for a woman as a beautiful sexual object. Beauvoir's diaries and letters show more frankly than her autobiography that in relationship to her peers, she wanted to be admired for her physical presence: "Tout le monde me trouve très belle avec ce nouveau pull-over bleu. J'ai été vaguement consciente de mon physique, de moi-même et de ma vie (passée) pendant l'exposé de la stagiaire et j'en ai été satisfaite" [Everyone thinks that I am very pretty in this new blue sweater. I was vaguely conscious of my physique, myself, and my life (past) during the intern's talk and I was quite satisfied with this].[25] The penalty was that a beautiful female object who bestowed her favors too easily was considered to be without morals and could not be taken seriously. As Beauvoir recounts in *Le deuxième sexe,* the French tended to think that liberated women were simply those with no sexual restraint:

> En France surtout on confond avec entêtement femme libre et femme facile, l'idée de facilité impliquant une absence de résistance et de contrôle, un manque, la négation même de la liberté. . . . Mais le dédain qu'affectent en France pour les "femmes qui couchent" les hommes mêmes qui profitent de leurs faveurs paralyse un grand nombre de femmes.
>
> [In France especially, people stubbornly confuse free women

> and easy women. The idea of easiness implies an absence of resistance and control, a lack, the very negation of freedom. But a great number of women are paralyzed by the disdain expressed for women who go to bed by the very men in France who take advantage of their favors.][26]

After the publication of *Le deuxième sexe,* many men severely criticized Beauvoir because she had spoken so openly about sex.[27] By the time she wrote her autobiography, she could freely talk about very few of her satisfying sexual relationships with men, because of their attachments to others. Her presentations of Algren, who was divorced and foreign, as a great sexual passion allowed her to display her heterosexuality in response to the French critics who attributed the writing of *Le deuxième sexe* to her frigidity or lesbian tendencies.[28] Furthermore, Beauvoir's substitute portrait of Algren as a mere passing fancy both stressed her attraction to males and allowed her to adopt the stereotypical male right to have a variety of sexual adventures: "Une femme qui se dépense, qui a des responsabilités, qui connaît l'âpreté de la lutte contre les résistances du monde, a besoin—comme le mâle—non seulement d'assouvir ses désirs physiques mais de connaître la détente, la diversion, qu'apportent d'heureuses aventures sexuelles" [A woman who expends her energy, who has responsibilities, who knows the bitterness of struggling against the world's resistances, needs—just like a male—not only to satiate her physical desires but to experience the relaxation and diversion provided by fulfilling sexual adventures].[29]

Both published and unpublished diaries confirm that Beauvoir frequently saw herself as a subject of scrutiny and was sensitive to the opinions of society. In her war diary, she mocks her own adherence to certain images, but this does not change her behavior: "Je vais me faire laver les cheveux, j'achète des ingrédients de toilette et je me fais belle, un peu par représentation de moi-même comme 'la femme qui ne se laisse pas aller' en temps de guerre" [I am going to have my hair washed, I have been buying beauty products and making myself look good, partly to project myself as "the woman who does not let herself go" in times of war]. She imagines herself as others might see her: "j'ai eu une vive représentation de moi comme 'entrant dans le "Dôme," avec des yeux encore gros de larmes,' ça m'a fait absolument nécessaire, c'était typiquement la femme en temps de guerre. Et c'était moi" [I had a vivid image of myself as "entering the Dome, my eyes brimming with tears"; this struck me as absolutely necessary. It was the typical woman in wartime. And it was me]. She reflects on her gift for changing herself for her audience: "Je me sens capable d'adaptation devant les gens et même habile. . . . jamais je ne cherche à donner une impression d'ensemble de moi; mais sur chaque conduite, chaque réplique, je cherche celle qui convient à l'interlocuteur" [I feel capable of adapting myself to people and even skilled at it. . . . never do I seek to give an overall impression of myself; but for each behavior, each reply, I seek what would best correspond to my interlocutor].[30] Her unpublished diary entries of her first outings with Sartre show careful attention to her physical presentation: "j'ai ma robe en crêpe de Chine et sans manches qui me va bien" [I am wearing my sleeveless crêpe de Chine dress which looks good on me] (26 July 1929). The question that is never explicitly answered in her diaries, letters, or theories is how a woman can acknowledge herself as a created object, please the masses, and still be true to others and herself.

Just as Beauvoir, the autobiographer, constructs herself to reconcile societal traditions, her desires, and her own ideals, so too she reinvents Algren in the same vein. Her 1927 diary confirms her tendency to intellectualize her passions for others and thereby maintain her freedom from them: "En réalité je ne désire pas Jacques. Je désire le désirer et je sais que sa seule présence m'apportera ce désir" [In reality, I do not desire Jacques. I desire desiring him and I know that only his presence causes this desire in me] (18 April). In the same diary, she reveals a propensity toward misjudging herself and Jacques (her significant other of the moment): "Si bien que souvent, quand je veux te juger du dehors, je suis injuste comme je le suis pour moi-même" [So well that often when I want to judge you as an outsider, I am unjust just as I am to myself] (18 April). Beauvoir met Algren in February 1947 while she was writing *Le deuxième sexe.* Parallels between her theoretical construct of the emancipated woman and her relationship with Algren indicate that many of the statements about women in general were also intensely personal for Beauvoir. Her portrait of the emancipated female includes the myriad problems faced by a woman trying to realize her freedom. Men rarely consider women as equals, and Algren's interviews and biography indicate that despite his many endearing qualities, he did not view Beauvoir as an equal.[31] Although woman's sexual appetites and needs often equal those of man, she becomes more easily attached to the being who gives her physical pleasure than does man. Likewise, because she is not brought up like a boy, she easily forgets her personal goals once a man enters her life.[32]

Beauvoir's expressed disdain for women who devote too much of themselves to love relationships and who rely too heavily on men seemingly camouflaged her fear of losing herself to love and caused her to minimize her feelings for Algren. Discourse about her friends, her country, or her adopted family members veiled aspects of Beauvoir's sexuality, her relationship with Algren, and the predominance of emotions in her own life. She portrayed everything as more important than her affective and physical needs:

> Cette histoire attrista encore une année qui, malgré mes travaux, des plaisirs et l'émotion que me donna la pièce de Sartre, fut pour moi mélancolique. Les gens étaient moroses: MacArthur limogé, on continuait tout de même à se battre en Corée et l'économie française en pâtissait. Aux funérailles de Pétain, vichystes et anciens collabos s'étaient manifestés avec éclat. . . . Sartre considérait sans gaieté les événements et sa situation, cela m'attristait. L'échec d'Olga me peina. Et j'avais du mal à liquider mon histoire avec Algren.
>
> [Lucienne's end made even sadder a year which, despite my work and the pleasure and excitement I got from Sartre's play, was for me melancholic. Even with MacArthur retired, we continued to fight in Korea and the French economy suffered from it. At Pétain's funeral, Vichyists and former collaborators had appeared with pride. . . . Sartre observed the events and his own situation without gaiety and this saddened me. Olga's failure distressed me. And I was having a hard time liquidating my story with Algren.][33]

Yet her choice of camouflage cannot hide the obsession with Algren that ends her paragraph and implies that the traditionally feminine longings of the "woman in love" filled her unconscious. Like Lucienne, her typist, she was being devoured by uncontrollable forces. Algren gave Beauvoir pleasure but evoked war within her. He made her doubt that independence was based on economy. Like the French, she was fighting (figuratively) in a foreign country for no reason, and her French economy of exchange with Algren was suffering. She was caught in the double bind of acting the part of a financially and emotionally independent woman (a feminist) while she (the erotic lover) unconsciously depended heavily on the affection of her lover for happiness. Like Olga, her friend and former lover turned actress, she could not be convincing in her role. Furthermore, her choice of the verb *liquider* to express the end of her liaison with Algren evokes the thought of liquid, a stereotypically feminine attribute, an erotic substance facilitating sexual and sensual play, and the source of life. *Le deuxième sexe* implies that an egalitarian love story—that is, one that a thirty-year-old woman would seek—would require that a man consider a woman to be his equal in all domains: "La femme de 30 ans est rejetée vers les mâles adultes. . . . Le problème quand elle souhaite une histoire, une aventure, où elle puisse engager son coeur avec son corps, c'est de rencontrer un homme qu'elle puisse considérer comme un égal sans qu'il se regarde comme supérieur" [The woman of thirty is thrown back to adult males. . . . The problem, when she wishes for an affair or an adventure in which she could involve both her heart and body, is to meet a man whom she could consider as an equal without his considering himself superior].[34] A more liquid story would thus be one between equals where there was a constant flow of give and take physically, emotionally, and intellectually. The word *liquider* suggests that whereas literally Beauvoir seeks to end her affair with Algren symbolically, she tries to make it one between equals. Yet she acknowledges that she cannot do either. Beauvoir's letters to Algren point to such an interpretation. She indicates her desire to experience everything in life: she wants to be both a woman and a man, to have many friends but delight in her solitude, to work a lot, to write good books, and to travel and enjoy herself. She longs to be both selfish and unselfish (2 July 1947). The keenly articulated awareness of her personal thirst to experience everything manifests itself in her portrait of the typical woman who struggles with conflicting desires. Her attempt to relegate Algren to his proper textual place mirrors her feminist philosophy that women with fruitful lives in the outside world will not view love as the ultimate end, but contradicts her ideal authentic woman by denying Algren's endearing qualities and importance to her.

Furthermore, gender stereotypes conflict with a woman's efforts to achieve a relationship of equality with a man. Fidelity is traditionally viewed as a feminine attribute. As Beauvoir explains it, "Le mariage traditionnel autorisait l'homme à quelques 'coups de canif dans le contrat'; sans réciprocité" [The traditional marriage allowed the man a few pocket knife thrusts into the marriage contract (a few illicit affairs) without reciprocity].[35] These pressures were, if anything, more intense during the 1920s and '30s: the French government, which feared population stagnation after the First World War, instituted campaigns and laws to increase population growth. The Catholic Church similarly took official stances to convince women that their proper role was to find mates and devote themselves solely to them.[36] In contrast, freedom was and is most often perceived as a masculine right. Beauvoir addresses these societal expectations in her critique of marriage in *Le deuxième sexe:*

> Aussi bien n'est-ce pas l'amour que l'optimisme bourgeois promet à la jeune épousée: l'idéal qu'on fait miroiter à ses yeux, c'est celui du bonheur, c'est-à-dire d'un tranquille équilibre au sein de l'immanence et de la répétition. . . . La vocation du mâle, c'est l'action; il lui faut produire, combattre, créer, progresser, se dépasser vers la totalité de l'univers et l'infinité de l'avenir; mais le mariage traditionnel n'invite pas la femme à se transcender avec lui; il la confine dans l'immanence.
>
> [Thus what bourgeois optimism offers the young bride is certainly not love; the bright ideal held up to her is that of happiness, which means the ideal of a peaceful equilibrium in a life of immanence and repetition. The male is called upon for action, his vocation is to produce, fight, create, progress, to transcend himself toward the totality of the universe and the infinity of the future; but traditional marriage does not invite woman to transcend herself with him; it confines her to immanence.] (2:228; 447–48)

Fidelity and independence, both closely linked to freedom, are important theoretical values for Beauvoir: her unpublished diaries and the description in *Le deuxième sexe* indicate that the emancipated woman must not be false to others or herself and must be self-sufficient and ambitious.

In her private journal of 1926, Beauvoir expresses worry that having a husband might make her sacrifice her real self to one that would better please him: "et je sais que je n'ai pas le droit de lui donner à ma place une image qui lui plaise, ni d'être infidèle réellement à ce que je suis" [and I know that I do not have the right to give him a pleasing image instead of myself, nor to be really unfaithful to what I am] (21 August 1926). Yet being true to herself raises problems for Beauvoir because she changes often: "Je voudrais mettre quelqu'ordre dans mes pensées. L'ennui c'est que dans 15 jours elles auront changé, n'importe" [I would like to put my thoughts in order. The problem is that in 15 days they will have changed; what does it matter] (5 November 1926). She refers to the two beings within her and concludes that she much prefers the ridiculous emotional one: "C'est étrange ces deux êtres en moi: l'un si pondéré, capable de jugement et se possédant somme toute fort bien, l'autre parfaitement inverse, ridicule et que je préfère tellement au premier!" [It's strange these two being in me: one so ponderous and capable of judgment, and overall very in control of itself, the other perfectly opposite, ridiculous and the one I much prefer to the other!] (12 August 1926). She indicates her attraction to the mysterious in her statements that a good writer should not seek to be understood immediately: "J'en conclus que, lorsqu'on écrit, il ne faut pas chercher à être compris tout de suite; la tendance première est de vouloir tout dire; mais comme dit Cocteau ce qui est intéressant, c'est ce qu'on lit entre les lignes" [I conclude that when one writes, one must not seek to be understood right away; the first tendency is to want to say everything; but as Cocteau says, what is interesting is what is read between the lines] (10 September 1926). Many of the contradictions found within the pages of her autobiography might derive from her occasional preference for her unreasonable, passionate side and her efforts to emulate her idea of this ideal writer. Her 1926 diary further shows that she imagines herself to be torn between two wishes. She desires a single soul mate with whom to share her life: "Et je sais qu'il n'est pas un être qui mieux que lui convienne à mon être! Je sais que si je ne l'épouse pas, jamais je n'épouserai personne; ça vaudrait mieux je crois! Mais ce serait si vide, si implacablement triste que je n'aurais pas non plus la force de faire grand chose" [And I know that not a single being suits me better than he (Jacques)! I know that if I do not marry him, I will never marry anyone; that would be better, I believe! But it would be so empty, so implacably sad that I would not have the strength to do much of anything else either] (23 October 1926). But she longs also to experience numerous love relationships: "Je veux *aimer* et de plus en plus chaque être, et de plus en plus nombreux les êtres" [I want: *to love* and more and more each being and more and more numerous the beings] (31 October 1926). One notices the same battle between independence and dependence throughout her unpublished diaries from 1926 to 1930. Each time that Beauvoir falls in love, whether it be with Jacques, Merleau-Ponty, Maheu, or Sartre, she oscillates between two basic ideas: either her man's absence makes her feel increasingly forlorn or it convinces her of her growing self-sufficiency. Her entries of September 1929 disclose her joy at meeting Sartre, who, thanks to his uniqueness, continually shook her out of her lassitude and encouraged her to experience life to the fullest in a way that no other man had:

> En tout cas, merci, cher Baladin, même si vous me plaquez dans un an je vous dirai merci d'être venu me chercher—m'arracher à l'enlisement—peut-être il eût été plus confortable de dormir près de J., un temps—mais j'aurais vu, trop tard, et souffert bien, bien plus—ou je n'aurais pas vu, pas vécu—c'eût été pire.
>
> [In any case, thank you, dear Buffoon, even if you dump me in a year I will say thank you for having come to get me—for tearing me out of my lassitude—maybe it would have been more comfortable to sleep next to Jacques for a while—but I would have seen too late and suffered a lot, a lot more—or I would not have seen, not have lived. That would have been worse.] (16 September 1929)

The battle to reconcile feminine and feminist tendencies as well as fidelity and freedom is particularly apparent in the discursive choices that Beauvoir makes in recounting her relationship with Algren in *La force des choses*. Her first introduction of him follows a long section concerning her travels in America and serves to manifest certain characteristics that she shares with the theoretical emancipated woman depicted in *Le deuxième sexe*. She portrays herself as an active and responsible female with an important job and self-assigned goals. She reminds the reader of her numerous travels and of her status as author and philosopher:

> Il me devint plus proche encore quand à la fin de mon séjour je me liai avec Nelson Algren. Bien que j'aie raconté—très inexactement—cette histoire dans *Les mandarins* j'y reviens, non par goût de l'anecdote mais pour regarder de plus près un problème que dans *La force de l'âge* j'ai pris trop aisément pour résolu: entre la fidélité et la liberté, y a-t-il une conciliation possible? A quel prix.
>
> [America became even closer to me when I became attached to Nelson Algren toward the end of my stay. Although I recounted the affair—very inaccurately—in *The Mandarins,* I return to it now, not out of any taste for trivial detail, but in order to examine more closely a problem that in *The Prime of Life* I too easily took to be resolved: Is there any possible reconciliation between fidelity and freedom? And if so, at what price?][37]

At this point of *La force des choses,* Beauvoir creates a slight ambiguity by not mentioning anyone's name in connection to her faithfulness or her freedom. A paragraph later she narrows her focus to Sartre: "Nombreux sont les couples qui concluent le même pacte, à peu près, que Sartre et moi: maintenir à travers des écarts une 'certaine fidélité'" [There are numerous couples who make approximately the same pact as Sartre and myself: to maintain a 'certain fidelity' when straying],[38] but her initial lapse suggests that at an unconscious level, it is the conciliation of freedom and her faithfulness to Algren that is problematic. This insertion of Algren into her autobiographical life minimizes Algren's humanity by reducing him to a "problem," thus downplaying her potential love for him, and maximizes her intelligence, which thereby shows her to be a modern thinking woman. She insists upon her skills of analysis, acknowledges that she has already recounted their story inaccurately in *Les mandarins,* and points out that she wants to review it again for philosophical reasons.

Her introduction of Algren also sets up a tension between emotion and intellect—or body and soul—that turns her love affair into a tale of pain and disharmony. According to *Le deuxième sexe,* woman in contemporary traditional society is stymied by her lack of rights; she thus pursues self-definition via such unsatisfactory means as narcissism, love, and religion. In contrast, the modern emancipated woman accepts masculine values such as thought, action, work, and creation (2:521; 679, and 2:562; 718). *Les mandarins* depicts the fictional Anne burning to make love to the physical presence and warmth of a man: "Ça semblait étrange de me retrouver sur mes jambes, réchauffée par ma seule chaleur, et que mon corps sût se mouvoir et qu'il occupât une place à lui; tout le jour, il n'avait été qu'une absence, un négatif: il attendait la nuit et les caresses de Lewis" [It seemed strange to find myself on my feet again, warmed by only my own heat, and that my body knew how to move and that it occupied a place of its own; all day long it had only been an absence, a negation: it waited for the night and Lewis's caresses].[39] In contrast, the autobiographical author-persona of *La force des choses* seeks rather to reveal her philosophy and downplay her feelings and desires through her relationship with Algren. Such erotic longings betray a woman's need for a man and potentially keep her from acting upon her goals. Beauvoir's unpublished diary suggests rather that the act of writing, in addition to embalming certain life events, falsifies and replaces emotional need. The autobiographical "I" (who is predominantly pure intellect) strongly evokes the first-person narrator Beauvoir created for her diary at the age of eighteen: "Comme j'ai peu besoin de lui parfois; comme j'ai peu besoin de personne. C'est à ces moments-là en général que j'écris, et c'est pourquoi ce cahier est si différent de moi-même" [How little I need him (Jacques) at times; how little I need anyone! It's at these times in general that I write and that is why this notebook is so different from myself] (24 October 1926). As the author of *La force des choses,* Beauvoir is momentarily distanced from Algren and cares little about the actual man; she wants rather to scrutinize their situation in the abstract to see if any conciliation is possible between fidelity and liberty. In thus presenting Algren, the autobiographical "I" denies him status as a flesh-and-blood lover or friend and reduces him to a variable in an equation. The use of the word *problème* in *La force des choses* in association with their relationship adds further insult and, paradoxically, reinserts the notion of potentially irrational and stereotypical sentiment by evoking a source of pain or vexation, which could be interpreted as her love for Algren. Beauvoir's 1926 diary confirms such an interpretation, for she associates love and friendship with suffering: "Je ne savais pas aimer avant cette année puisque j'ignorais le passionné désir de souffrir horriblement pour ceux qu'on aime" [I didn't know how to love before this year because I was ignorant of the passionate desire to suffer horribly for those one loves] (7 November 1926); "Il faut que je me résigne pour moi toute amitié sera une sanglante lutte" [I must resign myself to the fact that for me each friendship will be a bloody struggle] (14 October 1926). In her autobiography, she compares her love for Algren to torment and a page later blames this pain on her pact with Sartre to experience contingent loves: "nous avions voulu connaître des 'amours contingentes'" [we had wanted to experience "contingent loves"].[40] Yet the ambiguity created by her exclusion of Sartre from the paragraph introducing fidelity and freedom and her stress on her determination (*vouloir*) to experience contingent loves imply that the trouble is rather the result of her ambition to remain faithful to either Algren or Sartre while keeping her freedom.

The clash between liberty and fidelity mentioned in *La force des choses* between a paragraph about dependent American women and one about traditional marriages and Beauvoir's "certaine fidélité" (certain faithfulness) to Sartre takes on a broader meaning. In the terms of Beauvoir's theory, "fidélité" is directed toward oneself and one's work as a woman instead of toward a single man. *Le deuxième sexe* confirms that the reconciliation of freedom and fidelity is a problem for the independent woman. A liberated woman would have total economic autonomy, an occupation, a strong sense of herself as an active and responsible subject, and self-assigned goals and rights. For Beauvoir, woman's self-doubt, obsession with love, and lack of publicly valued achievements is due to societal structures that only a radical political change resulting in equal treatment and attitudes toward the sexes would remedy. Like a male, an emancipated female would have the right to sexual satisfaction where and when she chose (2:521–28; 679–86). She would not constantly doubt herself, not always have to prove herself to others, not always be afraid of criticism (2:542–49; 699–706). Raised like a boy, she would understand the importance and empowerment of solitude—she would experience herself as a unique and sovereign being who depends on nobody (2:556–57; 712–13). Overall, a woman must struggle to find her sense of self and to avoid becoming the traditional stereotyped female who never transcends her role as man's servant and mirror. Once she has achieved independence, she must not let the man of her life destroy it: "Pendant vingt ans d'attente, de rêve, d'espoir, la jeune fille a caressé le mythe du héros libérateur et sauveur: l'indépendance conquise dans le travail ne suffit pas à abolir son désir d'une abdication glorieuse" [During twenty years of waiting, dreaming, hoping, the young girl has cherished the myth of the liberating savior-hero: the independence she has conquered in her work is not enough to abolish her desire for a glorious abdication] (2:538; 695–96).

In retelling her tale with Algren, Beauvoir repeatedly underscores the theme of faithfulness to herself and underplays his importance in her life, whereas in reality she persistently wore the ring he gave her and even was buried with it on her finger. Disparaging portraits of lovesick females in *Le deuxième sexe* suggest that she kept his ring on her finger not only because she loved him, but also to remind herself of what she might have become, an *amoureuse* or a housewife, if she had accepted his marriage proposal. Her unpublished diaries, incongruities in her life, her autobiography, and her comments concerning her works also point to the refusal to become a traditional woman, which figures in Beauvoir's writing as early as the 1920s, before she met Sartre. Loose pages in her 1926 unpublished journal concern a woman who rejects marriage because she does not want to be loved for her hair, her dress, her way of dancing, or any image that has little to do with herself as a fully rounded person. But as the inconsistencies in Beauvoir's life and works indicate, refusing an idea on a theoretical level does not often transfer to reality. A reader of her unpublished letters and her fictionalized version of her affair with Algren is left with the impression that Beauvoir would indeed have married Algren if she could have kept her work, her life in Paris, and her daily meeting with Sartre. It also seems likely that she did not clearly offer this as a possibility to Algren because she had the idea that she should be ready to commit all to him if her love were true. In her 1926 diary Beauvoir comments on love: "C'est là qu'il faut accomplir le prodige de se donner tout en se réservant sans donner moins parce qu'on se réserve, sans se réserver moins parce qu'on se donne" [It is in this domain that one must achieve the wondrous task of simultaneously giving and keeping oneself, without giving any less because of the keeping and without keeping any less because of the giving] (21 August 1926). Her letter to Algren of 23 July 1947 slightly alters her 1926 view; she states, in the midst of a declaration of undying love, that she knows that whatever happens, she would never give everything to him and that she feels bad about it. This is perhaps why she contradicts herself—because she seeks an impossible relationship in which she grants everything to her beloved without losing anything of herself. In *La force des choses,* between the end of her love affair with Algren and the beginning of her romantic liaison with Lanzmann, Beauvoir offers an analysis of *Les mandarins* that suggests that she also anguished over the dangers of devoting everything to a man. She states that it was difficult to create Paule, the female character of *Les mandarins* who becomes insane when her lover leaves:

> je conçus Paule comme une femme radicalement aliénée à un homme et le tyrannisant au nom de cet esclavage. . . . Mieux qu'au temps du *Sang des autres* . . . je savais combien il est dangereux pour une femme d'engager tout de soi dans sa liaison avec un écrivain ou un artiste, buté sur ses projets: renonçant à ses goûts, à ses occupations, elle s'exténue à l'imiter sans pouvoir le rejoindre . . . s'il se détourne d'elle, elle se retrouve dépouillée de tout; j'avais vu quantité d'exemples de cette déchéance et j'avais envie d'en parler.
>
> [I conceived Paule as a woman radically alienated from herself by an exclusive attachment to one man, and tyrannizing him in the name of this slavery. . . . Even better than at the time of *The Blood of Others* . . . I understood how dangerous it is for a woman to invest all of herself in her liaison with a writer or an artist, obsessed by his work: giving up her tastes, her occupations, she exhausts herself in imitation of him without being able to catch up to him. . . . If he turns away from her, she finds herself stripped of everything; I had seen numerous examples of this degeneration and I felt like speaking of it.] [41]

Although Beauvoir attributes this new understanding to the stories others have told her, her experience with Algren also offers much reason for contemplation. He too was a writer and, as a foreigner who wanted her to marry him and remake her life in the United States, was in effect asking her to give up her life in order to embrace his. She had already clearly explained in her letters that she could not devote her life to him. Her statements concerning Anne's failure to find self-fulfillment establish work as standing in opposition to a love relationship with a man and do not include any possibility for reconciliation of work and love if a woman wants true freedom: "Anne se rapproche plus que les autres d'une vraie liberté; elle ne réussit tout de même pas à trouver dans ses propres entreprises un accomplissement" [Anne gets closer than the others to a true freedom; she nevertheless does not succeed in finding fulfillment in her own enterprises]. Beauvoir rejects Anne for not passionately embracing her work and for accepting herself as a secondary person: "Cependant elle n'a ni mes appétits, ni mes entêtements, ni surtout l'autonomie que me donne un métier qui me tient à coeur. . . . Faute d'avoir des buts et des projets à soi, elle mène la vie 'relative' d'un être 'secondaire'" [Yet she has neither my appetites nor my stubbornness, nor, above all, the autonomy that I get from a job that I love. . . . Due to a lack of goals and plans of her own, she leads the *relative* life of a *secondary* being].[42]

Beauvoir's ideas about the fictional Paule and Anne further suggest that she disfigures Algren to put an end to her own fascination with him; her tendency to forget herself entirely in her love relationships manifests itself in her brief discussion of Algren as a man with whom she experienced mutual attraction: "mais je n'ai pas dit quelle complicité s'était tout de suite établie entre nous, ni comme nous avions été déçus de ne pas pouvoir dîner ensemble" [but I did not mention the great complicity that was immediately established between us, nor how disappointed we were not to be able to have dinner together]. Momentarily, in her reweaving of their tale, her fascination with him becomes an uncontrollable force more closely approximating the emotions evoked by *Les mandarins;* only physical interference from someone else can separate her from this man: "Avant de partir pour la gare je lui ai téléphoné: ils ont dû m'ôter le récepteur des mains" [Before I left for the train station, I called him: they had to force the receiver out of my hands].[43] Ironically, in reconstructing Algren in *La force des choses* as feminine, exotic, and surrounded by emptiness once Beauvoir left,[44] the author Beauvoir saves her feminist self from the sorrows of dependency on a lover by attributing the same ugly fate to her partner in accordance with her theory: "chacun s'efforce d'en faire supporter par l'autre l'abjection et de s'en réserver l'honneur" [Each struggles to project the abject on to the other and to reserve the honor for oneself].[45] She puts Algren in the position of her fictional character Paule, who loses everything when her lover leaves.

Beauvoir subverts the patriarchal notions about love and sexuality with her creation of several different endings for this love story with Algren and in so doing also destroys Algren. She combats centuries of myths and legends, which promote a Prince Charming figure as the ultimate in every girl's life, with an analysis of just what such a prince might have brought to a princess. Beauvoir's analogies reduce Algren to nothing by considering not his inherent greatness but rather his effect on her. The question she asks herself at their parting suggests new ways for women to demystify love relationships, which do not in and of themselves provide the only reason to live. This does not mean that Beauvoir does not yearn for love or sexual passion and even believe in their importance. It suggests that she is struggling to reconcile feminism, eroticism, and exoticism and to protest against the male tradition carefully delineated in *Le deuxième sexe:* "Elle apprend que pour être heureuse il faut être aimée; pour être aimée, il faut attendre l'amour. La femme c'est la Belle au bois dormant, Peau d'Ane, Cendrillon, Blanche Neige, celle qui reçoit et subit. . . . La suprême nécessité pour la femme, c'est de charmer un coeur masculin" [She learns that to be happy she must be loved; to be loved, she must wait for love. Woman is Sleeping Beauty, Donkey Skin, Cinderella, Snow White, the one who receives and submits. . . . The supreme necessity for woman is to charm a masculine heart].[46] Thus, when Beauvoir learns that Algren is getting remarried and that she will probably never see him again, she uses the information to understand more about herself and her relationship to eroticism and exoticism. Instead of contemplating suicide, like Anne in *Les mandarins,* she reconstructs Algren as a function of his country (the exotic) and of the self she was with him (a foreigner): "Algren allait se remarier avec son ex-femme. . . . je pensais que plus jamais je ne le reverrais, ni la maison, ni le lac, ni ce sable où picoraient les petits échassiers blancs; et je ne savais pas ce que je regrettais le plus fort: un homme, un paysage ou moi-même" [Algren was going to remarry his ex-wife. . . . I thought that I would never again see him, the house, the lake, or the sand where the little white waders pecked about; and I didn't know which I missed more; a man, a countryside, or myself].[47] This question implies that she was not in love with him as a flesh-and-blood individual; rather, her attachment to him is more a symptom of her desire to rediscover America and the exotic. Her reaction highlights the importance of reinventing the healthy solitude, viewed in *Le deuxième sexe* as necessary to the emancipated woman. Living in another country allows one to discover a new and foreign self. Beauvoir's correspondence implies that it is the outlandish, more relaxed, more narcissistic, more sensual self that she allowed to blossom in the United States that she will miss. Loving an American who spoke no French, despite her efforts to teach him, allowed her new avenues of exploration with language as well as new modes of self-expression and self-creation, as the 352 letters that she wrote to him in English attest.[48] Some letters manifest her bewilderment at expressing herself in another language. On 4 June 1947 she bemoans the fact that love can't be put into words, especially since English ones are all that she has. On 21 October 1947, feeling misunderstood, she asks Algren if it is her English or her handwriting that he doesn't understand.[49] Other letters indicate her delight over writing on new topics in a foreign tongue. On 23 October 1947 she comments that she never really wrote love letters before and certainly never in English.[50]

As part and parcel of her quest to combine eroticism, exoticism, and feminism, Beauvoir, the autobiographical persona in *La force des choses,* must manifest her equality with males. To do so, she constructs oppositions between herself, Sartre, Algren, and Sartre's lover Dolores Vanetti Ehrenreich, who is referred to as "M." Sartre becomes the natural Other to prove her point. As Beauvoir describes it, not only does she herself have a contingent relationship like Sartre, but also his contingent lover M. is not his priority and thus must rearrange her life around Beauvoir's plans. Sartre and M. also camouflage Beauvoir's excitement concerning her four-month vacation with Algren: "Les lettres de M. étaient sombres; elle avait consenti de mauvaise grâce à passer quatre mois avec Sartre pendant que je voyagerais avec Algren" [M.'s letters were somber. She had grudgingly agreed to spend four months with Sartre while I traveled with Algren]. Furthermore, Beauvoir is infinitely more rational (more like the stereotypical male) in her even-tempered analysis of her own passions than M. Whereas M.'s letters are somber and her attitude toward Sartre bad-tempered, Beauvoir's desire to be near Algren again is intense: "J'avais une immense envie de me retrouver auprès d'Algren" [I had an immense desire to be back near Algren]. The strength of her passion is quickly negated, however, by numerous rationalizations that serve to accentuate her equality with men and to nullify any possible suggestion that she is a slave to her sexual needs: "mais enfin je n'avais vécu que trois semaines avec lui; je ne savais pas dans quelle mesure je tenais à lui: un peu, beaucoup ou davantage? . . . sachant que j'aurais pu rester avec Sartre je m'exposais à des regrets qui se tourneraient, sinon en rancune à l'égard d'Algren, du moins en dépit contre moi-même" [But after all I had lived with him for only three weeks; I didn't know how much he meant to me: a little, a lot, or more? . . . Knowing that I could have stayed with Sartre, I was opening myself up to regrets which could turn, if not into rancor against Algren, at least into resentment of myself].[51]

The construction of Beauvoir's narrative and her descriptions as she weaves Algren into her narrative prove her equality with men in general and Sartre in particular. The structure of her paragraphs merges Sartre's love life with her own. Her situation with Algren becomes Sartre's with M. as the same paragraph shifts from one to the other without a transition: "Je dis aussi que nous nous reverrions, mais nous ne savions ni quand, ni comment et j'arrivai à Paris, chavirée. Sartre aussi avait des ennuis" [I also said that we would see each other again but we knew neither when nor how and I arrived in Paris shattered. Sartre too had problems] (141; 126). She underlines her equality with Sartre by use of the word "too" (*aussi*), which links his problems (*ennuis*) to her own and by juxtaposition implies that Algren is like M. An analysis of the relationship between Sartre and M. continues in this same paragraph, starting with a full page on Algren and Beauvoir that can be read as a thinly veiled study of Beauvoir's own romantic liaison: "Si M. s'installait à Paris, sacrifiant sa situation, ses amitiés, ses habitudes, tout, elle serait en droit d'attendre tout de Sartre: c'était plus qu'il ne pouvait lui offrir. Mais s'il l'aimait, comment supporterait-il de ne pas la voir pendant des mois?" [If M. were to move to Paris, sacrificing her position, her friendships, her habits, everything, she would have the right to expect everything from Sartre. It was more than he could give her. But if he loved her how could he stand not seeing her for months?] (142; 127). Like M., Algren and Beauvoir could not give up their homes and sacrifice everything without losing their independence; yet it did not seem plausible to love someone and still agree to long periods of separation. The same link between couples is strengthened later in the text: Sartre's breakup with M. foreshadows the end of Beauvoir's affair with Algren and implies the benefits of Algren's refusal to live in Paris. Before narrating her last trip to the town of Miller as Algren's lover, Beauvoir includes a paragraph indicating the condition of Sartre's love life: "Sartre avait des soucis privés. En 49 il avait voyagé avec M. au Mexique et au Guatemala et vu aussi Cuba, Panama, Haïti, Curaçao. Ils ne s'entendaient plus bien. Malgré les résistances de Sartre, elle s'était fixée à Paris. Ils se querellèrent et finirent par rompre" [Sartre had private worries. In '49 he traveled with M. to Mexico and to Guatemala and also saw Cuba, Panama, Haiti, Caracas. They no longer got along well. Despite Sartre's resistance, she had come to live in Paris. They quarreled and ended up breaking things off]. This paragraph precedes the one about her return to Algren, which begins, "J'avais correspondu toute l'année avec Algren" [I had corresponded with Algren all year long], and thereby evokes how her rapport with Algren might have ended had he moved to France (243–44; 224).

These parallels between Algren, M., Beauvoir, and Sartre show that males, despite their tendency to emphasize only their public professional lives, also suffer and benefit from the necessary bond between their personal lives and their public careers. The careers of both Sartre and Algren, like that of Beauvoir, are thus shown, through *La force des choses,* to depend on their personal interactions.[52] Likewise, the textual parallel between couples illustrates Beauvoir's belief stated in *Le deuxième sexe* that men and women have similar sexual needs and attribute to their partners whatever qualities they refuse to accept in themselves:

> En vérité, l'homme est comme la femme une chair, donc une passivité, jouet de ses hormones et de l'espèce, proie inquiète de son désir; et elle est comme lui au sein de la fièvre charnelle consentement, don volontaire, activité. . . . c'est contre soi que chacun lutte, projetant en son partenaire cette part de lui-même qu'il répudie.
>
> [In truth, man is like woman, a flesh, therefore a passivity, victim of his hormones and his species, a worried prey to his desires, and she is like him in the midst of carnal passion consentment, voluntary gift, activity. . . . It is against oneself that each struggles, projecting onto the partner the part of oneself that one rejects.] (2 : 573; 728)

Her situation with Algren mirrors Sartre's situation with M., which fortifies her own ties with Sartre and denies specificity or distinct tenderness to Algren or M. (the contingent lovers). Beauvoir's analysis also contains a curious mixture of condemnation and justification of Sartre, and because she merged the boundaries between herself and Sartre, it also suggests her guilt (conveniently imputed to another of her partners) concerning her behavior toward Algren: "on peut estimer qu'il l'avait abusée dans la mesure où il lui était impossible de lui en communiquer l'évidence. De son côté d'ailleurs, elle ne lui avait pas dit qu'en s'engageant dans cette histoire, elle en refusait les limites" [one might conclude that Sartre had taken advantage of her (M.) in that it was impossible for him to communicate the obvious to her. As for her, she had not told him upon agreeing to have an affair with him, that she refused its limits].[53] Beauvoir's struggle with detachment ends on a note that defends Sartre and, by association, excuses herself for not wholeheartedly choosing Algren: "son excuse c'est que, tout en refusant d'altérer ses relations avec moi, il tenait violemment à elle et il avait voulu croire possible une conciliation" [His excuse is that he simultaneously refused to alter his relationship with me and cared immensely about her, and he had wanted to believe that it was possible to maintain the two relationships].[54]

As part of the gender reconstruction in *La force des choses,* Beauvoir stresses her own honesty and self-assertiveness, stereotypically masculine traits, and Algren's gullibility and ignorance, traditionally feminine traits: "Je lui dis, avant de le quitter, que ma vie était faite en France, pour toujours; il me crut sans rien y comprendre" [I told him before leaving him that my life was made in France forever; he believed me without understanding anything]. Showing herself and not Algren as the speaking party before their first separation, Beauvoir emerges as the dominant and active force in their relationship. The feminine parallel between Algren and M. continues as the narrative reveals that M. too has misunderstood the wishes of her lover: "Avant de s'embarquer pour la France, M. lui avait écrit avec franchise: 'Je viens, décidée à tout faire pour que tu me demandes de rester.' Il ne le lui avait pas demandé" [Before leaving on the boat for France, M. had written him frankly: "I am coming determined to do everything I can to make you ask me to stay." He hadn't asked her to do so] (141–42; 126).

Beauvoir's pretense of nonchalance about Algren's indifference to her also supports her political goal of re-creating an emancipated female self who neither suffers nor lies to herself to maintain her love relationships. Despite Algren's excuse of having too much work, one might easily interpret his refusal to have Beauvoir return to America as a potential rejection of the chance to deepen their relationship. According to this scenario, it is because of his lack of enthusiasm, which suggests that she is more emotional and dependent than he, and because his absence allows her to deny his freedom and ambiguity that she skillfully convinces herself and her reader that she was much better off without him: "J'en fus peinée: le travail n'était qu'un prétexte; mais je fus aussi soulagée: ces revoirs, ces départs, ces rebuffades, ces élans, me surmenaient. Pendant un mois à Paris, je travaillai, je lus, je vis mes amis" [I was hurt by this: work was only a pretext, but I was also relieved: these reunions, these departures, these rejections, these outbursts of passion overwhelmed me. For a month in Paris, I worked, I read, I saw my friends] (179; 162). In showing how easily she could fill her life with other pursuits, she illustrates that women are independent, intelligent, and creative beings whose lives do not revolve around men or love. Furthermore, her awareness that Algren's answer is a pretext serves to show that she is not the stereotypical woman in love willing to believe anything to save her pride, whom she describes in *Le deuxième sexe:* "Il faut donc qu'elle souffre ou qu'elle se mente" [Thus she must either suffer or lie to herself] (2:496; 659).

The examples offered in this study indicate that Beauvoir's portrayal of Algren and herself reveals her struggle between choosing her life consciously according to her philosophy and still being tortured as an adult by the patriarchal myths that formed her as a child. Both options remained problematic for in rejecting stereotypes Beauvoir also had to suppress, at least in her autobiography, the passionate way that she experienced life. Her published and unpublished diaries and letters confirm that intense emotion and a latent desire to be, at least occasionally, a traditional woman were also part of her daily life. Could she simultaneously be erotic, exotic, and feminist? The contradictions in *La force des choses* suggest that Beauvoir tried but never could totally abandon certain pleasures in favor of her feminist ideals, which were seemingly engendered as a reaction against the childhood myths that she tried to suppress. This struggle manifests itself in the structures used to insert Algren into the text and in the descriptions of him, which illustrate her financial autonomy, the importance of her profession and of her friends, and her self-confidence, motivation, and responsibility. She tries to maintain her sexual difference as an erotic female but denies the passivity and dependence usually attributed to this role. She repeats her goals and clarifies that she would rather lose a man than abandon her objectives, and this cancels out her erotic side instead of recasting it as part of her feminism. Solitude is depicted as a useful time for self-reflection. The parallel created by the relationship between Sartre and M. and Beauvoir and Algren illustrates the equality between both sexes who are similarly ruled by hormones and who simultaneously seek escape from their own irrationalities by blaming the opposite sex. The erasure of the differences between the sexes destroys her exoticism, for she can no longer be mysteriously irrational and foreign if her partners and rivals are also that way. Beauvoir's contradictory portrait of herself, Algren, and others who touched their relationship exemplifies the theoretical authentic erotic, exotic, feminist woman and shows that Beauvoir, despite her efforts, failed to be one when she transformed and embalmed the past with her writing. In contrast, her ideal woman simultaneously experiences herself as both subject and object and renews each relationship continuously in the hope of allowing each significant other the space to grow.

Overall, Beauvoir left a complicated sexual legacy for women, one that can best be defined in terms of what it was not. She left a variety of self-portraits in the form of diaries, letters, fiction, autobiography, philosophical essays, and even interviews, none of which can be privileged as the true version of her gender construction. Neither Sartre's victim nor wife, she seemingly constructed her public relationship with him to increase her freedom as a woman in society and to prove philosophical points concerning other women. Algren was not the one great love of her life, but one of a circle of many great loves that included a number of women. Her multiple portraits of Algren and her desire to be buried with his ring on her finger indicate primarily that she remained conflicted about her longing for him and that at least one part of her, which was perhaps also partially a construction for her public, remained his eternal lover. Beauvoir's multiple tellings of the same life in many forms bequeath to her public the notion that woman is a construct of society and of herself: she has the right to reformulate her existence as often as desired and as in as many ways as possible, for every portrait is a creation that contests some other equally valid version of reality. In the documentary about her life, which Beauvoir had hoped would help people to know her better, she offers a final excuse for the many contradictions she experienced and/or recorded and thereby suggests that the multiple and conflicting portraits of her life were left purposely as a way of exemplifying the impossibility of depriving a life of its ambiguity: "j'ai horreur du héros positif et les livres avec des héros positifs ne m'intéressent pas. . . . Un roman, c'est un problématique. L'histoire de ma vie . . . est une espèce de problématique et je n'ai pas à donner des solutions à des gens et les gens n'ont pas à attendre des solutions de moi" [I hate positive heroes and books with positive heroes do not interest me. . . . A novel poses a hypothetical problem. The story of my life . . . is a type of hypothetical problem and I do not have to give people solutions and people must not expect them from me].[55]

Notes

I am indebted to the Bibliothèque Nationale of France in Paris and the Ohio State University Libraries Special Collections for allowing me to study Beauvoir's manuscripts, and to Northern Kentucky University, the Southern Regional Grants Award Program, and the American Philosophical Society for funding my study. I thank Sylvie Le Bon de Beauvoir, Beauvoir's executor of estate, and Mauricette Berne, curator of the twentieth-century manuscript collection at the Bibliothèque Nationale of France, for facilitating my study of Beauvoir's early unpublished diaries. I am especially grateful to Sylvie Le Bon de Beauvoir, who allowed me to quote from these unpublished diaries in this article. I would like to acknowledge Melanie Hawthorne and the Northern Kentucky University Department of Literature and Language Writing Group for their insightful comments on earlier versions of this article.

1. Schwarzer, *After "The Second Sex,"* 85.

2. Many, for example, had patterned their lives on what Beauvoir had written they should be and felt betrayed upon reading her published diary. They faulted Beauvoir for bragging about her black-market bargains and for stating that she found the Germans in uniform quite handsome. Others, who rejected marriage and children because of Beauvoir's credos, blamed her for ignoring her own beliefs to cater to Sartre's whims (Bair, "Do as She Said," 32). Some stated that Beauvoir made negative comments, even in her private letters and diaries, about her female lovers, their bodies, and behaviors or suggested that Beauvoir took female lovers only to imitate Sartre or, worse, to control his relationships with them (Galster, "Une femme machiste et mesquine," 53–62). Ingrid Galster, unlike most critics, defends Beauvoir against these claims and encourages a reinterpretation of Beauvoir in the context of all of her writings.

3. Other reasons that Beauvoir camouflaged her sexuality have been explored in Klaw's "*L'Invitée* Castrated," "Sexuality in Beauvoir's *Les mandarins,*" and "Desire."

4. Schwarzer, *After "The Second Sex,"* 111.

5. Beauvoir, "Mon expérience d'écrivain," in *Les écrits,* 450. All translations, unless otherwise indicated, are my own and follow the original French text as closely as possible. For the reader's convenience, corresponding page numbers for the original French and the published English translations, when available, follow my translations.

6. Ibid., 454–55.

7. Beauvoir, *Journal de guerre,* 181. More current theories on autobiography similarly agree with Beauvoir that writing autobiography is a creative process and add that it also is one that informs memory. Patricia Spacks concludes that people remember less than they think they do, that they imagine part of what they believe they remember (*Imagining a Self,* 19). Roy Pascal points out that in re-creating their lives, autobiographers impose a logic on initially illogically occurring events and give meaning to their lives by establishing a sort of ideal image of the self beneath the personality that appears to the world (*Design and Truth in Autobiography,* 193).

8. In *Le deuxième sexe,* Beauvoir establishes a difference between male and female eroticism. One difference is that a male attains sexual pleasure by projecting himself toward the other without losing his autonomy, whereas for the female the normal sexual act puts her in a position of dependence upon the male (148–55; *The Second Sex,* 371–78).

9. *Shoah* (1985) is a nine and one-half hour documentary that shows the remains of the extermination camps and includes interviews with survivors of World War II to provide an oral history of the Holocaust.

10. Beauvoir, *La force des choses,* 177; *Force of Circumstance,* 160.

11. Ibid., 140–41; 125.

12. Qtd. in Weatherby, "The Life and Hard Times of Nelson Algren," 39; Algren, "The Question of Simone de Beauvoir," 136; Algren, "Simone à Go Go," 66.

13. Some of the more recent readings interrogate Beauvoir's autobiographical and theoretical prose to learn about her sexuality. Kathleen Woodward takes some of Beauvoir's autobiographical comments at face value and notes that changes in the human body such as the development of breasts and menstruation repelled Beauvoir, and finds it significant that Beauvoir spoke so little about her sexual relationship with her lovers: "Indeed, in four volumes of memoirs noteworthy for their frankness, we find next to nothing about her sexual life with Sartre or Algren or with Lanzmann, the only man with whom she ever shared living quarters. In short, it would seem that changes in the body in general arouse in her a deep-seated dislike of what is, for her, a sign of transformation as well as the thing itself" ("Simone de Beauvoir," 95).

14. John D. Raymer, for example, combines passages from the publications of both Beauvoir and Algren to re-create their love affair and its demise from both their points of view. With numerous references to Beauvoir's letters to Algren, the biography by Claude Francis and Fernande Gontier describes Beauvoir and Algren as being desperately, madly in love with each other (*Simone de Beauvoir,* 259), but still accepts at face value the portrait Beauvoir offers in her autobiography that Algren belonged to the

category of contingent loves and that this was a normal and beneficial situation for literary work (270). A 1990 essay by Leah Hewitt explores Beauvoir's interviews and the textual inconsistencies in her autobiographical works to postulate why readers often interpret Beauvoir too literally. With a focus on *Mémoires d'une jeune fille rangée* and *Tout compte fait,* Hewitt argues that Beauvoir's unconsciously feminine voice evidences itself through the numerous contradictions and incoherencies in the text (13–51). Armine Kotin Mortimer is one of the few critics who illustrated as early as 1991 that Beauvoir's autobiography contains numerous distortions and who recreates portions of Beauvoir's life based on the published letters and journals through which she and Sartre corresponded and the novel *L'invitée.* With a focus on *La force de l'âge,* Terry Keefe meticulously documents the discrepancies in the information provided by Beauvoir's published memoirs, letters, and diaries. Others explore Beauvoir's self-portrait in her published diary and letters. In an analysis of Beauvoir's construction of a fictional self in *Journal de guerre,* Emma Wilson suggests that Beauvoir writes for Sartre's consumption and to portray herself as his double in her relations with women. Christine Ann Evans similarly contends that Sartre mediated Beauvoir's relationship with women and that in her published diary and letters, it was her deference to his wishes and career that caused her descriptions of her relationships with women to be troubled.

15. Dayan and Ribowska, *Simone de Beauvoir,* 92. In 1994 Jean-Pierre Saccani recast the Beauvoir/Algren saga with Algren as the victim and Beauvoir as alternately dominated by Sartre or Algren. Deirdre Bair's 1990 biography portrays Algren as Beauvoir's true destiny: "He had given her what she never dreamed would be hers: passion, devotion, affection, and intellectual support" (*Simone de Beauvoir,* 353). Bair uses her conversation with Hélène de Beauvoir to question Beauvoir's presentation of the affair with Algren: when her sister asked her if she were sorry that Algren had died, Beauvoir replied, "Why should I [be]? . . . What did he feel for me, that he could have written those horrible things?" However, she continued to wear his ring (502–3). Bair also hypothesizes that Beauvoir may have used certain discourse in her letters and autobiography after 1960 because "the myth of the [Sartre/Beauvoir] couple was the dominant, paramount entity of her life" (372). Bair's generalization is undoubtedly true, but my goal is to show how the meaning of the myth of the couple as well as the other factors potentially influenced Beauvoir's construction of self and others. Margaret Crosland, who sees the fictional Lewis Brogan from Beauvoir's *Les mandarins* and Nelson Algren as interchangeable, also alludes to Algren's symbolic role for Beauvoir: "Beauvoir obviously needed a Brogan in her life, and if Algren had not appeared she would no doubt have found someone else" (*Simone de Beauvoir,* 382). In her 1989 biography of Algren, Bettina Drew postulates that Algren "must have been appalled to read Simone's *nonfictional* account of their affair" and claims that "the description of their affair was almost grotesquely self-serving" (*A Life on the Wild Side,* 332, emphasis added). How and why does Beauvoir manage to create such an effect? Toril Moi disagrees with the "far too positive assessment of the virtues of that liaison," but she focuses on Algren's negative points, not on Beauvoir's recapitulation of events (*Simone de Beauvoir,* 295). Some of the

lengthier book reviews concerning the publication of Beauvoir's letters to Algren include Acocella and Drew.

16. Beauvoir, *Le deuxième sexe,* 2:13; *The Second Sex,* 267.

17. A close reading of Beauvoir's writings reveals that in the tradition of most autobiographers (Allport, *The Use of Personal Documents,* 78), in order to produce her desired self, Beauvoir focuses on conflict and passes over the happy, peaceful periods of time.

18. Beauvoir, *Le deuxième sexe,* 2:133–34; *The Second Sex,* 374.

19. Beauvoir, *La force de l'âge,* 106–7; *The Prime of Life,* 86.

20. Bair, *Simone de Beauvoir,* 340.

21. Beauvoir, *Le deuxième sexe,* 2:168; *The Second Sex,* 402.

22. In order to realize Beauvoir's concepts of ambiguity and freedom, one must unceasingly choose not to confine oneself or the other to a single definition (*Pour une morale de l'ambiguïté,* 96–97; *The Ethics of Ambiguity,* 67).

23. Beauvoir, *Le deuxième sexe,* 2:167–68; *The Second Sex,* 402.

24. She alludes to her homoerotic urges in her *Journal de guerre* (23, 88) and argues in essays that women, who seek many of the same sensual joys as men, are even more naturally drawn to other females (*Le deuxième sexe,* 2:136; *The Second Sex,* 377). Simons attributes this refusal of a lesbian identity to Beauvoir's "refusal to deny herself and other women the possibility of relationships with men" ("Lesbian Connections," 140).

25. Beauvoir, *Journal de guerre,* 264.

26. Beauvoir, *Le deuxième sexe,* 2:532–33; *The Second Sex,* 690.

27. Beauvoir, *La force des choses,* 205; *Force of Circumstance,* 187. Beauvoir's first collection of short stories that deals extensively with female bodies and desires was rejected because her writing might offend Gallimard's patrons and critics (Bair, *Simone de Beauvoir,* 207).

28. Beauvoir, *La force des choses,* 205; *Force of Circumstance,* 187.

29. Beauvoir, *Le deuxième sexe,* 2:528; *The Second Sex,* 686.

30. Beauvoir, *Journal de guerre* 79, 83, 181.

31. Crosland, *Simone de Beauvoir,* 382; Drew, *A Life on the Wild Side,* 336.

32. Beauvoir, *Le deuxième sexe,* 2:536–38; *The Second Sex,* 693–96.

33. Beauvoir, *La force des choses,* 264; *Force of Circumstance,* 245.

34. Beauvoir, *Le deuxième sexe,* 2:535–36; *The Second Sex,* 693. Further references to this work and its English translation will appear in the text.

35. Beauvoir, *La force des choses,* 139; *Force of Circumstance,* 124.

36. Bell and Offen, *Women, the Family, and Freedom,* 306–10; 313–14.

37. Beauvoir, *La force des choses* 139; *Force of Circumstance,* 124.

38. Ibid.

39. Beauvoir, *Les mandarins,* 342; *The Mandarins,* 320.

40. Beauvoir, *La force des choses,* 140; *Force of Circumstance,* 125.

41. Ibid., 285; 266.

42. Ibid., 286–88; 268.

43. Ibid., 140; 125.

44. Ibid., 177; 160.

45. Beauvoir, *Le deuxième sexe,* 2:573; *The Second Sex,* 729.

46. Ibid., 2:40; 291.

47. Beauvoir, *La force des choses,* 269; *Force of Circumstance,* 250.

48. The translated and published version of these letters that reorganizes the manuscript pages numbered by Lauren Helen Pringle and housed at Ohio State University Libraries states that there are only 304 letters (1997).

49. In the translated version of the letters, the paragraph including this comment does not appear.

50. The translation slightly attenuates the force of this statement: "Vous savez, je n'ai jamais écrit des lettres d'amour en anglais" [You know I never wrote love letters in English] (90).

51. Beauvoir, *La force des choses,* 170; *Force of Circumstance,* 154. Further references to this work and its English translation will appear in the text.

52. See Eleanore Holveck ("Simone de Beauvoir"), who argues that Beauvoir uses her autobiography to develop her philosophy on the existing individual consciousness and its relations to others and to time, place, history, and death.

53. Beauvoir, *La force des choses,* 142; *Force of Circumstance,* 127. As previously stated, Beauvoir's letters to Algren show her anguish over her inability to devote everything to him (23 July 1947).

54. Beauvoir, *La force des choses,* 142; *Force of Circumstance,* 127.

55. Dayan and Ribowska, *Simone de Beauvoir,* 75.

6

Simone de Beauvoir on Henry de Montherlant

A Map of Misreading?

RICHARD J. GOLSAN

As a complement to and illustration of her analysis of masculine myths of women in part 3 of the first volume of *Le deuxième sexe* (The second sex), Simone de Beauvoir offers her assessment of the representation of women in the works of five male writers: D. H. Lawrence, Paul Claudel, André Breton, Stendhal (Henri Beyle), and Henry de Montherlant. Each author, she argues, is representative of a particular attitude toward woman which she considers "typical" to the degree that it conforms to a specific and persistent current of thought vis-à-vis woman in the Western cultural tradition. Thus the essay on D. H. Lawrence focuses on woman as sexual object, while in the work of Claudel woman's role is that of "handmaid of the Lord." In Stendhal, as one might predict, she becomes the object and embodiment of romantic desire, whereas in Breton she is linked to poetic inspiration.

Of the male writers treated in this section, Henry de Montherlant receives pride of place in that he is the first author discussed and the one to whom Beauvoir devotes the lengthiest analysis. He is, moreover, most representative in general terms of Beauvoir's discussion of masculine myths of women provided in the previous section, and for this reason, among others, Montherlant and his work are deserving of attention here.

Unlike the other writers discussed, Montherlant is not well known to Anglo-American readers, nor is he generally conceded to be a "canonical" figure in French literature today, although he was more widely read and discussed in France at the time *Le deuxième sexe* was written. The fact remains, however, that the choice of Montherlant as the male writer whose attitudes toward women are most deserving of the close scrutiny remains something of a mystery. This is so for several reasons. First, Montherlant's case was not typical in the sense clearly intended by Beauvoir in that he was not heterosexual but resolutely pederastic in his tastes throughout his life. The publication during the 1980s of posthumous works including novels and especially Montherlant's correspondence with Roger Peyrefitte confirms the nature and avidity of these appetites and the pursuit of their satisfaction even to the point of recklessness (Peyrefitte and Sipriot). Indeed, while residing in Marseilles during the early stages of the Occupation, Montherlant was arrested by Vichy authorities for soliciting a minor.[1] While Montherlant's pederasty was not widely known to the general public until the late 1960s, it was no secret to other Parisian literati, and it is hard to imagine that Beauvoir was not aware of Montherlant's preferences at the time of the writing of *Le deuxième sexe*. Under any circumstances, it will be necessary to weigh Montherlant's sexual proclivities in assessing the accuracy of Beauvoir's reading of his attitudes toward women as they manifest themselves in his life and works.

A second enigma concerning the choice of Montherlant is also implicit in the nature of Beauvoir's analysis. Toward the end of her essay entitled, appropriately enough, "Montherlant ou le pain du dégoût" (Montherlant or the bread of disgust), Beauvoir links Montherlant's misogyny with his right-wing politics and especially his collaborationism during the Occupation. According to Beauvoir, the need to dominate and humiliate the Other, in this case woman, finds its parallel in the Nazis' murderous abuse of inmates in the concentration camps (as well as, she insists, whites' treatment of African-Americans in the South). Thus, for Beauvoir, it is easy to imagine Inès de Castro, the murdered heroine of Montherlant's 1942 play *La reine morte* (The dead queen), as an inmate of Buchenwald, and the Portuguese king Ferrante, who orders her death, as "s'empressant à l'ambassade d'Allemagne par raison d'Etat" [officiously bustling about the German Embassy for reasons of state].[2] While Beauvoir's reading of the play is problematic for reasons to which we shall return, the broader issue concerns the choice of Montherlant as exemplary of the link between misogyny and right-wing and *fascisant* politics. Montherlant's political attitudes are more ambiguous or at least less consistent than Beauvoir allows. Reports as to the extent and nature of his collaborationism vary, and while his political sympathies were almost always on the right, he did not tie himself to right-wing or fascist parties or movements during the interwar years.[3] A more appropriate choice to illustrate Beauvoir's point would have been a writer such as Pierre Drieu la Rochelle, whose misogyny was more thoroughgoing and typical in the manner described by Beauvoir and whose politics were more resolutely and consistently fascistic and collaborationist than were Montherlant's. In the 1930s Drieu proclaimed his fascist sympathies in his essays and fiction and joined Jacques Doriot's fascist Parti Populaire Français during the latter part of the decade. During the Occupation Drieu edited the collaborationist *Nouvelle revue française* and contributed pro-German articles to numerous collaborationist newspapers and reviews. More important, in works such as the 1939 novel *Gilles* and the 1945 novel *Les chiens de paille* (Straw dogs) women are explicitly linked with left-wing politics and resistance and considered symptomatic of a cultural decadence that saps the virility of the (fascist) male.[4] Such links are occasionally evident in Montherlant, but they are hardly indicative of a consistently sexually and politically Manichaean vision, as is so obviously the case with Drieu.

If considerations such as these make Beauvoir's choice of Montherlant and his work as representative of male attitudes toward or myths of women somewhat curious, the reasons for that choice become clearer when one considers the extent to which her assessment of Montherlant is consistent with and in fact derives from the broader discussion of masculine representations of women throughout history. It is therefore helpful to turn to the particulars of Beauvoir's general argument as well her reading of Montherlant before any assessment of the accuracy of the latter can be made.

In situating woman in relation to man in masculine representations and myths, Beauvoir begins her analysis by first situating man in relation to nature and then in relation to his fellow man. On both counts, her analysis is essentially Hegelian in inspiration. Before encountering his fellow man, the Other, man first encounters Nature. Beauvoir characterizes this relationship as follows:

> il a prise sur elle, il tente de se l'approprier. Mais elle ne saurait le combler. Ou bien elle ne se réalise que comme une opposition purement abstraite, elle est obstacle et demeure étrangère; ou bien elle subit passivement le désir de l'homme et se laisse assimiler par lui; il ne la possède qu'en la consommant, c'est-à-dire en la détruisant. Dans ces deux cas, il demeure seul; il est seul quand il touche une pierre, seul quand il digère un fruit.
>
> [he (man) has some hold upon her (nature), he endeavors to mold her to his desire. But she cannot fill his needs. Either she appears simply as a purely impersonal opposition, she is an obstacle and remains a stranger; or she submits passively to man's will and permits assimilation, so that he takes possession of her only through consuming her—that is, through destroying her. In both cases he remains alone; he is alone when he touches a stone, alone when he devours a fruit.][5]

The only way out of this impasse and its attendant solitude is through the presence of the Other, that is, from a "consciousness separate from mine but identical to mine"—other men. But implicit in the presence of this Other is what Beauvoir labels, after Hegel, "la tragédie de la conscience malheureuse" [the tragedy of the unfortunate human consciousness]. Since "chaque conscience prétend se poser seule comme sujet souverain" [each separate conscious being aspires to set himself up alone as sovereign subject], he therefore "essaie de s'accomplir en réduisant l'autre en esclavage" [tries to fulfill himself by reducing the other to slavery]. The result is that human, or more precisely, masculine relations are doomed to incessant conflict. The life of man "n'est jamais plénitude et repos; elle est manque et mouvement, elle est lutte" [is never abundance and quietude; it is dearth and activity, it is struggle].[6]

Beauvoir allows for the possibility that this state of affairs can be transcended through friendship and generosity, but these are not, as she remarks, "facile virtues." And, moreover, man "n'aime pas la difficulté" [does not like difficulty]. He dreams "de quiétude dans l'inquiétude et d'une plénitude opaque qu'habiterait cependant la conscience" [of quiet in disquiet and of an opaque plenitude that nevertheless would be endowed with consciousness].[7] That dream, Beauvoir insists, is incarnated precisely in woman:

> elle est l'intermédiaire souhaité entre la nature étrangère à l'homme et le semblable qui lui est trop identique. Elle ne lui oppose ni le silence ennemi de la nature, ni la dure exigence d'une reconnaissance réciproque; par un privilège unique elle est une conscience et cependant il semble possible de la posséder dans sa chair. Grâce à elle, il y a un moyen d'échapper à l'implacable dialectique du maître et de l'esclave qui a sa source dans la réciprocité des libertés.
>
> [she is the wished-for intermediary between nature, the stranger to man, and the fellow being who is too closely identical. She opposes him with neither the hostile silence of nature nor the hard requirement of a reciprocal relation; through a unique privilege she is a conscious being and yet it seems possible to possess her in the flesh. Thanks to her, there is a means for escaping that implacable dialectic of master and slave which has its source in the reciprocity that exists between free beings.][8]

Nature "élevée à la translucidité de la conscience" [elevated to transparency of consciousness],[9] woman combines the virtues of being an adequate reflector of male sovereignty and posing no threat to it. Thus she serves as a "wondrous hope" to man by confirming his sense of his own freedom while not challenging it in any way.

But woman also serves a profoundly negative function. As the one who gives birth to man, she is also a constant reminder of his carnality, his mortality, and thus a foil to his aspirations to divinity. For Beauvoir, at least in this context, man is best defined through these godly aspirations, this flight from immanence, and he thus resents and indeed abhors the limitations of the flesh. Given his preference, he "voudrait telle Athéné, avoir surgi dans le monde adulte, armé de pied en cap, invulnérable" [would like to have sprung into the world, like Athena fully grown, fully armed, invulnerable],[10] but this is not possible. For this reason, according to Beauvoir, throughout history woman has inspired man with horror—the horror of his own carnal contingency, which he projects upon her.

Beauvoir's abstract and globalizing assessment of the fundamental dynamics of male-female relations as presented here could be challenged on any number of levels. Recent work in gender studies by critics such as Judith Butler and others has emphasized a nonessentialist approach to gender differences that would instead stress the performative aspect of such distinctions.[11] From a different angle, Tzvetan Todorov has recently questioned the validity of the Hegelian master-slave dialectic—so dear to Beauvoir and so crucial to her analysis—as constituting the basic dynamic according to which all human relations need to be defined.[12]

But what is most striking about Beauvoir's model is the degree to which, in some of its most important postulates, it resembles a number of recent efforts to theorize the attitude of the fascist male toward women. In her study of French literary fascism and its literary precursors, Alice Yeager Kaplan notes that the most striking feature of the Italian futurist (and fascist) Marinetti's fictional hero Mafarka is that he is not born of a woman but is instead constructed in a laboratory by his father. As such, he fulfills the masculine fantasy of transcending his own carnality and especially his fleshly origins in the womb of his mother.[13] In his massive two-volume study of fascist male desire, *Male Fantasies,* Klaus Theweleit explores in exhaustive and shocking detail the extent to which fascist violence is inextricably bound to a hatred and fear of the carnality and immanence represented by and embodied in women. The parallels between Beauvoir's model in *Le deuxième sexe* and these more recent assessments of fascist gender attitudes provide further evidence as to why Beauvoir's model would work well in analyzing works by figures such as Drieu, and why they illuminate at least some aspects of the work of a more ambivalently reactionary writer such as Montherlant.

Two significant modifications of the general model of male attitudes toward women presented in *Le deuxième sexe* are evident in the discussion of Montherlant. First, in the general model, the Other and woman constitute two different categories, whereas in Beauvoir's discussion of Montherlant they are collapsed into one: the woman becomes the Other—the one and only Other. As a result, she assumes a doubly negative charge in that she embodies the conflictual Other from which man generally seeks repose in woman, but, in her own right, she also embodies man's fear and resentment of his carnal origins, his inability to escape immanence. Given these modifications, it is not surprising that for Montherlant, in Beauvoir's reading, woman assumes none of the more positive attributes she assumes in the general model proposed in the previous section. She is not "Nature elevated to transparency of consciousness," nor does she offer the "wondrous hope" of man's fulfilling himself as being by carnally possessing another being while simultaneously confirming his own freedom through her docility.

Woman's destructiveness to man in Montherlant's vision is evident first in the fictional representation of the mother in his earliest play. Discussing *L'exil* (Exile), whose subject is a young man forbidden by his mother to go off to fight in World War I, Beauvoir notes that the mother's resistance in the play is not presented as protectiveness but as a "crime"; she wishes to "garder son fils à jamais enfermé dans les ténèbres de son ventre; elle le mutile afin de pouvoir l'accaparer et remplir ainsi le vide stérile de son être" [keep her son forever enclosed within the darkness of her body; she mutilates him so she can keep him all to herself and thus fill the sterile void in her being].[14]

In Montherlant's subsequent works, men fare no better with women in the roles of lovers, wives, and friends. Beauvoir analyzes a number of women characters in Montherlant's prewar fiction, especially the 1929 novel *La petite infante de Castille* (The little infanta of Castille) and the quartet of novels published in the mid-thirties under the general title *Les jeunes filles* (The young girls), in order to show not only the destructiveness of these women but the bankruptcy of Montherlant's notions of masculine freedom and sensuality. First, to the extent that woman is capable of love, she loves man not in his strength or happiness but in his weakness and misery. In this fashion, she discourages his higher Nietzschean aspirations and encourages his descent into wretchedness. She "lives on sensations" and "wallows in immanence" and attempts to persuade her lover to do the same. It is not surprising, then, that in representations of women as lovers in Montherlant, the imagery used to evoke them ranges from the excessively carnal—Montherlant emphasizes their bodily odors, their perspiration—to the outright grotesque. Describing a mistress hanging on her lover's arm on a stroll through the Bois de Boulogne, Montherlant likens the woman to a slug attached to its host.

Woman as wife fares no better. She combines all the physical repugnance of the mistress, but in placing even greater demands on the husband's time and energies, she not only saps his virility but distracts him from his "glorious" and creative solitude. There is, moreover, very little benefit in exchange. In the quartet of novels *Les jeunes filles* the central plot line concerns whether the hero, the novelist Pierre Costals, will succumb to the temptation to marry Solange Dandillot and accept a perfectly bourgeois situation. Although Costals belabors the issue through several hundred pages, it is clear that all Dandillot has to offer Costals is occasional but meaningless sensual gratification. Beauvoir notes that to the extent that there is a distance between Montherlant and his protagonist, it is that the latter is less aware of the nothingness of the women with whom he consorts than is his creator. The ironic style of the novel thus derives from this additional level of disdain.[15]

As Beauvoir remarks, it is not surprising that, given attitudes such as these, Montherlant should consider historical epochs that idealize women to be decadent, whereas he sees more masculine and virile cultures as much superior by comparison. For Montherlant, the latter include especially imperial Rome and the Italian Renaissance.[16] This is not to suggest, however, that there is no place for woman in Montherlant's ideal universe. Having assumed all the attributes of the Other, she is essential to the male to make him conscious of his own being and especially his freedom. But to suit his purposes precisely, to be "ideal" in Montherlant's scheme, she must be "parfaitement stupide et parfaitement soumise; elle est toujours prête à accueillir l'homme, et ne lui demande jamais rien" [perfectly stupid and perfectly submissive; she is always ready to accept the male and never makes any demands upon him].[17] It is in this sense that, according to Beauvoir, Montherlant's statement to the effect that what he seeks in the woman is the child needs to be understood. It is not the innocence, freshness, or purity of the child he seeks, but rather a perfect docility and acquiescence to his superior will. Although Beauvoir does not mention it, it is perhaps this aspect of Montherlant's attitude toward women that explains the real core of his sexuality, his pederasty.

If, in Beauvoir's view, Montherlant's fictional representations of women tell us a great deal about his attitude toward woman, they tell us a great deal about what might be described as his emotional and spiritual bankruptcy as well. The denigration and condemnation of woman, and through her, the Other *tout court,* suggests a monstrous egotism that admits to no real, genuine human contacts—no intersubjectivity—and indeed to no other consciousness outside itself. As Montherlant affirmed in his 1935 essay "Service inutile" (Futile service), "I have only the idea I create of myself to sustain me on the seas of nothingness."[18] Beauvoir notes that in his later works and in his personal life Montherlant increasingly avoids competition with others because this would be admitting to an equal, sovereign Other outside the self, and this is something that Montherlant's self-perception and self-image simply cannot stand.

Under such circumstances, notions such as personal freedom, human emotions, and even sensuality lose all authenticity—they are shams. As Beauvoir notes, Montherlant's cherished freedom is meaningless because it has no object—it consumes itself in a sterile and unproductive self-contemplation. Human emotions are limited to what Montherlant feels about himself as he observes himself exercising a meaningless sovereignty. Finally, even Montherlant's cherished sensuality can never be genuine because to indulge it truly would be to admit to one's own immanence. This would constitute not only a descent from Montherlant's self-assigned superiority but a descent to a level of equality in abjectness with others.

Some six years after the publication of *Le deuxième sexe,* in two lengthy articles in *Les temps modernes* called "La pensée de droite, aujourd'hui" (Right-wing thought today), Beauvoir expands upon the analysis of Montherlant just described and applies it to virtually all the major French right-wing intellectuals and writers of the twentieth century. Along with Montherlant, they can admit to no other conscience but their own, no other value outside themselves. Living in an atomized universe in which they alone are sovereign, they praise an immutable "nature" while denying history, deliberately "mutilating" its dialectic, since any progress or *dépassement* would compromise their own sovereignty. Similarly, as writers and intellectuals, they haughtily affirm their truths and admit to no debate, since to discuss their affirmations would be to acknowledge an equal, something that their worldview and system of values simply do not allow. As Beauvoir notes, to demonstrate or prove one's truths would be to lower oneself.[19] This explains, moreover, why right-wing writing tends incessantly toward the aphoristic, the affirmative. Finally, although Beauvoir does not concern herself in these essays with the right-wing male's attitudes toward women and sexuality, it is obvious from the analysis she offers that they are virtually identical to those she attributes to Montherlant. Real love and sensuality are, therefore, accessible only to those on the left.

Implicit in Beauvoir's analysis is a kind of de-gendering or de-sexualizing of the "man of the right," who becomes little more than a dis-incarnate, solipsistic ego consumed with affirming its own empty superiority. As is the case with Jean-Paul Sartre's famous discussion of the French collaborator with the Nazis, for Beauvoir as well, political condemnation is thus linked to a similar condemnation along the lines of gender and sexuality. While for Sartre political acquiescence to fascism is tied to sexual deviancy, Beauvoir goes one step further: political reaction is inseparable from a sexual and romantic sterility bordering on the inhuman. To the degree, then, that "political correctness" for Sartre and Beauvoir appears to be grounded in a "healthy" heterosexuality, both are engaged in the writings under discussion here in elaborating countermyths to Nazi and fascist myths of virility. The dangers of both the myths and the countermyths are not difficult to discern.[20]

It is fair to say that given the examples she uses, Beauvoir argues convincingly for the sterility of Montherlant's solipsistic egotism, an egotism that depends on and derives from the denigration of and disdain for the Other. But does Beauvoir's essay deal adequately with the representation of women in the entirety of his work, or is her reading of Montherlant over-determined by the general and theoretical model she proposes at the outset? Moreover, doesn't Montherlant's homosexuality, or more precisely, his pederasty, have to be taken into account if all the factors that affected his attitudes toward women are to be understood?

In dealing with the first concern, it is perhaps safe to say that especially in relation to Montherlant's novels and plays written during and after the Occupation, Beauvoir's move to collapse woman and the Other into a single obstacle is ultimately not tenable. In fact, in many of these texts, woman—whether young or old, wife or lover—is singled out as the locus of certain forms of purity and wisdom that ultimately reveal to many of the male protagonists the sterility and futility of their own projects and aspirations, whether they be political, religious, or spiritual. This is not to say that these women serve as or are dismissed as obstacles, but rather that their innate superiority ultimately undermines the pretensions of the male protagonists or simply underscores for the spectator the vacuousness of these pretensions. Examples of such women in Montherlant's work include the "mad" Queen Jeanne in the 1960 play *Le cardinal d'Espagne* (The cardinal of Spain), who deflates the protagonist's political and religious aspirations through the wisdom of her supposed madness. Similarly, in the 1963 novel *Le chaos et la nuit* (Chaos and the night), the protagonist Celestino's daughter serves as an excellent foil for the political and emotional excesses of her anarchist father.

It could be argued that these works were written subsequent to Beauvoir's analysis of Montherlant in *Le deuxième sexe* and thus represent a later and more positive stage in the development of Montherlant's attitudes toward women and perhaps even the Other in more general terms. But the fact is that in two of the works that Beauvoir does discuss, the plays *La reine morte* and *Le maître de Santiago* (The master of Santiago), produced in 1948, precisely the same representations of women and personal dynamics obtain. Despite Beauvoir's dismissive comparison of Inès de Castro in *La reine morte* to an inmate at Buchenwald—a comparison that reduces her to the status of helpless and humiliated victim—the fact is that she plays a much more important role in the play than the comparison allows, especially in relation to the play's protagonist, King Ferrante. While it is true that Inès is ultimately murdered at Ferrante's behest, her murder does not occur until her championing of marital and maternal love—precisely those intersubjective relations Montherlant supposedly abhors—reveals to Ferrante the emptiness of his own political machinations and ambitions. Moreover, when both Inès and Ferrante lie dead at the end of the play, it is Inès around whom the people of Portugal gather, thus sanctifying *her* person and *her* values and not those of the dead king. To conclude, as Beauvoir seems to, that Ferrante alone embodies the haughty, egocentric, and "masculine" virtues that Montherlant supposedly admires ignores the presence in the play of another, purer exemplar of these virtues, the Infanta of Navare. That a woman should embody these masculine virtues in their purest form suggests a level of "gender trouble" in the play for which Beauvoir's model cannot account.

Although Mariana, the daughter of Alvaro, the protagonist of *Le maître de Santiago,* is not the object of such adulation as Inès receives at the end of *La reine morte* for having championed love, and is in fact defeated in her aspirations, her mere presence nevertheless serves as a clear reminder of the sterile egotism of her father and the futility of his disdain.

Does the representation of women and their impact on both plot and thematics in Montherlant's later plays and novels then serve to undermine Beauvoir's reading? A preliminary response would appear to be "yes," a yes that is amplified by a final consideration that must be taken into account both in relation to the later plays and novels just mentioned as well as the prewar works upon which Beauvoir bases the bulk of her analysis: Montherlant's pederasty. To link directly Montherlant's fictional women to an ideal or archetypal conception of woman is to ignore the complexity and subterfuges of Montherlant's own sexuality and the various ways in which that sexuality emerged in Montherlant's fictional worlds. In his biography of Montherlant published in two parts during the 1980s and '90s and entitled, appropriately enough, *Montherlant sans masque* (Montherlant unmasked), Pierre Sipriot painstakingly documents the cases of numerous women characters in Montherlant's fiction who were based on real male adolescent lovers. Similarly, the recurrent figures of wayward sons, evident in several of Montherlant's novels and plays and not discussed by Beauvoir in *Le deuxième sexe,* also were adolescent lovers who, through various miscues, failed to live up to their "father's" expectations. Sipriot also notes in relation to Montherlant's contemplation of marriage in the mid-thirties that contrary to the account of the affair dramatized in *Les jeunes filles,* the real-life relations between Montherlant and his fiancée were hardly carnal. Montherlant indulged his appetite for male adolescents throughout the affair, and only entertained thoughts of marriage in the first place to satisfy the bourgeois conventions dear to his family.[21]

The intricate relationship between the heterosexuality of Montherlant's heroes and his own homosexuality is too complex to be analyzed in detail here, but it clearly creates serious difficulties for Beauvoir's reading of Montherlant and his protagonists as unproblematically heterosexual in their leanings. More important for our purposes, it would be naïve to assume that Montherlant's sexual proclivities did not affect in significant ways his own attitudes toward women and his representations of them in his fiction and essays.

Regardless of his sexual inclinations, it is important to stress that Montherlant's representations of *le féminin,* especially in his works produced in the thirties, bear a striking resemblance to similar, largely negative representations of women in the works of heterosexual right-wing writers such as Drieu as well as left-wing writers, artists, and intellectuals, including the likes of André Malraux and, occasionally, filmmakers such as Jean Renoir and Marcel Carné. Indeed, the cinematic aesthetic of poetic realism often draws much of its dramatic power from images of women and le féminin as dangerous and destructive to man in precisely the way Beauvoir describes in her general discussion of masculine representations of women.

In all the cases just cited, it is not female sexuality per se that threatens men but a highly gendered notion of le féminin, itself the cornerstone of the interwar preoccupation with decadence that is at issue. The obsessive hold of this preoccupation, moreover, affected those on the right *and* left, regardless of their sexual preferences. If Beauvoir's reading of Montherlant, his sexuality, and his attitudes toward and representations of women is unreliable, it serves nevertheless as an accurate diagnosis of a malady he shared with many of those of his generation and that manifests itself in his work, especially between the wars. Beauvoir may well misread Montherlant on numerous occasions, but, perhaps unintentionally, she reads the cultural climate that produced many of his most important works with frightening precision.

Notes

1. Sipriot, *Montherlant sans masque,* 2:141–43.
2. Beauvoir, *Le deuxième sexe,* 1:330; *The Second Sex,* 213.
3. See Golsan, "Henry de Montherlant."
4. For further discussion of the links between women, femininity, and decadence in the works of fascist writers during the interwar period, see Loselle in Hawthorne and Golsan, *Gender and Fascism in Modern France,* 101–18.
5. Beauvoir, *Le deuxième sexe,* 1:231; *The Second Sex,* 139–40.
6. Ibid., 1:231–32; 139–40.
7. Ibid., 1:232; 140.
8. Ibid., 1:232–33; 140–41.
9. Ibid., 1:233; 141.
10. Ibid., 1:240–41; 147.
11. Butler, *Gender Trouble,* 6.
12. See the special issue of *New Literary History* (27.1 [1996]) devoted to Todorov's ideas along these lines.
13. Kaplan, *Reproductions of Banality,* 76–87.
14. Beauvoir, *Le deuxième sexe,* 1:312; *The Second Sex,* 199–200.
15. For an excellent discussion of the quartet *Les jeunes filles* and its relation to Montherlant's personal life, see also Michel Raimond, *Les romans de Montherlant.*

16. As for works inspired by these historical periods, see especially the plays *La guerre civile* (The civil war) and *Malatesta.*

17. Beauvoir, *Le deuxième sexe,* 1:316; *The Second Sex,* 203.

18. Montherlant, *Essais,* 598, author's translation.

19. Beauvoir, "La pensée de droite, aujourd'hui," 2221.

20. For a discussion of Sartre's sexist reading of the collaborator, for example, see Andrew Hewitt, "Sleeping with the Enemy," in Hawthorne and Golsan, *Gender and Fascism in Modern France,* 119–40.

21. See Sipriot, *Montherlant sans masque,* 2:68–102, and Raimond, *Les romans de Montherlant.*

7

"Le Prototype de la Fade *Répétition*"

Beauvoir and Butler on the Work of Abjection in Repetitions and Reconfigurations of Gender

LIZ CONSTABLE

Academic Reception Contexts and Their Discontents

WE all probably have participated in discussions of academic feminism where a specific feminist critical perspective has become the target of an "Oh, but that's so [name the decade]" put-down. These forms of intellectual rebuff enclose modes of feminist thought within appropriate or inappropriate historical reception contexts. They treat feminism as if it had a "sell by" date, and as if our supposedly "dated" perspectives ought to make us feel out of place, out of a shared intellectual place, and excluded by the terms of an implicit, contemporary intellectual contract. Such incidents point clearly, first, to the need to remind ourselves of the multiplicity of reception contexts in academic feminism. They point also to the complex temporalities, geographies, historical, and cultural contexts that have activated, and will continue to reactivate, the reception of feminist thought. Finally, such rebuffs foreground the ease with which we inadvertently universalize particular contemporary feminist theoretical concerns as the only pertinent, relevant, and legitimate reception context for readers. As if we feel bashful about our feminist pasts, we inadvertently embarrass others into valorizing a single developmental time line of academic feminism. In so doing, our disdainful dismissals of critical datedness brush away the historicity of feminist interventions as well as their potential for historically deferred effects in new reception contexts.[1]

In our contemporary context of academic feminism, such intellectual rebuffs often occur during dialogues about the commonality or distinctiveness of methodologies and priorities of feminist and/or queer theorists. I would suggest that key elements of this implicit dialogue between and among feminists and queer theorists can be productively addressed by undertaking a critical rereading of Simone de Beauvoir's *Le deuxième sexe* (1949; The second sex) as much more than simply one of the important starting points for Judith Butler's landmark poststructuralist work on "troubling" or denaturalizing gender.[2] Poststructuralist perspectives, which have so compellingly questioned the subject-based, humanist modalities of change reliant upon the emancipation from oppressive power regimes, inevitably consider Beauvoir and existentialist philosophical frameworks to have far exceeded their intellectual "sell by" date.[3] In the context of French poststructuralist feminism (Cixous, Irigaray, Kristeva), the intellectual shunning of Beauvoir stems from a feminist reception context that, particularly in Irigaray's case, explores differentialist rather than egalitarian, models of feminism. In turn, this has resulted in these theorists having had "very little to say about the author of *The Second Sex,*" as Toril Moi puts it.[4] Therefore, it is to Butler's credit that she gives Beauvoir such a significant place in her own early work. In so doing, she troubles those intellectual genealogies that make existentialist philosophy and Beauvoir's work part of the necessarily excluded background for the emergence of poststructuralist projects in feminism and queer theory.

Nevertheless, what does this mean in terms of the significance of Beauvoir's text today for feminists and/or queer theorists? None of us can deny the presentist voices that would make of Beauvoir at best a significant, but superseded, stage of feminism. None of us can deny those voices who would ask the following types of question: "If we, and our students of feminist theory, have read Judith Butler's *Gender Trouble* (1990), doesn't that paradigm-shifting text, together with Butler's more recent work, make the context of Beauvoir's earlier denaturalizing of femininity in *Le deuxième sexe* appear limited for today's readers since it focuses primarily on disclosing the oppressively asymmetrical formations of heterosexuality for women? What, then, does the rereading of Beauvoir offer queer theorists and feminists as we approach a new millennium?"

In the analysis I take up here, I suggest that Beauvoir's work on shame and abjection as intersubjective relational identity-forming processes finds a renewed relevance in a post-Butler context, one where Butler's contribution has itself been so pivotal in disclosing the discursive abjecting and shaming strategies at work in formations of gendered identity. A critical reading of Beauvoir's *Le deuxième sexe,* one of the most provocative and enduring early "trouble-making texts" in the theorizing of gender and sexuality, throws light in turn on some of the theoretical inclusions and exclusions implicit in Butler's subsequent work on gendered identity formation. The theoretical exclusions I will focus on can be divided into three interrelated areas all dealing with abjection and gendered identity formation, areas that end up somewhat easily obscured if we hold on to a presentist genealogical perspective, from where we see Butler radicalizing Beauvoir's work and where Beauvoir's analysis of "becoming woman" is left behind as a stage on the way to poststructuralist feminism and queer theory.[5]

I would suggest that something is left out when the weight of critical energy today focuses first on the constructedness and contingency of heteronormative power structures and then, in Butler's terms, on their potential rearticulation from other non-normative, nonhegemonic subject positions. What ends up eclipsed is the continued analysis of the nonetheless effective, or "successful," workings of abjection as one of the ways masculinity constructs itself in relation to its others within heteronormativity, precisely the work undertaken by Beauvoir. This eclipse has both specific and more general sources. In specific terms, although Butler's critical focus has always been on exposing the "regulatory fictions" naturalizing both masculinity and heteronormativity, she herself has developed her work on abjection much more extensively in the latter context. And in broader terms, queer theory's critical focus, and the centrality of the axes of shame and pride in queer activist politics, has given greater momentum to the contemporary shift toward analyses of abjection and shame as the degrading processes producing the insides and outsides of heteronormativity, rather than the power asymmetries *within* heteronormativity.

Second, I would suggest that we sometimes lose sight of the fact that our positionality as queer subjects does not remove us from the reception contexts where we—as women—are still interpellated as simply the others of masculinity, where masculinity is still the operative term, and where important differences between us as women collapse in the face of our interpellation by others as women, plain and simple. Here, I'll borrow Butler's terms from *Gender Trouble* in order to shift them away from her emphasis on the production of one's gender and toward the emphasis I want to give to *reception* and *production* of one's gender as mutually constitutive. "Taking up" the signifying tools of gender does not do away with the ways in which our practices are taken up or not taken up by others through reception contexts bristling with heteronormative affective asymmetries. Even when we refuse what Beauvoir describes as the abject feeling of inevitably failing at femininity, this does not mean that as queer women we function outside of others' literal and figurative shaming looks, or shaming indifference—an important part of the construction of masculinity analyzed by Beauvoir and one that interpellates us as women first and foremost.

The value of readjusting Butler's focus on production of gender toward a more Beauvoirian focus on reception, and on the contextualization of the affective dimension of intersubjective encounters, is doubly important. At a level of feminism as critical tool, Butler's work from *Gender Trouble* onward has questioned effectively (un)critical feminisms that take the category of woman as a unifying sign, a presumed universal subject of feminism. However, Butler's troubling of complacent assumptions that limit the theoretical potential of feminist work (what we do in the name of women) needs to be separated in our analyses from what gets done to a group of subjects imagined by others as unified through their identity as women. Here, how we are taken up, what affective reception is given to us, is a distinct facet of feminist analysis precisely because it is inseparable in the everydayness of lived situations from the identities we take up as gendered subjects.

Finally, if Butler's work is seen today as an inevitable radicalizing of Beauvoir's suggestive concept that becoming one's gender is an open-ended process, it is precisely because of the energetic possibilities for change heralded in her concept of the social and political force of resignification or recontextualization of identificatory terms that have a history of shaming or abjecting subjects (e.g., queer, nigger). By contrast, Beauvoir's work has seemed weighed down by the detailed analysis of the constraints and limits on becoming one's gender any way other than through the abjection implicit in situations where woman is equated with femininity. A superficial comparison suggests that the weight of limitations and limited prospects for change in Beauvoir contrasts sharply with the apparent scope of possibilities for change in Butler's work. However, this narrative of Beauvoir's limits and Butler's possibilities also calls for some revisions.

Common Contexts for Beauvoir and Butler

One could argue that what links Beauvoir's and Butler's respective bridges between philosophy and feminism goes beyond their shared critical wariness concerning some of the unifying assumptions within the term "feminism."[6] More significant for my analysis here is the common ground they share through their respective sustained inquiries into the capacity of contexts or situations to shape notions of the cultural legitimacy and legibility of the enactments of gender and sexuality that in turn endorse implicit social-sexual contracts. Beauvoir examines femininity as an artificial construct testifying to what she refers to as women's abject position in relation to masculinity within the context of heterosexuality's social contract. In *Gender Trouble,* subsequently in *Bodies That Matter* (1993), and most recently in *The Psychic Life of Power: Theories in Subjection* (1997), Butler analyzes a different type of abjection: the shaming of queer desires, bodies, and sexual relations (the abject discontents) that results from state and social sanctions reinstituting heterosexuality as the only legitimate, albeit contingent, context for understanding sex, gender, and sexuality.[7] Analogous to Wittig's concept of the "heterosexual contract," the heterosexual matrix for Butler defines heterosexuality as the prevailing interpretive filter (or context) that has had the effect of dictating that sex, gender, and sexual identity are to be understood as coherent, continuous, stable, and interlocking facets of identity.[8] Abjection, for Butler, functions as the reiterated invocation and reinstatement of the originary exclusions constitutive of heterosexual subjects. Both theorists, then, attribute powerful agency to contexts, what Butler calls "the cultural conditions for articulation" as the prime forces in authorizing, as well as constraining, enactments of one's gender and sexuality.[9]

Both theorists also make abjection (the process of casting something away, or repudiating it, and the feeling of being cast away or shamed) a central concept in their analyses of the relationship between social context and the regulation of gender norms and, therefore, implicit social-sexual contracts. For both Beauvoir and Butler, the processes of abjection produce the definers and defined, the figure and ground, of social-sexual contracts; abjection names the very demarcating, differentiating, and disconnecting processes by which relations of figure and ground are instituted in social-sexual contracts. For Beauvoir, masculinity figures itself against the ground of an abjected femininity, and for Butler, heteronormativity produces itself as the defining term through abjecting nonheteronormative bodies and desires. And yet, while processes of abjection ground their projects, there are significant divergences between Beauvoir's emphasis on abjection as the intersubjective impact of affective power in contextualized situations and Butler's work. Butler focuses, instead, on the psychoanalytic concept of abjection (or repudiation), transferred to the social context, where it describes a Foucauldian exercise of discursive power producing the context itself of heteronormativity by making homosexuality its constitutive outsideness. Affects in Beauvoir contrast with discourse in Butler, and the production of masculinity in Beauvoir contrasts with the production of heteronormativity as the defining and definers' term for Butler. It is to the implications of these distinctions that I now turn, with the reminder that just as the contexts defining gender norms end up naturalizing themselves through abjecting others, so too do academic theoretical contexts. What is gained or lost when we move from Beauvoir to Butler, from affect to discourse, from masculinity to heteronormativity, and from intersubjective to psychic abjection as the central terms?

Repetition and Abjection: Getting beyond Abjection?

When Butler inscribes her denaturalizing of gender in the trajectory of Beauvoir's *Le deuxième sexe,* the project common to these two theorists lies in their contention that the maintenance of unchanging, repetitive enactments, or embodiments, of gender constitutes an illusion of biologically determined, normative gendered identities—masculinity and femininity—yoked together in heterosexuality. Clear tensions exist between Beauvoir's existential-phenomenological approach and Butler's poststructuralist perspective (particularly in their understandings of the subject, subjectivity, and modes of agency). However, it is also precisely Beauvoir's rerouting of the phenomenological notion of constitutive acts, and of Jean-Paul Sartre's notion of the body as transitivity—that is, as a way of situating oneself in the world, as a project to be maintained and extended continuously through such acts—that gives Butler an important impetus in her work on resignifying gender. Although Butler refuses the existentialist concept of a prediscursive subject behind the deeds, both theorists understand gendered identity as a nonteleological process where, as Butler puts it, "the 'doer' is variably constructed in and through the deed."[10] Where Beauvoir observes that "On ne naît pas femme: on le devient" [One is not born, but rather becomes, a woman],[11] Butler gives a strong reading to Beauvoir's choice of the verb "become." Becoming one's gender—the transitivity of the process—suggests to Butler not only that this process is an "activity incessantly renewed," but also that it is an open-ended process, and one where the subject in question is active in gender constitution, unlike other constructionist perspectives that present the subject as a passive object constructed by cultural conventions: "The strength of Beauvoir's analysis is that it shows us the contingency at the foundation of gender, an uneasy but exhilarating fact that *it is not necessary* that we become the genders we have in fact become."[12]

Thus, for both Beauvoir and Butler, polarized, discrete gender identities do not represent, or give expression to, preexisting embodied materialities, but rather materialize gender through a process of cumulatively, collectively endorsed enactments of gender. They both suggest that the consistent and unchanging repetition of such enactments is a collective regulation of what Butler, referring to heterosexuality, describes as just "one possible signifying and contingent signifying practice" among many others.[13] Both theorists analyze the naturalizing of femininity as an effect of repetitive, fixed, signifying practices that pass themselves off as causally or deterministically linked to biological femaleness. And for both theorists, femininity's "failure" is an optimistic sign that it is possible to become one's gender differently. When we read Butler's argument that gender norms are failed copies of nonexistent originals, that preexisting originals are in fact "effects" (Butler's reworking of Derrida's concept of the citationality of the sign), we retrieve Beauvoir's notion in writing that "Bien que certaines femmes s'efforcent avec zèle de l'incarner, le modèle n'en a jamais été déposé" [however zealously women may try to embody femininity, the original has never been patented].[14] And yet, what does each theorist make of the potent possibilities for change in her respective observation that femininity is an enactment of gender as unlikely as it is artificial, a paradoxically repetitive approximation of a nonexistent normality?

In the area of horizons of change, an initial glance at the projects of Beauvoir and Butler suggests overwhelmingly that it is Butler who holds the trump card of turning the failure of gender norms into the very means, and tools, of their successful resignification from nonheteronormative positions. The failure of femininity becomes a site of contestatory strength through what Butler describes as "working the weakness of the norm."[15] By contrast, repetition for Beauvoir can only reenact and reentrench past enactments of gender. Moreover, the failure of femininity, the concept with which Beauvoir opens the first volume of *Le deuxième sexe,* is a failure that becomes potent with possibilities for different enactments of one's gender only, Beauvoir writes, if women have social, economic, and sexual rights equivalent to those of men, at which point "entre les sexes naîtront de nouvelles relations charnelles et affectives dont nous n'avons pas idée" [new affective and carnal relationships, of which we have no idea at present, will emerge between the sexes].[16] Since it is only in the final pages of *Le deuxième sexe* that Beauvoir gestures toward other configurations of gender and sexuality, and since there is a striking discrepancy between the grandiosely utopic scope of such statements and Beauvoir's underdeveloped treatment of the means of their implementation, this seems to leave a rather sketchy profile of Beauvoir's vision of the horizons of change.

Such sketchiness is not helped by the fact that throughout the text, Beauvoir's argument hinges on a series of stark oppositions, binaries heavy with the baggage of existentialist subject-based theories of social change, which sound alarm bells in our contemporary poststructuralist context, and which seem to suggest that her horizons of change entail simple reversals or mere structural repetitions of the same. Passive repetition is contrasted with active invention, enslavement is opposed to liberation, dependence is distinguished from autonomy, immanence opposed to transcendence, uniformity contrasted with singularity, contingency opposed to sovereignty and shame distinguished from dignity. These oppositions structure the ways Beauvoir defines women's life-defining task of overcoming contingency through projecting their lives beyond their lived contingency or secondarity, beyond the "inessential" position projected onto them and in turn internalized by them. Her choice of terms suggests that she defines women's responsibility as the arrogation of rights to self-definition, rights that have only come to appear unwarranted for women as a result of generations of repetitions of their role as a *personnage imaginaire* (imaginary personage) in the cultural *comédie* (histrionics) of femininity.[17] Women's responsibility, writes Beauvoir, is to "créer positivement des situations neuves" [try positively to create new situations],[18] to exercise their freedom and "la projeter par une action positive dans la société humaine" [project it through positive action into human society].[19]

The discrepancy I pointed to earlier between such a utopic range for change and such rudimentary treatment of the means for change cannot but prompt us to conclude, at first, that Beauvoir's apparent shortcomings are complemented, retrospectively, by Butler's strengths in getting beyond abjection and in envisaging horizons of change in enacting one's gender. And yet, this critical narrative of shortcomings and strengths, a feminist genealogy where Butler's work supersedes that of Beauvoir, is precisely the one that calls for some revisions when we examine the two writers' respective treatments of abjection and contingency.

Butler: "Working the Weakness of the Norm"

In our contemporary theoretical context, Butler's poststructuralist emphasis on the foundational contingency, or instability, afflicting all the signs of gender (especially those signs accepted as norms) has contributed enormously to reshaping the ways we understand queerness. To adopt David Halperin's terms, queerness is a question of "positionality" and not "positivity."[20] Butler's combination of Derridian notions of the iterability of the sign with Foucault's concept of power as productive, rather than repressive, has provided queer theory with indispensable theoretical levers through which to depathologize the stigma of sexual deviancy and its accompanying determination of queerness as an object of knowledge (its putative positivity). Instead, thanks to the work of Butler and others, we see such abjecting strategies as the effects of productive power enacting, and reinforcing, the meaning-making mechanisms on which fictions of gender stability and normativity depend in institutional, pedagogic, juridical contexts. Such fictions repeatedly mark and situate other bodies with the evidence of their own disavowed semiotic instability. The marking process disguises the instability and contingency of its own fictions by conjuring up deviant subjects out of semiotic instability. Halperin refers to this Foucauldian exercise of discursive power as one where homosexuality becomes the "semiotic dumping ground"[21] for projections that rely on universalizing one possible determinate context for signs—heteronormativity—as *the* determinate, and determining, context for societally acceptable meaning, or what Butler has referred to, from the time of *Gender Trouble* onward, as cultural intelligibility.

In terms of Butler's impact on academic feminism and queer theory, more significant has been her emphasis on the contestatory—though always ambivalent and aleatory—potential for subjects to rearticulate naturalized gender norms through expropriating terms from their context, through exposing the heteronormative context of meaning as just that: not the only context, but one context. As she puts it in *Bodies That Matter:* "the transferability of a gender ideal or gender norm calls into question the abjecting power it sustains. For an *occupation* or *reterritorialization* of a term that has been used to abject a population can become the site of resistance, the possibility of an enabling social and political resignification."[22]

The possibilities of expropriating terms from their naturalized context and of taking them over, "occupying" or "reterritorializing" them, as Butler puts it, are the possibilities held within Butler's concept of contingent foundations. Where Beauvoir's phenomenological take on contingency designates woman's secondarity, her inessential position in socio-sexual contracts, Butler's reframes contingency through a poststructuralist lens, as the very contingency of the supposedly foundational grounds of gender norms. This contingency makes gender norms vulnerable to contestatory resignification. That is, contingent foundations produce provisional contexts for

Butler. And yet, it is on the question of contexts, and recontextualization of signs as the sites of change, that Butler's project, as she herself recognizes, not only finds its greatest theoretical potential but also encounters its greatest material limits.

A little background to Butler's term "reterritorialization" is called for here. For Butler, identity needs to be seen in terms of a reversal of cause and effect, where the subject traditionally assumed to be initiating turns out, on the contrary, to be produced after the fact, as an effect of its repeated enactments of gendered identity. The reversed causality here implies that the process of gendered identifications follows a metaleptic structure.[23] Working with such a metaleptic notion of gendered bodies, Butler focuses on signification (signifying practices), rather than epistemology, to analyze resistance to the shaming or abjecting of queer desires, bodies, and sexual relations. Butler draws on Derrida's notion of the originary iterability, or citationality, of signs (linguistic and nonlinguistic) to disclose the primary terms (masculinity, heteronormativity) as usurpers, those who have territorialized, taken possession, as if they were authorized to permanent and exclusive—rather than contingent—political power. In this way, her project taps the originary secondarity in language to counter the culturally and historically contingent secondarity to which certain gendered bodies and sexual identities have been relegated. The most effective contestation of degrading or oppressive social regulation of gender and sexuality takes place not through opposing these modalities of power, but instead from within, through turning the same signs of power against themselves and reworking their potential signification, by reterritorializing them. In *Gender Trouble,* Butler writes:

> The subject is not *determined* by the rules through which it is generated because signification is *not a founding act, but rather a regulated process of repetition* that both conceals itself and enforces its rules precisely through the production of substantializing effects. In a sense, all signification takes place within the orbit of the compulsion to repeat; "agency," then, is to be located in a variation on that repetition. If the rules governing signification not only restrict, but enable the assertion of alternative domains of cultural intelligibility, i.e., new possibilities for gender that contest the

> rigid codes of hierarchical binarisms, then it is only *within* the practices of repetitive signifying that a subversion of identity becomes possible.[24]

Butler sees the potential for change through repetition that operates through recontextualizing the signs of gendered bodies. For contexts are indeed both potentially illimitable—as Derrida puts it, resistant to "empirical saturation," "without any center or absolute anchorage"[25]—and yet also limited by the conventions, conditions, and circumstances prevailing on the reception(s) of any particular recontextualization.

Butler's recontextualization, as a process of "working the weakness of the norm," is close to the process that Ernesto Laclau, also drawing on Derrida, refers to as "radical contextualization."[26] For both Butler and Laclau, identity formation understood in these terms is always partial, for contingency marks the historicity implicit in the moment of the enunciation of identities. It is also always relational, dependent on the very forces that it excludes, and that oppose it (its constitutive outside). Thus, identities and contexts are inseparable, and the illusion of full identities (as opposed to relational, partial, incomplete identities), as Laclau puts it "necessarily presupposes the repression of that which is excluded by [their] establishment."[27]

But if the recognition of this exclusionary, differentiating formation of identity for what it is—simply a strategic and provisional closure—is to carry the contestatory potential of resignification, Butler's project gets into trouble of a less productive kind. The exclusionary formation of identity she discloses as always a contingent foundation, even when it passes itself off as natural, is the same identity formation that through radical misappropriation of signs occupies and territorializes the signs of power through repudiation, foreclosure, and abjection all over again. The structural logic remains unchanged; only the context changes. The question I am raising is not "How do we read or interpret the resignification as distinct from its original enunciation?" The constitutive ambivalence and aleatory nature of resignification is one Butler points to throughout her work. She is quite clear about this when she signals that resignification cannot be in and of itself positive, but is instead the unaccountable and ambivalent site of agency within the matrices of power. Indeed, the unaccountability, the "wild card" dimension of resignification, is inevitably for her both its strength and its weakness.

Here, instead, it is the exclusionary formation of identity—both the problem (when assumed to be foundational) and the solution (when recognized as provisional)—that I want to focus on. Butler's choice of terms—"occupation" and "territorialization"—suggests that the recontextualization of an abjected identity position (e.g., queerness) has to make the same claims to an illusory full identity, or "cultural intelligibility"—that is, the same exclusive significatory occupation of its grounds—as do the identities it opposes. Just as hegemonic identities found and ground themselves as if they are independent of the relational matrix through which they emerge, and just as such identities seek to appear independent of the meanings others may confer upon them, it would seem difficult to see how resignified identities can separate themselves from abjection as an exclusionary identity formation.

To a certain extent, Butler is conflating two different meanings of abjection in her work on identity formation, a perhaps inevitable pitfall of the boldly thought-provoking combinations of theoretical frameworks she works with. As she herself comments, her arguments on differentiating or exclusionary processes of identity formation draw on "psychoanalysis and the relation between kinship, psychic formation and language."[28] As a result, her abjection draws on an intrapsychic model, a differentiating process of identity formation operating discursively at individual and collective levels; and yet, abjection also names, though less frequently in her work, the intersubjective mechanisms of shaming and degrading of the identities whose existence seems to threaten one's own. Where abjection as an interpsychic differentiating mechanism might prove unavoidable, abjection as an intersubjective mechanism is clearly avoidable—hence the problems that we see surface, with some equivocation on Butler's part, in her written dialogue with feminist critic Nancy Fraser over the levels at which abjection operates. She writes in response to Fraser's questions about the exclusionary formation of identities: "It might be clarifying, then, to consider that whereas every subject is formed through a process of differentiation, and that the process of becoming differentiated is a necessary condition of the formation of the 'I' as a bounded and distinct kind of being, that there are better and worse forms of differentiation, and that the worse kinds try to abject and degrade those from whom the 'I' is distinguished."[29] Here Butler outlines a continuum between better and worse forms of differentiation, and in that move takes us away from psychic models of abjection and toward intersubjective ones. This move is followed later in the same response by Butler's call for "the development of forms of differentiation which lead to fundamentally more capacious, generous, and 'unthreatened' bearings of the self in the midst of community,"[30] a more fully intersubjective approach to abjection and a goal on which she sees her work aligned with Fraser's projects. My objective is not to suggest that Butler is unaware of the problems implicit in a model of resignification reliant on "abjection anew," that is, an exclusionary formation of identity; on the contrary, I would suggest that she steers clear of using the shame-pride axis of gay activism in her writing precisely because of her awareness of the risks of endorsing reverse-abjection to counter abjection. However, it is at the point where her work tries to combine psychic models of abjection as the tools to understand discursive structures with intersubjective understandings of affective abjection that the theoretical exclusions of her project become clearer. It is also at this point that Beauvoir's work on abjection finds a renewed relevance.

Not only are the different levels of analysis confusing in Butler's work; so too are the different subjects of abjection. In what ways is the abjection exercised against queer subjects distinct from, or similar to, that exercised against women, or against any other group? The construction of masculinity is, as Butler notes, a "politically consequential permutation of the exclusionary formation of the subject," and masculine subjects, when "understood as figures of mastery and instrumental will, have conventionally . . . required the de-subjectivation of the feminine."[31] And yet, where Butler touches on such a significant point, as on the permutations of exclusionary formations of the subject, she also quickly moves away again. She adds legitimately, yet unhelpfully, to her comment on the political consequences of masculinity as an exclusionary formation of the subject, "but it [masculinity] is not the only one."[32] As we noted from the outset, the asymmetries within heteronormativity get short shrift in Butler's approach, and the contestatory energy of recontextualization offers limited ways of restructuring the relational matrices within contexts, or social situations, and limited ways of envisaging gendered identity other than through discursive processes of abjection.

Whose Shame Are We Talking About, Anyway?

In turning to Beauvoir, looking back, so to speak, is also a way of seeing beyond, certain of the impasses of Butler's work. For Beauvoir, when women repeat culturally endorsed norms of femininity, they give up their potential to redefine the connections between gender and sexual practices through opening up nonoppressive, reciprocal relationships. Such an abdication condemns the woman to the fate of becoming a passive "prototype de la fade répétition" [prototype of rapid recurrence],[33] an artificial product of past enactments of gender, and also the unfortunate model for younger women's future submission to cultural norms. Women thereby repeat a given script of femininity, not in the theatrical sense but rather in the sense of being conscripted into adherence to a series of rules for predicting, interpreting, responding to, and controlling one's life. Learned or internalized femininity Beauvoir describes as a passive self-alienation, most dramatically concretized in the institution of marriage: "c'est-à-dire d'un tranquil équilibre au sein de l'immanence et de la répétition" [which means the ideal of quiet equilibrium in a life of immanence and repetition], "la conservation paisible du passé, le *statu quo*" [the peaceful conservation of the past, the maintenance of the *status quo*], "la monotone répétition de la vie dans sa contingence et sa facticité" [the monotonous repetition of life in all its mindless factuality].[34]

Yet what are the processes governing women's internalizing of a script of femininity described by Beauvoir as woman's experience of herself as sexually self-conscious, shameful, passive "prey," limited by her corporeality? What, for Beauvoir, are the clues, instructions, prompts, or pressures to which boys and girls are subject, and that inform them about culturally endorsed enactments of masculinity and femininity in the adult world? What are the formative elements isolated by Beauvoir to explain that the situations in which young women find themselves engender the sense of themselves as split between their vocation to be feminine (docile, passive, impotent, frivolous) and their status as real human beings?

Beauvoir's response suggests that women's passivity results from a combination of three elements: the preponderance of idealized images of the female body, an awareness of the cultural penalties attached to transforming the terms of the script of femininity, and affective responses to the female body as a sexualized body. It is this final element, the affective environment, one marked predominantly by the sense of strangeness and self-consciousness it produces in young girls, to which she gives most weight, both in its own right and as a medium for the other formative elements. For example, the idealizing images of the rhetoric of purity implicit in commercial and familial pressures on the teenage girl make her changing pubescent body feel to her strangely at fault:

> Car, une des contraintes qui pèsent le plus odieusement sur elles, c'est celle de l'hypocrisie. La jeune fille est vouée à la "pureté," à l'innocence précisément au moment où elle découvre en elle et autour d'elle les troubles mystères de la vie et du sexe. On la veut blanche comme l'hermine, transparente comme un cristal, on l'habille d'organdi vaporeux, on tapisse sa chambre avec des tentures couleur de dragée.
>
> [For one of the constraints that bear upon them most odiously is that of hypocrisy. The young girl is dedicated to "purity" and "innocence" just when she is discovering in herself and all around her the mysterious stirrings of life and sex. She is supposed to be white as snow, transparent as crystal, she is dressed in filmy organdy, her room is papered in dainty colors.][35]

Here, we encounter one of the most disputed aspects of Beauvoir's presentation of women's relationship to their bodies and their sexuality in *Le deuxième sexe,* namely, her emphasis on the self-consciousness, embarrassment, and disgust that women internalize from their affective environment and that in turn shape their experience of their growing bodies. She presents these feelings as instrumental in precipitating women's passive capitulation to the sequence of repetitive reenactments of femininity. As the copious criticism of *Le deuxième sexe* attests, it is the shameful self-consciousness that Beauvoir locates as causally central to formations of femininity that has triggered critical reactions of feminist despair and disgust with the text itself. Just as many readers' aversion to the work has expressed itself through collapsing interpretations of the text back into Beauvoir's life, and through reading her philosophical insights on gender as "tainted" by those of Sartre, so too have readers objected to what they consider the contaminating traces of Sartre's misogynist perspectives on sexuality and the female body in Beauvoir's descriptions.[36]

And yet, the causal relationship Beauvoir discloses between affective experiences of strangeness, shame, and humiliation and women's capitulation to the script of femininity should not be dismissed so quickly on the grounds that it evinces biographical influences inimical to feminist critique. Whose concept of shame is this, anyway? As I will suggest, Beauvoir's understanding of the workings of shame transforms the Sartrian existentialist concept of "being-in-situation" away from its universalizing of masculine subjects and away from his definition of shame in *L'être et le néant* (Being and nothingness), to make of her intersubjective contextualization of shame (the conjunction of shame and social situations) the very theoretical tool through which to analyze the asymmetrical engendering of subjects.

In Beauvoir's analysis of the familial and cultural environment in which children are raised, she stresses that although the interest, joy, and affirmation manifested toward boys' developing sexual bodies remain constant throughout their adolescence, this contrasts sharply with the situation of little girls: "l'anatomie masculine constitue une forme forte qui souvent s'impose à la fillette; et *littéralement elle ne voit plus* son propre corps" [The male anatomy constitutes a powerful formation that often impresses itself upon the little girl's attention; and she *literally no longer sees* her own body].[37] She internalizes the insignificance those around her accord her body, and this self-shaming is compounded as the young woman enters puberty by other intersubjective encounters, whose effect Beauvoir describes as a shame resulting from interruptions to otherwise close, sustained communication: e.g., mothers who reproduce their own shame toward their bodies by avoiding communication with their daughters about menstruation or sexuality. For Beauvoir, the cumulative result of such minimal communication, absence of feedback, and negative reception of women's embodied sexuality magnifies their sense of shameful self-consciousness, specifically the strangeness of their own bodies: "Oppressée, submergée, elle devient étrangère à elle-même du fait qu'elle est étrangère au reste du monde" [Overburdened, submerged, she becomes a stranger to herself because she is a stranger to the rest of the world].[38]

Most pertinent, for our examination of the interrelatedness of production and reception of gender, Beauvoir observes that the feelings of shameful self-consciousness result not, predictably, from the other's judging or invasive gaze, nor from the explicit contempt or disgust expressed by others. Self-consciousness and embarrassment emerge from the intermittency, or withholding, of responses to the self, an absence of communication from others, which Beauvoir suggests is as potently injurious as the more explicitly contemptuous forms of shaming responses. As a feeling of invisibility—a sense of others' lack of interest—self-consciousness in turn expresses itself as a tormented sense of one's heightened visibility, but as Beauvoir presents it, a feeling of being "out of place" or strange. Abject self-consciousness, in Beauvoir's analysis, is the mortifying or humiliating feeling experienced by the little girl who has no sense that others respond to the "real" body she inhabits.

Experiencing shameful self-consciousness and abjection through an absence of others' response, as Beauvoir defines it, shifts the definition of shame away from Sartre's terms, where instead the subject's sense of shame is marked by the other's overwhelming presence, by a resulting sense of violation of the self, and a visibility defined as the vulnerability of being-for-others: "shame is only the original feeling of having my being *outside,* engaged in another being and as such without any defense, illuminated by the absolute light which emanates from a pure subject."[39] And it is here that we start to see clearly Beauvoir's rewriting of Sartrian shame—the vulnerability the self reluctantly finds exposed in being-for-others—which makes of shame instead the affect experienced in the face of nonrecognition. Shame here is the affect engendered through the construction of masculinity and therefore an affective asymmetry that structures the intersubjective situations, which in turn engender women through abjection.

When Beauvoir defines a constitutive split, or lived contradiction, in the process of becoming woman, between taking on "the vocation of femininity" and becoming a "real human being," she reroutes significantly Sartre's distinction between the two categories of embodiment: the in-itself (facticity, brute objectness) and the for-itself, the latter defining the meaning the Sartrian subject gives to facticity by exercising freedom through not merely desirable but essential syntheses of the in-itself and the for-itself. The achievability and accessibility of those essential syntheses are what Beauvoir genders through attributing their relative accessibility to the respective positions of men and women in situations. For Sartre, one of the major impediments to achieving such syntheses is the objectifying look of the other; to be objectified, Sartre explains, is to be exposed to the demeaning or shaming look of an other and to be reduced to being-for-others. Self-consciousness and embarrassment color the affective register of such passing moments for the Sartrian subject, yet they are dispelled when the subject returns to being-for-itself and when the subject returns the objectifying look in a Sartrian version of a masculine face-off. Penelope Deutscher clarifies some of the implications of Beauvoir's reinterpretation of this face-off:

> Sartre's discussion of the Look as a real, but only a fleeting, loss of freedom is substantially modified by Beauvoir. She describes the way in which women internalize a social status as beings-for-others. . . . Because it is sustained by an inequitable social and economic situation, women do not have an equal ability to shrug off their being-for-others by "returning the look." Beauvoir's theory of sex oppression is generated partly through her expansion of the concept of being-for-others. . . . Being-for-others is no longer a fleeting phenomenon. It is seen as persistently determining women as "other," so that women's loss of freedom is more than temporary.[40]

Deutscher skillfully points to the way in which Beauvoir makes being-for-others constitutive of the process of becoming woman, a form of permanent social and cultural pressure and not simply a passing ordeal; in turn, she points to the centrality of that process in Beauvoir's definition of oppression.[41] However, Deutscher leaves out the significantly different inflection Beauvoir gives to the form of shame experienced by woman. This is not simply a variant of Sartre's being-for-others, under the "burning presence of the Other's look,"[42] where the neutral or genderless subject becomes an object and is thereby reduced to facticity. Instead, women feel a shameful self-consciousness, an Otherness implicit in being objectified through an absence of response, an absence of the look of another that would confer acknowledgement and value.

At this point, we see Beauvoir significantly shifting her analysis of the distribution and affective experience of shame in the direction of what we might refer to today as the construction of masculinities. Her analysis addresses the following questions: Who gets to shame whom? How do subjects experience shame differently according to their positionality in relation to masculinity? One way of defining masculinity—be it embodied in biological men, or women—is as a form of self-defining authority that seeks to remain indifferent or invulnerable to the meanings that others' looks may confer on it. Here, Susan Bordo's work on the construction of masculinity draws directly on Beauvoir's suggestive departure from Sartre:

> there is a provocative difference in the way that Sartre and Beauvoir approach the subject [of vulnerability]. For Sartre, our vulnerability to the objectifying and defining look of the Other is an occasion for shame, is the "hell" that other people represent. But strikingly Beauvoir describes that vulnerability as a necessary condition of self-worth—for women. . . . Perhaps Sartre's recoil from The Look of the Other—described by Sartre as a "possession" of him, and "stealing" of his being (445)—is better understood, not the way Sartre presents it, as a universal feature of the human condition, but as a consequence of an ideology of masculinity that abhors being gazed at, because of the passive femininity which it entails.[43]

Bordo's observation is significant in the way in which it reinforces a key argument made by Michèle Le Doueff that Beauvoir's work in *Le deuxième sexe* radically shifts Sartre's existentialist framework from a systematic one to that of a point of view or perspective[44]—and furthermore, I would add, that Beauvoir's point-of-view approach discloses that the differential affective distribution and experiences of shame have everything to do with becoming one's gender.

If, as we have seen for Beauvoir, producing oneself as a gendered body is inseparable from the reception of others' reactions, such taking in of reactions or the lack thereof and the taking up of a role as a gendered body work together. The woman takes up and enacts femininity in abjection, a response Beauvoir contrasts with the culturally endorsed pride and dignity that the little boy internalizes and learns to manifest in his own identity and eroticized body. Yet, given the obvious limitations of the invulnerability and pride she identifies in this construction of masculinity, what does Beauvoir offer as ways of becoming a gendered subject other than through shame and pride?

Here, as we have noted, Beauvoir's work is incomplete. This is not necessarily a shortcoming that finds its response in Butler's work on resignifying gender norms. For Beauvoir, abjection does not find its solution in the abjecting all over again of other subjects, nor in adopting (masculine) pride. Furthermore, the links Beauvoir makes at different points between social and economic inequalities and the resulting affective asymmetries take us in a productive direction. In the concluding paragraphs of *Le deuxième sexe,* commenting on the power plays in erotic encounters, she writes,

> Dans ces combats où ils croient s'affronter l'un l'autre, c'est contre soi que chacun lutte, projetant en son partenaire cette part de lui-même qu'il répudie; au lieu de vivre l'ambiguïté de sa condition, chacun s'efforce d'en faire supporter par l'autre l'abjection et de s'en réserver l'honneur.
>
> [In those combats where they (men and women) think they confront one another, it is really against the self that each one struggles, projecting into the partner that part of the self which is repudiated; instead of living out the ambiguities of their situation, each tries to make the other bear the abjection and tries to reserve the honor for the self.] [45]

When Beauvoir so insistently denounces the reworking of what Butler condemns as the exclusionary formation of identities, there is, to borrow Butler's term, a radical potential in Beauvoir's detailed analyses of the contextualization of these intersubjective asymmetries first as susceptible to change through an acknowledgment of the ambiguities of identity—as opposed to Butler's call for new forms of cultural intelligibility—and second as being formed through taking in, as well as taking up, one's gender. The role Beauvoir gives to responses, information taken in, as constitutive of the processes shaping one's gendered identity can be productively brought into dialogue with affect theory as a nonpsychoanalytic framework for understanding the histories of affects, or emotions. Here I evoke American psychologist Silvan Tomkins, whose recently republished work on affects—and specifically shame—is richly suggestive in its intersubjective emphasis on the ways in which the subject's affective identity becomes more highly sensitized and complex through the processing of feedback within an interdependency between affects and their objects. The dialogue would be especially important since Tomkins's model is somewhat universalizing and lacks Beauvoir's insights into the connections between affective asymmetries and becoming one's gender. When Beauvoir comments that only after women have social, economic, and sexual rights equivalent to those of men that "entre les sexes naîtront de nouvelles relations charnelles et affectives dont nous n'avons pas idée" [new affective and carnal relationships, of which we have no idea at present, will emerge between the sexes],[46] not only is there a prospect of becoming one's gender other than through abjection. Where Butler's recontextualized sites of resistance require a cultural intelligibility that suggests a regrounding of gendered identity through abjection all over again, this leaves queer theory with tools that risk reproducing the relational matrix that has reified the context of the heterosexual matrix. Beauvoir's emphasis, instead, on the need to rethink those relations within contexts (at a social, economic, and affective level) gains a renewed significance. And where Butler's emphasis on productive repetition as resignification is undercut by its repetition of an abjecting logic, the theoretical energy it bestows on (gender's) failure as its (resistant) success is also undercut by its avoidance of the affective and intersubjective toll of failing through abjection. These exclusions suggest that looking back to Beauvoir's *Le deuxième sexe* might well be a way of looking forward for both feminism and queer theory.

Notes

1. See Ruth Evans's excellent introductory essay to *Simone de Beauvoir's "The Second Sex"* for an analysis of the ways in which rereading the text today produces "untimely" effects, forms of deferred action that Evans defines as the text's postmodernity in a Lyotardian sense.

2. I will be referring to Judith Butler's work throughout this chapter as "poststructuralist" and not "postmodern," for, as she points out in her article "Contingent Foundations," the very nebulousness of the term "postmodernism" leaves it as predominantly the term of detractors or "onlookers" who denounce a congeries of ideas lumped loosely together as attacks on the subject, reduction of reality to representation, deconstruction, nihilism, and so on. As Butler comments, its function as a favorite term for intellectual mud-slinging is clear in the fact that it operates predominantly to designate other positions, rather than as a category scholars take up to locate their own work.

3. On this point, see Sonia Kruks, "Introduction," where she points to the ways in which Beauvoir's existentialist phenomenology would seem to make her work part of the very Enlightenment approaches to concepts of the subject and of modalities of

change out of which, and against which, Foucault and Derrida developed their own positions resulting in the eclipse of phenomenological perspectives in favor of poststructuralist ones. See also Anna Alexander, who observes that in poststructuralist hostility to the humanist subject, it is Sartre's existentialist ego that "absorbed the hostility" ("The Eclipse of Gender," 114).

4. Moi, *Feminist Theory,* 26.

5. I use the verb "radicalize" here because of the frequency with which Butler uses the qualifier "radical" to describe her understanding of modalities of change; it also reflects the influence on Butler's work of Chantal Mouffe and Ernesto Laclau's project of rethinking radical democracy through a Derridian understanding of the constitution of political fields as articulations. See *Hegemony and Socialist Strategy.*

6. Here, Toril Moi's comment on Beauvoir's ambivalent position vis-à-vis feminism is worth quoting: "By taking as her point of departure a story of historical and social transformation, or in other words: by giving feminism an end, by imagining a society in which there would be no longer any need to *be* a feminist, Beauvoir provided women all over the world with a vision of change. . . . The great virtue of narratives is that they come to an end: *The Second Sex* helps me remember that the aim of feminism is to abolish itself" (*Simone de Beauvoir,* 213).

7. See the introduction to *Bodies That Matter.* Here Butler explains her uses of abjected identities in a social context through analogy with the psychoanalytic notion of foreclosure, or the repudiation of elements in the subject that constitute the unconscious. Transferring this concept to a social context, Butler defines these abjected identities as the sexual identities that are unintelligible within the heterosexual matrix, yet whose unintelligibility is essential to the maintenance of that same core matrix since they form its constitutive outsideness.

8. For Butler, the heterosexual matrix operates through making identification and desire mutually exclusive: that is, in this logic, if one identifies as a woman, one desires a woman, and vice versa, reinforcing the notion that there is a determining structure aligning polarized gender identities and sexuality. For Wittig's concept of the heterosexual contract, see "On the Social Contract" in *The Straight Mind.*

9. Butler, "For a Careful Reading," 129.

10. Butler, *Gender Trouble,* 142.

11. Beauvoir, *Le deuxième sexe,* 1:13; *The Second Sex,* 267.

12. Butler, "Gendering the Body," 255.

13. *Gender Trouble,* 144. See Karen Vintges for a convincing interpretation of Beauvoir's perspective on women's oppression as one that emphasizes woman's secondarity as the result of historically and culturally contingent processes, and not of biology: "Beauvoir's thesis is that woman has been the *historic* (contingent) Other, but in no way the inevitable (necessary) Other" (56).

14. Beauvoir, *Le deuxième sexe,* 1:12; *The Second Sex,* xiii, translation modified.

15. Butler, *Bodies That Matter,* 237.

16. Beauvoir, *Le deuxième sexe,* 2:575; *The Second Sex,* 730, translation modified.

17. Ibid., 361; 543.

18. Ibid., 420; 594.

19. Ibid., 157; 678.

20. Halperin, *Saint Foucault,* 62.

21. Ibid., 45.

22. Butler, *Bodies That Matter,* 231, emphasis added.

23. Butler understands the reversed causality of enacting one's gender in a similar way to the operation of metalepsis in subject-formation proposed by de Man's reading of Nietzsche, "Rhetoric of Persuasion (Nietzsche)" in *Allegories of Reading:* "The 'truth' of identity, which was to become established in the future that follows its formulation, turns out to have always already existed as the past of its aberrant 'position'" (124). De Man develops this later by commenting that "the fiction of a 'subject-substratum' for the act is explicitly called secondary as compared to the prior fiction of the act itself" (128).

24. Butler, *Gender Trouble,* 145.

25. Derrida, "Signature, Event, Context," 12.

26. Laclau, "New Reflections," 23.

27. Ibid., 38.

28. Butler, "For A Careful Reading," 139.

29. Ibid., 140.

30. Ibid.

31. Ibid., 139.

32. Ibid.

33. Beauvoir, *Le deuxième sexe,* 2:44; *The Second Sex,* 295.

34. Ibid., 2:228, 430; *The Second Sex,* 447, 604.

35. Ibid., 2:74–75; *The Second Sex,* 322. Most strikingly and consistently in *The Second Sex,* Beauvoir attributes women's resigned passivity—the definition of what it is to "become woman"—not to direct sanctions or prohibitions, but rather to the internalizing of the reception context of their upbringing, which produces a constant discrepancy between idealized femininity and the reality of their bodies and which, in turn, results in women seeing their changing bodies as foreign, strange, or unfamiliar: "dans les glaces elle se reconnaît mal; elle se sent 'drôle,' les choses ont un air 'drôle'" [she hardly recognizes herself in mirrors; she feels "funny," things seem "funny"] (2:55; 305).

36. Greene, "Sartre, Sexuality," 199–211. See Toril Moi's excellent survey of the reception given to Beauvoir, which has far too often been a question of "reducing the Book to the Woman" (27) and "using the personal to discredit the political" (33), in "Politics and the Intellectual Woman: Clichés in the Reception of Simone de Beauvoir's Work," *Feminist Theory and Simone de Beauvoir,* 21–60.

37. *Le deuxième sexe,* 2:23; *The Second Sex,* 277.

38. Ibid., 2:82; 330.

39. Sartre, *Being and Nothingness,* 384.

40. Deutscher, *Yielding Gender,* 186, 189.

41. See also *Pour une morale de l'ambiguïté* for Beauvoir's analysis of oppression, where she writes:

> une liberté qui ne s'emploie qu'à nier la liberté doit être niée. Et il n'est pas vrai que la reconnaissance de la liberté d'autrui limite ma propre liberté: être libre, ce n'est pas avoir le pouvoir de faire n'importe quoi; c'est pouvoir dépasser le donné vers un avenir ouvert; l'existence d'autrui en tant que liberté définit ma situation et elle est même la condition de ma propre liberté.
>
> [A freedom which is interested only in denying freedom must be denied. And it is not true that the recognition of the freedom of others limits my own freedom: to be free is not to have the power to do anything you like; it is to be able to surpass the given towards an open future; the existence of others as a freedom defines my situation and is even the condition of my own freedom.] (127; 91)

42. Sartre, *Being and Nothingness,* 361.

43. Bordo, "Can a Woman Harass a Man?," 59–60.

44. Ibid., 104.

45. Beauvoir, *Le deuxième sexe,* 2 : 573; *The Second Sex,* 728.

46. Ibid., 2 : 575; 730, translation modified.

Bibliography

Acocella, Joan. "The Frog and the Crocodile: Love Letters from the Woman behind *The Second Sex*." *New Yorker* (Aug. 24 and 31, 1998): 144–52.

Ainslie, Ricardo C. *The Psychology of Twinship*. Lincoln: Univ. of Nebraska Press, 1985.

Aldrich, Robert. "Homosexuality in France." *Contemporary French Civilization* 7.1 (1982): 1–19.

Alexander, Anna. "The Eclipse of Gender: Simone de Beauvoir and the *Différance* of Translation." *Philosophy Today* (1997): 112–22.

Algren, Nelson. "The Question of Simone de Beauvoir." *Harper's Magazine* 230 (May 1965): 134–35.

———. "Simone à Go Go." *Ramparts Magazine* 4 (Oct. 1965): 65–67.

Allport, Gordon W. *The Use of Personal Documents in Psychological Science*. New York: Social Science Research Council, 1942.

Asher, Carol A. *Simone de Beauvoir: A Life of Freedom*. Boston: Beacon Press, 1981.

Bair, Deirdre. "Do as She Said, Not as She Did." *New York Times Magazine* (Nov. 18, 1990): 32, 34.

———. *Simone de Beauvoir: A Biography*. New York: Summit, 1990.

Barnes, Hazel E. "Simone de Beauvoir's Letters: A Poisoned Gift?" *Simone de Beauvoir Studies* 8 (1991): 13–29.

———. *The Story I Tell Myself: A Venture in Existentialist Autobiography*. Chicago: Univ. of Chicago Press, 1997.

Barreca, Regina, and Deborah Denenholz Morse, eds. *The Erotics of Instruction*. Hanover NH: Univ. Press of New England, 1997.

Bassnett, Susan, and André Lefevere, eds. *Translation, History, and Culture*. London: Pinter Publishers, 1990.

Beauvoir, Simone de. "Carnets de jeunesse: 1926–1930." Ms. Bibliothèque Nationale de France, Paris.

———. *La cérémonie des adieux*. Paris: Gallimard, 1981. Trans. *Adieux: A Farewell to Sartre* by Patrick O'Brian. New York: Pantheon, 1984.

———. *Le deuxième sexe*. 2 vols. Paris: Gallimard, 1949. Trans. *The Second Sex* by H. M. Parshley. New York: Knopf, 1952.

———. *La femme rompue*. Paris: Gallimard, 1967. Trans. *The Woman Destroyed* by Patrick O'Brian. New York: Putnam's Sons, 1969.

———. *La force de l'âge*. Paris: Gallimard, 1960. Trans. *The Prime of Life* by Peter Green. Cleveland: World Publishing Co., 1962.

———. *La force des choses*. Paris: Gallimard, 1963. Trans. *Force of Circumstance* by Richard Howard. New York: G. P. Putnam's Sons, 1965.

———. *L'invitée*. Paris: Gallimard, 1943. Trans. *She Came to Stay* (anon.). Cleveland: World Publishing Co., 1954. Trans. *She Came to Stay* by Yvonne Moyse and Roger Senhouse. London: Flamingo, 1984.

———. *Journal de guerre: Septembre 1939–janvier 1941*. Paris: Gallimard, 1990.

———. Letters to Nelson Algren. Ms. The Ohio State University Libraries Special Collections, Columbus.

———. *Lettres à Sartre*. 2 vols. Ed. Sylvie Le Bon de Beauvoir. Paris: Gallimard, 1990. Trans. *Letters to Sartre* by Quentin Hoare. New York: Little, Brown and Co., 1991.

———. *Les mandarins*. 2 vols. Paris: Gallimard, 1954. Trans. *The Mandarins* by Leonard M. Friedman. Cleveland: World Publishing Co., 1956.

———. *Mémoires d'une jeune fille rangée*. Paris: Gallimard, 1958. Trans. *Memoirs of a Dutiful Daughter* by James Kirkup. Cleveland: World Publishing Co., 1959.

———. "Mon expérience d'écrivain." Lecture given in Japan. 11 Oct. 1966. In *Les écrits de Simone de Beauvoir.* Claude Francis and Fernande Gontier. Paris: Gallimard, 1979. 439–57.

———. *Une mort très douce*. Paris: Gallimard, 1964. Trans. *A Very Easy Death* by Patrick O'Brian. New York: G. P. Putnam's Sons, 1966.

———. "La pensée de droite, aujourd'hui." *Les temps modernes* 112–13 (1954): 1539–75, and 114–15 (1954): 2219–61.

———. *Pour une morale de l'ambiguïté*. Paris: Gallimard, 1947. Trans. *The Ethics of Ambiguity* by Bernard Frechtman. New York: Philosophical Library, 1948.

———. *Privilèges*. Paris: Gallimard, 1955. Trans. *Must We Burn Sade?* by Annette Michelson. New York: Grove, 1953.

———. *Quand prime le spirituel*. Paris: Gallimard, 1979. Trans. *When Things of the Spirit Come First* by Patrick O'Brian. New York: Pantheon, 1982.

———. *Le sang des autres*. Paris: Gallimard, 1945. Trans. *The Blood of Others* by Roger Senhouse and Yvonne Moyse. New York: Knopf, 1948.

———. *Tout compte fait*. Paris: Gallimard, 1972. Trans. *All Said and Done* by Patrick O'Brian. London: André Deutsch and Weidenfeld and Nicolson, 1974.

———. *A Transatlantic Love Affair: Letters to Nelson Algren*. New York: New Press, 1998. Trans. *Lettres à Nelson Algren* by Sylvie Le Bon de Beauvoir. Paris: Gallimard, 1997.

Bell, Susan Groag, and Karen M. Offen. *Women, the Family, and Freedom: The Debate in Documents*. Vol. 2, 1880–1950. Stanford: Stanford Univ. Press, 1983.

Benhabib, Seyla, Judith Butler, Drucilla Cornell, and Nancy Fraser, eds. *Feminist Contentions: A Philosophical Exchange*. New York: Routledge, 1995.

Bergoffen, Debra B. *The Philosophy of Simone de Beauvoir: Gendered Phenomenologies, Erotic Generosities.* Albany: SUNY Press, 1997.

Bernheim, Cathy. *L'amour presque parfait.* Paris: Editions Le Félin, 1991.

Bordo, Susan. "Can a Woman Harass a Man? Towards a Cultural Understanding of Bodies and Power." *Philosophy Today* (1997): 51–66.

Bradley, Marion Zimmer. "Feminine Equivalents of Greek Love in Modern Fiction." *International Journal of Greek Love* 1.1 (1965): 48–58.

Brosman, Catharine Savage. *Simone de Beauvoir Revisited.* Boston: Twayne, 1991.

Butler, Judith. *Bodies That Matter: The Discursive Limits of "Sex."* New York: Routledge, 1993.

———. "The Body You Want." *Artforum* 31.3 (Nov. 1992): 82–89.

———. "Contingent Foundations: Feminism and the Question of 'Postmodernism.'" In *Feminists Theorize the Political.* Ed. Judith Butler and Joan W. Scott. New York: Routledge, 1992. 3–21.

———. "For a Careful Reading." In *Feminist Contentions: A Philosophical Exchange.* Ed. Seyla Benhabib, Judith Butler, Drucilla Cornell, and Nancy Fraser. New York: Routledge, 1995. 127–43.

———. "Gendering the Body: Beauvoir's Philosophical Contribution." In *Women, Knowledge, and Reality: Explorations in Feminist Philosophy.* Ed. Ann Garry and Marilyn Pearsall. Boston: Unwin Hyman, 1989. 253–62.

———. *Gender Trouble: Feminism and the Subversion of Identity.* New York: Routledge, 1990.

———. "Performative Acts and Gender Constitution: An Essay in Phenomenology and Feminist Theory." *Theater Journal* 40.4 (1988): 519–31.

———. *The Psychic Life of Power: Theories in Subjection.* Stanford: Stanford Univ. Press, 1997.

———. "Sex and Gender in Simone de Beauvoir's *Second Sex.*" *Yale French Studies* 72 (1986): 35–50.

———. *Subjects of Desire: Hegelian Reflections on Twentieth-Century France.* New York: Columbia Univ. Press, 1987.

———. "Variations on Sex and Gender: Beauvoir, Wittig, Foucault." In *Feminism as Critique.* Ed. Seyla Benhabib and Drucilla Cornell. Minneapolis: Univ. of Minnesota Press, 1987. 128–42.

Castle, Terry. *The Apparitional Lesbian: Female Homosexuality and Modern Culture.* New York: Columbia Univ. Press, 1993.

Cesarani, David. *Arthur Koestler: The Homeless Mind.* London: William Heinemann, 1998.

Cockburn, Alexander. "The Rapist and the Snitch." *The Nation* (Nov. 23, 1998): 9.

Cook, Blanche Wiesen. *Eleanor Roosevelt.* Vol. 1, 1884–1933. New York: Viking, 1992.

Cordero, Anne. "Simone de Beauvoir Twice Removed." *Simone de Beauvoir Studies* 7 (1990): 49–56.

Courtivron, Isabelle de. *Violette Leduc.* Boston: Twayne, 1985.

Crosland, Margaret. *Simone de Beauvoir: The Woman and Her Work.* London: Heinemann, 1992.

Dayan, Josée, and Malka Ribowska. *Simone de Beauvoir: Un film.* Paris: Gallimard, 1979.

DeJean, Joan. *Fictions of Sappho, 1546–1937.* Chicago: Chicago Univ. Press, 1989.

De Man, Paul. "Rhetoric of Persuasion (Nietzsche)." In *Allegories of Reading: Figural Language in Rousseau, Nietzsche, Rilke and Proust.* New Haven: Yale Univ. Press, 1979. 119–34.

Derrida, Jacques. "Signature, Event, Context." In *Limited Inc.* Evanston: Northwestern Univ. Press, 1988. 1–24.

Deutscher, Penelope. *Yielding Gender: Feminism, Deconstruction and the History of Philosophy.* New York: Routledge, 1997.

Donohue, H. E. F. *Conversations with Nelson Algren.* New York: Hill, 1964.

Drew, Bettina. *A Life on the Wild Side.* Austin: Univ. of Texas Press, 1989.

———. "Love between the Lines." *The Nation* 267.13 (Oct. 26, 1998): 28–31.

Duchen, Claire. *Feminism in France since May 1968 until Mitterand.* London: Routledge, 1986.

———. *Women's Rights and Women's Lives in France, 1944–1968.* London: Routledge, 1994.

Evans, Christine Ann. "'La Charmante Vermine': Simone de Beauvoir and the Women in Her Life." *Simone de Beauvoir Studies* 12 (1995): 26–32.

Evans, Martha Noel. *Masks of Tradition: Women and the Politics of Writing in Twentieth-Century France.* Ithaca: Cornell Univ. Press, 1987.

———. "Murdering *L'Invitée:* Gender and Fictional Narrative." *Yale French Studies* 72 (1986): 67–86.

Evans, Ruth, ed. *Simone de Beauvoir's "The Second Sex": New Interdisciplinary Essays.* Manchester: Manchester Univ. Press, 1998.

Fallaize, Elizabeth. *The Novels of Simone de Beauvoir.* London: Routledge, 1988.

———, ed. *Simone de Beauvoir: A Critical Reader.* New York: Routledge, 1998.

Farrère, Claude. *Mademoiselle Dax, jeune fille.* 1907. Rpt. Paris: Flammarion, 1916.

Flotow, Luise von. "Translating Women of the Eighties: Eroticism, Anger, Ethnicity." In *Culture in Transit: Translating the Literature of Quebec.* Ed. Sherry Simon. Montreal: Véhicule Press, 1995. 31–46.

———. *Translation and Gender: Translating in the "Era of Feminism."* Manchester UK and Ottawa, Canada: St. Jerome Publishing and Ottawa Univ. Press, 1997.

Forster, Penny, and Imogen Sutton, eds. *Daughters of de Beauvoir.* London: Women's Press, 1989.

Francis, Claude, and Fernande Gontier. *Les écrits de Simone de Beauvoir.* Paris: Gallimard, 1979.

———. *Simone de Beauvoir.* Paris: Librairie Académique Perrin, 1985. Trans. *Simone de Beauvoir: A Life . . . A Love Story* by Lisa Nesselson. New York: St. Martin's, 1987.

Fraser, Nancy. "Pragmatism, Feminism, and the Linguistic Turn." In *Feminist Conten-*

tions: A Philosophical Exchange. Ed. Seyla Benhabib, Judith Butler, Drucilla Cornell, and Nancy Fraser. New York: Routledge, 1995. 157–71.

———, and Sandra Lee Bartky, ed. *Revaluing French Feminism: Critical Essays on Difference, Agency, and Culture*. Bloomington: Indiana Univ. Press, 1992.

Fullbrook, Kate, and Edward Fullbrook. "Sartre's Secret Key." In *Feminist Interpretations of Simone de Beauvoir*. Ed. Margaret A. Simons. University Park: Pennsylvania State Univ. Press, 1995. 97–111.

———. *Simone de Beauvoir and Jean-Paul Sartre: The Remaking of a Twentieth-Century Legend*. New York: Basic Books, 1994.

Fuss, Diana. *Identification Papers*. New York: Routledge, 1995.

Gallop, Jane. *Feminist Accused of Sexual Harassment*. Durham: Duke Univ. Press, 1997.

———, ed. *Pedagogy: The Question of Impersonation*. Bloomington: Indiana Univ. Press, 1995.

Galster, Ingrid. "'Une femme machiste et mesquine': La réception des écrits posthumes de Simone de Beauvoir dans la presse parisienne." *Lendemains* 61 (1991): 53–62.

———. "Simone de Beauvoir face à l'Occupation allemande: Essai provisoire d'un réexamen à partir des écrits posthumes." *Contemporary French Civilization* 20.2 (Summer/Fall 1996): 278–93.

Galzy, Jeanne. *La cavalière*. Paris: Gallimard, 1974.

———. *Jeunes filles en serre chaude*. Paris: Gallimard, 1934.

Garber, Marjorie. *Vice Versa: Bisexuality and the Eroticism of Everyday Life*. New York: Simon and Schuster, 1995.

Golsan, Richard J. "Henry de Montherlant: Itinerary of an Ambivalent Fascist." In *Fascism, Aesthetics, and Culture*. Ed. Richard J. Golsan. Hanover NH: Univ. Press of New England, 1992. 143–63.

Greene, Naomi. "Sartre, Sexuality and the *Second Sex*." *Philosophy and Literature* 4.2 (1980): 199–211.

Groult, Benoîte. *Les vaisseaux du coeur*. Paris: Grasset et Fasquelle, 1988.

Haggerty, George E., and Bonnie Zimmerman, eds. *Professions of Desire: Lesbian and Gay Studies in Literature*. New York: Modern Language Association of America, 1995.

Halperin, David. *Saint Foucault: Towards a Gay Hagiography*. New York: Oxford Univ. Press, 1995.

Hawthorne, Melanie, and Richard J. Golsan, eds. *Gender and Fascism in Modern France*. Hanover NH: Univ. Press of New England, 1997.

Hermans, Theo, ed. *The Manipulation of Literature: Studies in Literary Translation*. London and Sydney: Croom Helm, 1985.

Hewitt, Andrew. "Sleeping with the Enemy: Genet and the Fantasy of Homo-Fascism." In *Gender and Fascism in Modern France*. Ed. Melanie Hawthorne and Richard J. Golsan. Hanover NH: Univ. Press of New England, 1997. 119–40.

Hewitt, Leah D. *Autobiographical Tightropes: Simone de Beauvoir, Nathalie Sarraute, Marguerite Duras, Monique Wittig, and Maryse Condé*. Lincoln: Univ. of Nebraska Press, 1990.

Holveck, Eleanore. "Simone de Beauvoir: Autobiography as Philosophy." *Simone de Beauvoir Studies* 8 (1991): 103–10.

Irigaray, Luce. *Le corps-à-corps avec la mère.* Ottawa: Les Editions de la Pleine Lune, 1981.

———. "Equal of Different?" In *The Irigaray Reader.* Ed. Margaret Whitford. London: Blackwell, 1991. 30–33.

Jaeggy, Fleur. *Les années bienheureuses du châtiment.* Trans. from Italian by Jean-Paul Manganaro. Paris: Gallimard, 1992. Trans. *Sweet Days of Discipline* by Tim Parks. New York: New Directions, 1993.

Jardine, Alice. "Death Sentences, Writing Couples, and Ideology." *Poetics Today* 6.1–2 (1985): 119–31.

———. "An Interview with Simone de Beauvoir." *Signs* 5.2 (1979): 37–49.

Joseph, Gilbert. *Une si douce Occupation: Simone de Beauvoir, Jean-Paul Sartre, 1940–1944.* Paris: Albin Michel, 1991.

Julienne-Caffié, Serge. *Simone de Beauvoir.* Paris: Gallimard, 1966.

Kaplan, Alice Yeager. *Reproductions of Banality: Fascism, Literature, and French Intellectual Life.* Minneapolis: Univ. of Minnesota Press, 1986.

Keefe, Terry. "Another Silencing of Beauvoir? Guess What's Missing This Time." *French Studies Bulletin* 50 (Spring 1994): 18–20.

———. "Autobiography and Biography: Simone de Beauvoir's Memoirs, Diary, and Letters." In *Autobiography and the Existential Self.* Ed. Terry Keefe and Edmund Smyth. Liverpool: Liverpool Univ. Press, 1995. 61–81.

Klaw, Barbara. "Desire, Ambiguity, and Contingent Love: Simone de Beauvoir, Sexuality, and Self-Creation or What Good Is a Man Anyway?" *Symposium* 51.2 (Summer 1997): 110–23.

———. "*L'Invitée* Castrated: Sex, Simone de Beauvoir, and Getting Published or Why Must a Woman Hide Her Sexuality?" *Simone de Beauvoir Studies* 12 (1995): 126–38.

———. "Sexuality in Simone de Beauvoir's *Les Mandarins.*" In *Feminist Interpretations of Simone de Beauvoir.* Ed. Margaret A. Simons. University Park: Pennsylvania State Univ. Press, 1995. 193–221.

Kristeva, Julia. *Les samouraïs.* Paris: Fayard, 1990. Trans. *The Samurai* by Barbara Bray. New York: Columbia Univ. Press, 1992.

Kruks, Sonia. "Introduction: A Venerable Ancestor? Re-Reading Simone de Beauvoir." *Women and Politics* 11.1 (1991): 53–60.

Laclau, Ernesto. "New Reflections on the Revolution of Our Time." In *New Reflections on the Revolution of Our Time.* London: Verso, 1990. 3–85.

———, and Chantal Mouffe. *Hegemony and Socialist Strategy.* London: Verso, 1990.

Lacoin, Elisabeth. *Zaza: Correspondance et carnets d'Elisabeth Lacoin, 1914–1929.* Paris: Seuil, 1991.

Lacoste, Guillemine. "Elisabeth Lacoin's Influence on Simone de Beauvoir's Life: What Might Have Been." *Simone de Beauvoir Studies* 11 (1994): 64–75.

———. "An Intricate Relationship: Simone de Beauvoir and Bianca Lamblin." *Simone de Beauvoir Studies* 11 (1994): 105–10.

Lamblin, Bianca. *Mémoires d'une jeune fille dérangée.* Paris: Editions Balland, 1993. Trans. *A Disgraceful Affair: Simone de Beauvoir, Jean-Paul Sartre, and Bianca Lamblin* by Julie Plovnick. Boston: Northeastern Univ. Press, 1996.

Le Doeuff, Michèle. *L'étude et le rouet: Des femmes, de la philosophie, etc.* Paris: Seuil, 1989.

———. "Simone de Beauvoir: Falling into (Ambiguous) Line." In *Feminist Interpretations of Simone de Beauvoir.* Ed. Margaret A. Simons. University Park: Pennsylvania State Univ. Press, 1995. 59–65.

Leduc, Violette. *La Bâtarde.* Paris: Gallimard, 1964. Trans. *La Bâtarde* by Derek Coltman. New York: Farrar, Straus, and Giroux, 1965.

———. *Ravages: Roman.* Paris: Gallimard, 1955.

———. *Thérèse et Isabelle.* Paris: Gallimard, 1966. Trans. *Thérèse and Isabelle* by Derek Coltman. New York: Farrar, Straus, and Giroux, 1967.

Loselle, Andrea. "Paul Morand's Gendered Eugenics." In *Gender and Fascism in Modern France.* Ed. Melanie Hawthorne and Richard J. Golsan. Hanover NH: Univ. Press of New England, 1997. 101–18.

Lotbinière-Harwood, Susanne de. *Re-belle et infidèle: La traduction comme pratique de réécriture au féminin/The Body Bilingual: Translation as a Rewriting in the Feminine.* Montreal and Toronto: Editions du remue-ménage and Women's Press, 1991.

Mahyère, Eveline. *Je jure de m'éblouir.* Paris: Buchet-Chastel, 1958. Trans. *I Will Not Serve* by Antonia White, 1959. Rpt. with introduction by Georgina Hammick. London: Virago, 1984.

Mallet-Joris, Françoise. *La chambre rouge.* Paris: Julliard, 1955.

———. *Le rempart des Béguines.* Paris: Julliard, 1951. Trans. *The Illusionist* by Herma Briffault. New York: Farrar, Straus & Young, 1952.

Margadant, Jo Burr. *Madame le Professeur: Women Educators in the Third Republic.* Princeton: Princeton Univ. Press, 1990.

Marks, Elaine. "It Is a Question of What I Find Exciting and What I Find Tedious, Even Boring." *Chronicle of Higher Education* (Dec. 15, 1993): B5.

———. "Lesbian Intertextuality." In *Homosexualities and French Literature: Cultural Contexts/Critical Texts.* Ed. George Stambolian and Elaine Marks. Ithaca: Cornell Univ. Press, 1979. 353–77.

———. "Memory, Desire, and Pleasure in the Classroom: *La Grande Mademoiselle.*" *MLA Newsletter* 25 (1993): 3–4.

———. "Transgressing the (In)cont(in)ent Boundaries: The Body in Decline." *Yale French Studies* 72 (1986): 181–200.

———, and Isabelle de Courtivron, ed. *New French Feminisms.* New York: Schocken Books, 1981.

Mayeur, Françoise. *L'enseignement secondaire des jeunes filles sous la troisième république.* Paris: Presse de la Fondation Nationale des Sciences Politiques, 1977.

McPherson, Karen S. *Incriminations: Guilty Women/Telling Stories.* Princeton: Princeton Univ. Press, 1994.

Meijer, Irene Costera, and Baukje Prins. "How Bodies Come to Matter: An Interview with Judith Butler." *Signs* 23:2 (Winter 1998): 275–86.

Moberg, Åsa. *Simone och jag: Tankar kring Simone de Beauvoir.* Stockholm: Norstedts, 1996.

Moi, Toril. "Beauvoir's Utopia: The Politics of *The Second Sex*." In *South Atlantic Quarterly* 92.2 (Spring 1993): 322–60.

———. *Feminist Theory and Simone de Beauvoir.* Oxford UK: Blackwell, 1990.

———. *Simone de Beauvoir: The Making of an Intellectual Woman.* Oxford UK: Blackwell, 1994.

Monferrand, Hélène de. *Les amies d'Héloïse.* Paris: Editions de Fallois, 1990.

———. "Campagne pour faire rééditer Jeanne Galzy." *Lesbia Magazine* 104 (Apr. 1992): 15.

———. *Les enfants d'Héloïse.* Paris: Double Interligne, 1997.

———. *Journal de Suzanne.* Paris: Editions de Fallois, 1991.

Monteil, Claudine. *Simone de Beauvoir: Le mouvement des femmes. Mémoires d'une jeune fille rebelle.* Montreal: Stanké, 1995.

Montherlant, Henri de. *Essais.* Paris: Gallimard, 1963.

Mortimer, Armine Kotin. *Plotting to Kill.* New York: Peter Lang, 1991.

Morton, Donald, and Mas'ud Zavarzadeh, eds. *Theory/Pedagogy/Politics: Texts for Change.* Urbana: Univ. of Illinois Press, 1991.

New Literary History 27.1 (1996). "Living Alone Together." Special issue on Todorov.

Ozouf, Mona. *Les mots des femmes: Essai sur la singularité française.* Paris: Fayard, 1996. Trans. *Women's Words: Essay on French Singularity* by Jane Marie Todd. Chicago: Univ. of Chicago Press, 1997.

Paidika: The Journal of Paedophilia 8 (1992).

Pascal, Roy. *Design and Truth in Autobiography.* Cambridge: Harvard Univ. Press, 1960.

Patterson, Yolanda Astarita. *Simone de Beauvoir and the Demystification of Motherhood.* Ann Arbor: UMI Research Press, 1989.

———. "Who Was This H. M. Parshley?: The Saga of Translating Simone de Beauvoir's *The Second Sex*." *Simone de Beauvoir Studies* 9 (1992): 41–47.

Peters, Hélène. *The Existential Woman.* New York: Peter Lang, 1991.

Peyrefitte, Roger, and Pierre Sipriot, eds. *Henry de Montherlant–Roger Peyrefitte correspondance.* Paris: Laffont, 1983.

Pilardi, Jo-Ann. "Feminists Read *The Second Sex*." In *Feminist Interpretations of Simone de Beauvoir.* Ed. Margaret A. Simons. University Park: Pennsylvania State Univ. Press, 1995. 29–44.

Pringle, Lauren Helen. *An Annotated and Indexed Calendar and Abstract of the Ohio State University Collection of Simone de Beauvoir's Letters to Nelson Algren.* Diss. Ohio State University. Ann Arbor: UMI, 1985.

Raimond, Michel. *Les romans de Montherlant.* Paris: CEDES, 1982.

Raymer, John D. "Nelson Algren and Simone de Beauvoir: The End of Their Affair at Miller, Indiana." *Old Northwest* 5 (1979–80): 401–7.

Reval, Gabrielle. *Les Sévriennes.* Paris: A. Michel, 1900.

Robinson, Christopher. *Scandal in the Ink: Male and Female Homosexuality in Twentieth-Century French Literature.* London: Cassell, 1995.

Saccani, Jean-Pierre. *Nelson et Simone.* Paris: Rocher, 1994.

Sartre, Jean-Paul. *Carnets de la drôle de guerre: Novembre 1939–mars 1940.* Paris: Gallimard, 1983. Trans. *The War Diaries of Jean-Paul Sartre: November 1939/March 1940* by Quintin Hoare. New York: Pantheon, 1984.

———. *L'être et le néant.* Paris: Gallimard, 1938. Trans. *Being and Nothingness: An Essay in Phenomenological Ontology* by Hazel E. Barnes. New York: Washington Square Press, 1966.

———. *Lettres au Castor et à quelques autres.* 2 vols. Paris: Gallimard, 1983. Trans. *Witness to My Life: The Letters of Jean-Paul Sartre to Simone de Beauvoir, 1926–1939* by Lee Fahnstock and Norman MacAfee. New York: Scribner's, 1992; and *Quiet Moments in a War: The Letters of Jean-Paul Sartre to Simone de Beauvoir, 1940–1963* by Lee Fahnstock and Norman MacAfee. New York: Scribner's, 1993.

———. *La nausée.* Paris: Gallimard, 1938. Trans. *Nausea* by Lloyd Alexander. Norfolk CT: New Directions, 1949.

Schoppmann, Claudia. *Im Fluchtgepäck die Sprache: Deutschsprachige Schriftstellerinnen im Exil.* Berlin: Orlanda Frauenverlag, 1992.

Schwarzer, Alice. *After "The Second Sex": Conversations with Simone de Beauvoir.* Trans. Marianne Howarth. New York: Pantheon, 1984.

———. "Beauvoir und die Frauen." *Emma* 5 (Sept./Oct. 1994): 104–7.

Scott, Gail. *Spaces Like Stairs.* Toronto: Women's Press, 1989.

Sedgwick, Eve Kosofsky, and Adam Frank, eds. *Shame and Its Sisters: A Silvan Tomkins Reader.* Durham: Duke Univ. Press, 1995.

Simon, Sherry. *Gender in Translation: Cultural Identity and the Politics of Transmission.* New York: Routledge, 1996.

Simons, Margaret. "Beauvoir and Sartre: The Philosophical Relationship." *Yale French Studies* 72 (1986): 165–79.

———. *Beauvoir and "The Second Sex": Feminism, Race, and the Origins of Existentialism.* Lanham MD: Rowman and Littlefield, 1999.

———. "Lesbian Connections: Simone de Beauvoir and Feminism." *Signs* 18.1 (Autumn 1992): 136–61.

———. "The Silencing of Simone de Beauvoir. Guess What's Missing from *The Second Sex.*" *Women's Studies International Forum* 6.5 (1983): 559–64.

———, ed. *Feminist Interpretations of Simone de Beauvoir.* University Park: Pennsylvania State Univ. Press, 1995.

Sipriot, Pierre. *Montherlant sans masque.* Vol. 1, "L'enfant prodigue, 1895–1932." Paris: Laffont, 1982. Vol. 2, "Ecris avec ton sang, 1932–1972." Paris: Laffont, 1990.

Spacks, Patricia Meyer. *Imagining a Self: Autobiography and Novel in Eighteenth-Century England.* Cambridge: Harvard Univ. Press, 1976.

Spivak, Gayatri. "French Feminism Revisited." In *Outside in the Teaching Machine.* New York: Routledge, 1992. 141–71.

Suleiman, Susan Rubin. "Life-Story, History, Fiction: Simone de Beauvoir's Wartime

Writings." In *Risking Who One Is: Encounters with Contemporary Art and Literature.* Cambridge: Harvard Univ. Press, 1994. 179–98.

———. "Writing and Motherhood." *The (M)Other Tongue: Essays in Feminist Psychoanalytic Interpretations.* Ed. Shirley Nelson Garner, Claire Kahane, and Madelon Sprengnether. Ithaca: Cornell Univ. Press, 1985. 352–77.

Theweleit, Klaus. [1977] *Male Fantasies.* Vol. 1, *Women, Floods, Bodies, History.* Minneapolis: Univ. of Minnesota Press, 1987. Translated from German by Chris Turner.

———. [1978]. *Male Fantasies.* Vol. 2, *Male Bodies: Psychoanalyzing the White Terror.* Minneapolis: Univ. of Minnesota Press, 1989. Translated from German by Chris Turner.

Tidd, Ursula. *Simone de Beauvoir, Gender and Testimony.* Cambridge: Cambridge Univ. Press, 1999.

Todd, Olivier. *Un fils rebelle.* Paris: Grasset, 1981.

Tompkins, Jane. *A Life in School: What the Teacher Learned.* Reading MA: Addison-Wesley, 1996.

Vance, Carole S. "Pleasure and Danger: Toward a Politics of Sexuality." In *Pleasure and Danger: Exploring Female Sexuality.* Ed. Carole S. Vance. Boston: Routledge and Kegan Paul, 1984. 1–27.

Venuti, Lawrence, ed. *Rethinking Translation: Discourse, Subjectivity, Ideology.* New York: Routledge, 1992.

Vicinus, Martha. "Distance and Desire: English Boarding School Friendships." *Signs* 9.4 (1984): 600–622.

Vintges, Karen. "*The Second Sex* and Philosophy." In *Feminist Interpretations of Simone de Beauvoir.* Ed. Margaret A. Simons. University Park: Pennsylvania State Univ. Press, 1995. 45–58.

Virmaux, Alain and Odette, eds. *Colette at the Movies: Criticism and Screenplays.* New York: Ungar, 1980.

Waelti-Walters, Jennifer. *Feminist Novelists of the Belle Epoque: Love as a Lifestyle.* Bloomington: Indiana Univ. Press, 1990.

Weatherby, W. J. "The Life and Hard Times of Nelson Algren." *The Times of London* (May 17, 1981): 39.

Wilson, Emma. "Daughters and Desire: Simone de Beauvoir's *Journal de Guerre.*" In *Autobiography and the Existential Self.* Ed. Terry Keefe and Edmund Smyth. Liverpool: Liverpool Univ. Press, 1995. 83–98.

Winterson, Jeannette. *Oranges Are Not the Only Fruit.* New York: Atlantic Monthly Press, 1987.

Wittig, Monique. *The Straight Mind and Other Essays.* Boston: Beacon Press, 1992.

Woodward, Kathleen. "Simone de Beauvoir: Aging and Its Discontents." In *The Private Self: Theory and Practice of Women's Autobiographical Writings.* Ed. Shari Benstock. Chapel Hill: Univ. of North Carolina Press, 1988. 90–113.

Yale French Studies 72 (1986). "Simone de Beauvoir: Witness to a Century." Ed. Hélène Vivienne Wenzel.

Contributors

Liz Constable teaches in the French and Italian departments and the Critical Theory Program at the University of California, Davis. She is the co-editor of a collection of interdisciplinary approaches to decadence entitled *Perennial Decay: The Politics and Aesthetics of Decadence in the Modern Era* (University Park: Pennsylvania State Univ. Press, 1999). She is particularly interested in women writers' approaches to gender and sexuality in the late nineteenth and early twentieth centuries, and has published articles in *L'Esprit Créateur, MLN,* and the *Journal for the Psychoanalysis of Society and Culture.*

Luise von Flotow is an associate professor of translation studies at the University of Ottawa. She is also a literary translator (German and French to English) and has published on Canadian/Quebec literature, feminist translation, and gender issues in translation. She is the author of *Translation and Gender: Translating in the "Era of Feminism"* (Manchester UK and Ottawa, Canada: St. Jerome Publishing and Ottawa Univ. Press, 1997).

Richard J. Golsan is professor of French at Texas A&M University and editor of the *South Central Review.* In addition to publishing monographs on Henry de Montherlant (*Service Inutile* [University MS: Romance Monographs, 1988]), René Girard (*René Girard and Myth* [New York: Garland, 1993]), and the memory of Vichy in modern France (*Occupation, Preoccupation: History and Counterhistory in French Culture since 1945* [Lincoln: Univ. of Nebraska Press, 2000]), he is the editor of *Fascism, Aesthetics, and Culture* (Hanover NH: Univ. Press of New England, 1992) and *Memory, the Holocaust, and French Justice: The Bousquet and Touvier Affairs* (Hanover NH: Univ. Press of New England, 1996). He has worked extensively on the Occupation, and has co-edited special issues of *L'Esprit Créateur* and the *Journal of European Studies* on this theme. He is the co-editor, with Melanie Hawthorne, of *Gender and Fascism in Modern France* (Hanover NH: Univ. Press of New England, 1997).

Melanie C. Hawthorne is associate professor of French at Texas A&M University and is affiliated with the Women's Studies Program there. She has written extensively on the decadent writer Rachilde and is currently competing a biography. Her translation of Rachilde's *The Juggler* appeared in 1990 (New Brunswick NJ: Rutgers Univ. Press). She is the co-editor, with Richard J. Golsan, of *Gender and Fascism in Modern France* (Hanover NH: Univ. Press of New England, 1997). She has published in journals such as the *French Review* and *L'Esprit Créateur* on topics ranging from nineteenth- and twentieth-century French literature to contemporary issues in women's studies.

Serge Julienne-Caffié is the author of *Simone de Beauvoir* (Paris: Gallimard, 1966). He lives in the United States and teaches contemporary French and francophone literature in Philadelphia.

Barbara Klaw is associate professor of French at Northern Kentucky University. Her numerous articles on Beauvoir appear in a variety of journals and books. Her first book, *Le Paris de Beauvoir/Beauvoir's Paris,* was published in Paris by Syllepse in 1999. She is currently working on an English translation and analyses of Beauvoir's unpublished diaries from 1926 to 1930.

Åsa Moberg's book on Simone de Beauvoir, *Simone och jag* (Simone and I), was published in Sweden in 1996; the book concerns Beauvoir's influence on the author's life, a theme that she extends in her article for this volume. A novelist and translator, a columnist for *Aftonbladet* since 1968, and formerly an advice columnist on love and sex in a weekly magazine for young women, Moberg is currently working on the first complete Swedish translation of *The Second Sex.*

Index

"Simone de Beauvoir" is abbreviated as "SB" in index entries.